THE PERSONAL VOICE IN BIBLICAL INTERPRETATION

Reading and interpreting the Bible, whether as an 'ordinary' or 'critical' reader, has always been strongly influenced and shaped by a person's unique character and life-story. Personal voice criticism takes seriously into account and makes explicit the role of the interpreter's personal voice within the process of deciding on the meaning of a text.

This composite, postcolonial volume contains the original essays of distinguished Jewish and Christian scholars of the Hebrew Bible and the New Testament from all continents and a variety of social locations and biographical backgrounds. The contributions testify to the pivotal role of real readers in reader-response criticism and in cultural studies and present some explicit autobiographical interpretations. They offer challenging new perspectives on the ancient biblical books and individual texts of the Torah, the Prophets, the Gospels, (Pauline) letters, and Revelation.

The Personal Voice in Biblical Interpretation makes evident the multiplicity and legitimacy of different interpretations and breaks new ground in the ongoing debate of the hermeneutics and methods in biblical scholarship on its way into the twenty-first century.

Ingrid Rosa Kitzberger is a Lise Meitner Research Fellow at the University of Münster. She has published widely in feminist interpretation and reader-response criticism.

THE PERSONAL VOICE IN BIBLICAL INTERPRETATION

Edited by Ingrid Rosa Kitzberger

London and New York

First published 1999
by Routledge
11 New Fetter Lane, London EC4P 4EE

Simultaneously published in the USA and Canada
by Routledge
29 West 35th Street, New York, NY 10001

Typeset in Garamond by
J&L Composition Ltd, Filey, North Yorkshire
Printed and bound in Great Britain by
T.J. International Ltd, Padstow, Cornwall

British Library Cataloguing in Publication Data
A catalogue record for this book is available from the British Library

Library of Congress Cataloging in Publication Data
The personal voice in biblical interpretation/edited by Ingrid Rosa
Kitzberger.
p. cm.
Includes bibliographical references and index.
1. Bible–Criticism, interpretation, etc. 2. Reader-response
criticism. I. Kitzberger, Ingrid R.
BS476.P47 1998
220.6–dc21 98–34313
CIP

ISBN 0–415–18099–6 (hbk)
ISBN 0–415–18100–3 (pbk)

Spell it out: I am not giving you anything fixed,
present or past, to theorize.
If you think you can theorize what I've given you,
you're a simpleton.
I am creating something ahead of me,
something I can work towards,
something that may help you work towards
your own model.
It's a praxis, a process. Not a static thing.

Nicole Ward Jouve,
White Woman Speaks with Forked Tongue.
Criticism as Autobiography

CONTENTS

vii

CONTENTS

CONTRIBUTORS

Maria Anicia Co is Lecturer in New Testament at Maryhill School of Theology and Loyola School of Theology, Quezon City, Philippines, and Lecturer in Old Testatment at San Carlos Seminary in Guadalupe, Makati.

J. Severino Croatto is Professor of Old Testament, Hebrew and Phenomenology of Religions at the Instituto Superior Evangélico de Estudios Teológicos, Buenos Aires, Argentina.

Mayer I. Gruber is Associate Professor in the Department of Bible and Ancient Near East at Ben-Gurion University of the Negev in Beersheva, Israel.

Ingrid Rosa Kitzberger is a Lise Meitner Research Fellow at the University of Münster, Germany.

Bernard C. Lategan is Professor of Biblical Studies and Dean of the Faculty of Arts and Social Sciences of the University of Stellenbosch, South Africa.

Francis J. Moloney is Professor of New Testament and Foundation Professor of Theology at the Australian Catholic University at Victoria, Australia.

Stephen D. Moore is Senior Lecturer in New Testament at the University of Sheffield, England.

Daniel Patte is Professor of New Testament and Chair of the Department of Religious Studies, and Professor of New Testament and Early Christianity at The Divinity School, Vanderbilt University, Nashville, TN.

Fernando F. Segovia is Professor of New Testament and Early Christianity at The Divinity School, Vanderbilt University, Nashville, TN.

Jeffrey L. Staley is Visiting Professor of Religion at the Department of Religion, Pacific Lutheran University, Tacoma, WA.

CONTRIBUTORS

Jan Gabriel van der Watt is Professor and Head of the Department of New Testament at the University of Pretoria, South Africa.

Maria Gemma Victorino is Lecturer in New Testament at Maryhill School of Theology, Quezon City, Philippines.

James W. Voelz is Professor of New Testament and Director of Graduate Studies at Concordia Seminary, St Louis, MO.

ACKNOWLEDGEMENTS

It is my sincere wish to extend my heartfelt gratitude to several people who, in their own unique ways, have had their share in the coming-into-existence of this volume.

Vicky Peters inspired and encouraged me with her enthusiasm to venture out on this project. Without her and without the great mystery that engendered our first encounter in Edinburgh in 1994 this volume would not be.

Richard Stoneman welcomed my project with great interest and openness and supported it through the official stages.

Coco Stevenson accompanied me during the various preparatory stages with her excellent and charming cooperation.

Jeffrey L. Staley encouraged me with his courage at one point and lended his expertise and generous help at another.

Edgar V. McKnight from Furman University, Greenville, SC, informed me, during his sabbatical at Münster University, that I needed e-mail before I knew it myself. His prophetic foresight and gentle introduction to the world of cyberspace later enabled me to carry out this project so effectively.

Rosemary Brown (from Edinburgh), with her unique talent of reading stars, me, and papers, assisted me in birthing this book.

Rosa Suiter supported me with love and concern through all the stages of the inner and outer process.

All those colleagues who, through their kind willingness to participate and their stimulating motivation, contributed to this volume made it possible in the first place. Those who supported the project through their interest and concern affirmed that I am barking up the right tree.

Daniel Patte, through his listening to my personal voice (without co-opting me) and his 'speaking with' me, has been a constant source of strength and empowerment.

Fernando F. Segovia has encouraged me 'in the struggle' and in the difficult though rewarding process of moving out of old orbits into a liberating universe.

Their generous invitation to a guest lecture at Vanderbilt University in

November 1996 provided a wonderful setting for the presentation of a first and still very shy version of my personal reading of the Samaritan woman's story. The affirmation as well as critique from an appreciative and challenging audience has greatly influenced and shaped my further development of personal voice criticism and of voicing myself. Encountering Amy-Jill Levine, Musa W. Dube, and Leticia Guardiola-Sáenz has been of special importance in this process.

THANK YOU!

INTRODUCTION

Mars and project/ions

From the surface of Mars — where the sky is salmon and Earth is a blue morning star — you probably would have noticed the spaceship coming. It may have been the noise the thing made that caught your attention; although the Martian atmosphere is spent and shredded, it's not too tenuous to carry sound. And it's certainly not too tenuous to make anything that tries to punch through it pay the price, causing the interloper to glow like a meteor as it plunges toward a touchdown somewhere on the ancient world. That you could not have missed.

There was, of course, no one in Mars' Ares Vallis floodplain to mark the moment when NASA's 3-ft.-tall Pathfinder spacecraft dropped into the soil of the long-dry valley. But there was a planet more than 100 million miles away filled with people who were paying heed when it landed, appropriately enough, on July 4.[1]

* * *

On the night of the Fourth, when we landed on Mars, I walk the beach and watch the fireworks compete with the stars in the enormous black sky. This is Independence Day, and I am alone. So are we all. This is what we discover at times like these — the first flight around the moon, the moon walk, the probe of Jupiter, the Viking missions, and now this amazing, take-your-breath-away event. Errands into space lift us out of ourselves and return us to ourselves. They tell us that we are alone in the universe, and how terrible and how wonderful an idea that is. [. . .]

What one man calls cosmic loneliness, another might see as being part of a system in which everything is at once lonely and companionable — rocks, beaches, people. Out there is Mars with its wasted territory. Around here are oceans and a gaseous atmosphere that turns the sky blue. The only justification for our loneliness is that we feel it. Did the Neanderthals experience cosmic loneliness? Is that why they kept quiet?[2]

* * *

1

On the same Fourth of July 1997, down here on the planet earth a contract was signed in London, appropriately enough, for the book that you, dear reader, are holding in your hands right now.

The Personal Voice in Biblical Interpretation testifies to the irruption of the 'I' within the critical task and to the insertion of a personal point of view and personal involvement in a discipline that has for long been dominated and shaped by a (supposedly) apersonal, objective paradigm.

Projecting the human point of view onto a planet 100 million miles away from us and with no life on it, as Jeffrey Kluger does in his wonderful article, is both startling and fascinating because it demonstrates the need for the personal dimension within such a cosmic enterprise as the Mars mission. The experience of both loneliness *and* relatedness, which Roger Rosenblatt notes in his equally fascinating article, calls forth our personal voices. Unlike the Neanderthals, we human beings did *not* remain silent. 'The Rock Festival on Mars', about which Leon Jaroff reported with a good deal of humour a week later,[3] made this human quest for the personal even more obvious. Nicknaming rocks on Mars and describing them as well as the Sojourner vehicle in the most human terms, as the Pathfinder scientists did, demonstrates the startling projection of the human quest for the personal even in, or perhaps because of, the highest degree of objective data and scientific perfection.

When I launched the project on *The Personal Voice in Biblical Interpretation* in April 1996, the enthusiastic and encouraging reactions from colleagues around the globe were overwhelming and inspiring. It seemed to me that many had just waited for a chance to utter their personal voices more clearly within biblical criticism and to reflect consciously on the impact of the personal on the critical task. Like the dried-up valley on Mars, valleys in biblical criticism and in biblical critics themselves have been dried up by a prevailing paradigm that has demanded the critic distance him- or herself from their 'objects' – the biblical texts – and thus created a split between the critical task and the personal self. These valleys, it appeared, desired to be filled again with living waters.

Although muted and suppressed, the personal voice of the critic has always been present in biblical criticism and has influenced the interpretive process even within the historical–critical paradigm. 'Objective' and 'neutral' criticism has never existed, and never will. To be sure, the hidden personal voices of interpreters have exercised *over*-powering effects on the readers.

With the rise of new paradigms the 'I' of the critic has come slowly but gradually into focus. Within *reader-response criticism* (McKnight 1985, 1988; Fowler 1991) the shift of focus from the 'implied reader' (Iser 1990: 50–67; Staley 1988), the 'intended readers', or constructed first readers (Kitzberger 1994, 1994a, 1995) to real, flesh-and-blood readers (Segovia 1996, 1998) on the one hand, and the rise of *cultural studies* with its focus on the social

2

location and thus contextualization of real readers (Segovia 1995b; Segovia and Tolbert 1995a, 1995b) on the other, have increasingly contributed to the ongoing paradigm shift within the discipline (Segovia 1995a). Explicit *autobiographical biblical criticism*, which has only begun recently (Staley 1995), intensifies the issues that are at stake in a personally defined and orientated criticism. The preparation of the *Semeia* volume on *Taking it Personally: Autobiographical Biblical Criticism* (Anderson and Staley, 1995, published January 1997) coincided – by chance or not? – with the launching of the project for this volume. Thus, the *kairos* seemed to have come for voicing the personal more expressively, consciously and creatively in the field of biblical criticism, and thus progressing further with the new hermeneutical discourse implied in such an endeavour. The *em*-powering effect of personal voice criticism on both the critics themselves as well as on their readers points to a future yet to come.

Books continue each other

It was early in the afternoon on a hot summer's day in July 1995. In the convention centre on the hill of Buda, overlooking the city of Budapest, we had just listened to a paper on cultural studies presented by Fernando F. Segovia during the Society of Biblical Literature International Meeting.

Inspired by this paper, we continued our previous conversation on the impact of the critic's personality on the interpretation of ancient texts. Vicky Peters was then in the process of evaluating and working on a proposal by Judith P. Hallett and Thomas Van Nortwick for a volume entitled *The Personal Voice in Classical Scholarship*, and shared her enthusiasm with me. In return, I shared with her my long-term commitment to feminist biblical interpretation and my experiences as a member of the seminar 'The Role of the Reader in the Interpretation of the New Testament', later 'Hermeneutics and the Biblical Text', at the annual meetings of the Studiorum Novi Testamenti Societas, chaired by Bernard C. Lategan and James W. Voelz. Within this encounter in Budapest the fascination with the personal in criticism that had been kindled in both of us in different contexts sparked off the idea for this present volume. Neither of us could have conceived this idea on her own. Thus, looking back it was obviously meant that we met the first time almost exactly a year before that memorable day, during the annual meeting of the Studiorum Novi Testamenti Societas in Edinburgh, in August 1994.

Vicky Peters' interest in my work continued when we met again in November 1994 in London. When introducing me to somebody as a future author for Routledge we both had no idea that this would come true so soon. Just as ideas continue each other and are able to create something new out of a transformative encounter, so it is with books. The timely proposal by Hallet and Van Nortwick inspired Vicky Peters and me to think about a volume on *The Personal Voice in Biblical Interpretation*. Thus, it proved true what Virginia Woolf noted about women's writing in *A Room of One's Own*, namely, that 'books continue each other, in spite of our habit of judging them separately', and 'have a way of influencing each other' (Woolf 1945: 79, 107). Therefore, the two editors of the 'predecessor' volume have also, though unconsciously, engendered this present volume; my gratitude for their right timing is extended to them.

Intertextual symphony

Both *intertextuality* and *interpersonality* have engendered and shaped the contributions in this volume. Coming from very different backgrounds, social locations, personal and professional affiliations, with very different life stories and biographies, we – thirteen biblical scholars of both the Hebrew Bible and the New Testament – Jewish and Christian, from all continents, have joined in this project on the personal voice in our discipline. Our contributions are as diverse as we are different from each other as people. Each one addresses the issue at stake in a unique way and with a unique stance, and thus contributes unique and at times controversial perspectives. Thereby, a symphony of personal voices is composed whose music is of a different quality from the sounds of the individual voices. The order in which the musicians are placed has been carefully considered on several criteria, yet it is not binding. You, dear reader, are invited to listen to these voices by following your own interest and intuition. Thus, the symphony of this volume will be unique for each reader, yet the intertextual context influences whatever reading strategy and procedure you choose.

The essays may be viewed in the light of those three 'categories' of personal voice criticism within biblical scholarship already outlined, that is, *reader-response criticism*, *cultural studies*, and *autobiographical criticism*. However, the borders between them are open, and this testifies to the fluidity that arises once the personal is introduced. The best way to approach this volume is, therefore, to listen to each contribution in its own right and uniqueness.

Listening to each other's voices and daring to speak with one's own personal voice calls forth and engenders equality, justice, and respect. Therefore, personal voice criticism is, by its very nature, *a democratic enterprise*. Thus, from its very beginning, the project was designed as *postcolonial* (Segovia 1995a; Spivak 1990; Brett 1996b; Donaldson 1996). By acknowledging the subjectivity and otherness of oneself and of the others, speaking *with* others becomes possible and speaking *for* others is overcome in the process (Patte 1995: 23–5, 1996: 389–96; West and Dube 1996; Alcoff

1991). Therefore, no attempt is made here to 'summarize' the following essays, in spite of common practice within introductions. Let everyone speak with her/his own tongue and let every reader listen to them with his/her own ears and respond in their own ways! Personal criticism is both an 'outspoken involvement on the part of the critic with the subject matter, and an invitation extended to the potential reader to participate in the interweaving and construction of the ongoing conversation this criticism can be, even as it remains a text' (Caws 1990: 2).

Hermeneutics and ethics

Personal voice criticism in its various forms is a praxis, a process, not static and fixed. Yet while it escapes the grasp of pure theory (Jouve 1991: 11) it calls for a hermeneutical discourse. What is at stake in this kind of criticism? How can it be situated within literary criticism in general and biblical criticism in particular?

To address the first question, let me recall a personal experience. 'Why did you choose this female first reader?', I was asked by Fernando F. Segovia in the discussion following the presentation of my reader-response paper on 'Mary of Bethany and Mary of Magdala' (Kitzberger 1995) in the seminar 'Hermeneutics and the Biblical Text' at the annual meeting of the Studiorum Novi Testamenti Societas in Chicago in the summer of 1993. Without thinking about it, I immediately responded, 'because it makes me less vulnerable'. At this point in the discussion, following on from Elisabeth Struthers Malbon's response paper, it had become obvious already how much a (first) reader construct and the actual reading of a text are shaped by one's own self.

What is at stake in personal voice criticism is *nothing less than the self of the critic* and it 'requires a certain intensity in the lending of oneself (Caws 1990: 2). By exposing oneself the critic makes herself/himself vulnerable, and that is always a risky endeavour. Some of the risk-takers in this volume have pointed out this first and foremost implication. But at the same time, the courage to voice oneself can and has been experienced as a liberating and *em*-powering experience, both on the part of the critics and of the (potential) readers.

Personal voice criticism always implies an *intertextual reading or interpretation*. The 'meaning' of the text, whether ancient or contemporary, emerges and is constructed in the encounter between the written text on the one hand and the critic as text on the other (Voelz 1995; Aichele and Phillips 1995; Kitzberger 1994, 1994a). In narrative–critical terms, the story-world proposed by the text and the story-world brought to the text by the reader influence, inform, and transform one another in a dynamic fashion. Thus, 'reading is a two-way process – *reading a text* in terms of our experience and *reading* our *experience* in terms of the text,' and this 'means that critical biblical studies needs to include the assessment of *both* the way in which we interpret the text from the perspective of specific contexts *and* the way in which the text interprets our contexts' (Patte 1998). It is 'through the dialectic tension that exists between text and experience that new understanding emerges' (Lategan, this volume). The essays in this volume bear witness to both ways of reading and to the dialectic between text and reader or interpreter. However, they also show that apart from these intertextual encounters, which are often based on interpersonal encounters, the choices of certain texts or books of the Bible for interpretation are already the result of such a two-way process as described by Daniel Patte. As much as we have chosen certain texts or certain biblical books, they have chosen us.

Personal voice criticism makes explicit that *no text is an autonomous and self-sufficient entity*, but is always open, literarily and pragmatically. Each texts calls for the reader's presence and activity in order to be realized and come alive. And it is especially the fragmentary nature of texts, the gaps and open ends (Victorino; Croatto), the silence created between and around the words, that enable, whether consciously or not, the personal voice of the reader or interpreter to enter into the text and construct it in a unique way, or – in musical terms – to compose the 'end' for an 'unfinished literary symphony' (Croatto).

Personal voice criticism makes explicit that all *critical readings are actually based on ordinary readings*; by affirming their legitimacy and multi-dimensionality a non-hierarchical relationship between them is established and the competence of each reader is acknowledged (Patte 1995: 76–107; West and Dube 1996). Each given reading and interpretation is based on the effect a text has on its readers. This also holds true for those critics who consider themselves 'purely objective' and 'neutral'.

Personal voice criticism takes seriously into account that there is not just one possible reading of a given text but that each interpretation implies *a choice from among the various meaning (producing) dimensions of a text* (Patte 1995; 1996). As a result, the process of any interpretation may be highlighted and the rich potential of any text is made visible. The surplus of meaning transcends the confinement of any chosen reading or interpretation.

Personal voice criticism, by its very nature, intensifies the *ethical dimension of all interpretations*, our responsibility for our interpretations and their effect on others (Schüssler Fiorenza 1988; Patte 1995; 1998; Fewell and Phillips 1998). The more personal our interpretations are, the more we are forced to claim and acknowledge them as such. But, at the same time, the ethical dimension of reading readings is at stake.

Genre and criticism by/of the 'I'

Personal voice criticism raises the issue of genre and the mode of critical discourse in a more pointed fashion than more traditional criticisms. As will become evident simply by reading the thirteen essays in this volume, the sheer *variety of genres* and also, in one or two cases, the impossibility of attributing an essay to any known genre calls for a new way of thinking about genre within criticism. It also shows that a new mode of criticism brings forth new genres that may be as individual and as creative as the respective critics. Besides prose, poetry, for example, may become a language of the critics.

Corresponding to the new paradigm in terms of genre, *the mode of critical discourse* in academic discipline becomes a critical issue that makes conscious what is at stake in any critical discourse. Certainly, personal voice criticism raises the issue of how to respond to it, that is, how to criticize this kind of criticism. This question was one of the most vigorously discussed within the session on the *Semeia* volume on autobiographical criticism at the AAR/SBL Annual Meeting in San Francisco last November. For sure, personal voice criticism and even the most intimate variant of it, autobiographical criticism, must be open to criticism, to 'critical interrogation' (Alcoff 1991: 25), if it claims to be criticism. However, this provokes questions about the object of such 'critical interrogation': is it the text, the reading of the text, or the reader's personal self and experience? A response like 'I am sorry about your divorce' (O'Brien 1995) doesn't do justice either to the critic or her piece of personal/autobiographical criticism. Thus, it is neither the experience nor the self of the reader that is put to criticism, but the way it is expressed within the critical task that is evaluated according to the contribution it makes or can make to the hermeneutical and methodological discourse and the practice of biblical scholarship. However, in dealing with personal voice criticism critics need to reflect and revise their praxis of criticism and the ethical stance involved with it. Thus, besides the ethics of reading, *the ethics of reading readings* comes to the fore. Criticism and respect certainly do not exclude each other, and, as should be demonstrated in any critical discourse, it's the piece and not the person that is put to scrutiny.

Personal plurals and the plurality of readers

'Who am I?' is the basic question underlying personal voice criticism and it is the question elaborated upon in the first essay of this volume. Pondering that question and reading the readings in this volume, it will become obvious that there is no easy and single answer. One reason for this is that the 'I' of each person, and thus of a critic alike, is always multi-dimensional, just like the texts we interpret. It is the 'personal plurals'

(Braund 1997) that make up the 'I', and real readers are several readers at the same time (Long 1996: 90–2). The question about one's identity becomes further complicated by the fact that our self is fleeting, as is well expressed by Bonhoeffer's words referred to by Patte in his essay: 'I am one person today, and tomorrow another. Am I both at once?' Thus, any personal voice criticism reflects the self as constituted and expressed at a given moment in time, but also as constituted in relations. Furthermore, the issue of the constructedness or re-constructedness of the self in the act of reading becomes an issue. No personal voice criticism presents the critic's self in total. It always implies a choice of what is communicated to the readers, which is just as legitimate as it is necessary.

'Is personal or especially autobiographical biblical criticism better than any other criticism?' That question still rings in my ears, as does Jeff Staley's answer during the previously mentioned session, 'it is simply different'.

The personal plural of each individual author and of all contributors together within this symphonic concert are voiced and you, dear readers, are invited to listen to them. With a plurality of readers in view, the interaction will definitely engender a variety of reading experiences. Such is the nature of personal voice criticism.

Encountering the 'I' over and over again in this volume, it is my hope and wish that you will not be as bored as Virginia Woolf when reading a man's personal writing, in which the dominance of the letter 'I' overshadowed everything so that nothing could grow there. Different from the 'impediment in Mr A's mind which blocked the fountain of creative energy', and his 'being honest as the day and logical as the sun', thus showing that he used only the 'male side of his brain', a writing in which both sides of the brain, the female and the male side, are activated, as for example, in Coleridge the creative energy 'explodes and gives birth to all kinds of other ideas' (Woolf 1945: 98–100). May this collection of essays by both women and men who have written with the left and right sides of their brains (to put it in a gender-neutral way) give birth to all kinds of ideas in you, our readers, or, in the words of Nicole Ward Jouve, 'help you work towards your own model'.

Ingrid Rosa Kitzberger
Münster, Pentecost 1998

Notes

1 Thus began Jeffrey Kluger's article 'Uncovering the Secrets of Mars', *Time* magazine, 14 July 1997, 40–1.
2 Roger Rosenblatt, 'Visit to a Smaller Planet', *Time* magazine, 14 July 1997, 47.
3 Leon Jaroff, 'Rock Festival on Mars', *Time* magazine, 21 July 1997, 72–4.

References

Aichele, G. and Phillips, G. A. (eds) (1995) *Intertextuality and the Bible*, *Semeia* 69/70, Atlanta, GA: Scholars.

Alcoff, L. (1991) 'The Problem of Speaking for Others', *Cultural Critique* 1991–2: 5–32.

Alter, R. (1989) *The Pleasures of Reading in an Ideological Age*, New York: Simon and Schuster.

Anderson, J. Capel and Staley, J. L. (eds) (1995) *Taking It Personally: Autobiographical Biblical Criticism*, *Semeia* 72, Atlanta, GA: Scholars.

Blount, B. K. (1995) *Cultural Interpretation. Reorienting New Testament Criticism*, Minneapolis, MN: Fortress.

Braund, S. Morton (1997) 'Personal Plurals', in Hallett and Van Nortwick (eds) *Compromising Traditions*, 38–53.

Brett, M. G. (1996a) 'The Ethics of Postcolonial Criticism', in Donaldson (ed.) *Postcolonialism and Scriptural Reading*, 219–28.

—— (ed.) (1996b) *Ethnicity and the Bible*, Biblical Interpretation Series, 19, Leiden: Brill.

Caws, M. A. (1990) *Women of Bloomsbury. Virginia, Vanessa, and Carrington*, London and New York: Routledge.

Croatto, J. S. (1995) *Biblical Hermeneutics. Toward a Theory of Reading as the Production of Meaning*, Maryknoll, NY: Orbis Books (3rd edn).

Culpepper, R. A. and Segovia, F. F. (eds) (1991) *The Fourth Gospel from a Literary Perspective*, *Semeia* 53, Atlanta, GA: Scholars.

Donaldson, L. E. (ed.) (1996) *Postcolonialism and Scriptural Reading*, *Semeia* 75, Atlanta, GA: Scholars.

Dube, M. W. (1996) 'Reading for Decolonization (John 4:1–42)', in Donaldson (ed.) *Postcolonialism and Scriptural Reading*, 37–59.

Easthope, A. (1991) *Literary into Cultural Studies*, London and New York: Routledge.

Fewell, D. Nolan and Phillips G. A. (eds) (1998, forthcoming) *Ethics, Bible, Reading as If*, *Semeia* 77, Atlanta, GA: Scholars.

Fowler, R. M. (1991) *Let the Reader Understand: Reader-Response Criticism and the Gospel of Mark*, SBL Dissertation Series, 54, Chico, CA: Scholars.

—— (1995) 'Taking It Personally: A Personal Response', in Anderson and Staley (eds) *Taking It Personally*, 231–8.

Hallett, J. P. and Van Nortwick, Th. (eds) (1997) *Compromising Traditions. The Personal Voice in Classical Scholarship*, London and New York: Routledge.

—— (1997a) 'Introduction', in Hallett and Van Nortwick (eds) *Compromising Traditions*, 1–15.

Iser, W. (1980) 'The Reading Process: A Phenomenological Approach', in Tompkins (ed.) *Reader-Response Criticism*, 50–69.

—— (1990) *Der Akt des Lesens. Theorie ästhetischer Wirkung*, UTB, 636, München: Wilhelm Fink (3rd edn).

Jouve, N. Ward (1991) *White Woman Speaks with Forked Tongue. Criticism as Autobiography*, London and New York: Routledge.

Kitzberger, I. R. (1994) 'Love and Footwashing: John 13:1–20 and Luke 7:36–50 Read Intertextually', *Biblical Interpretation* 2: 190–206.

Kitzberger, I. R. (1994a) '"Wasser und Bäume des Lebens" – eine feministisch-intertextuelle Interpretation von Apk 21/22', in H.-J. Klauck (ed.) *Weltgericht und Weltvollendung. Zukunftsbilder im Neuen Testament*, Quaestiones Disputatae, 150, Freiburg i.Br.: Herder, 206–24.

—— (1995) 'Mary of Bethany and Mary of Magdala – Two Female Characters in the Johannine Passion Narrative. A Feminist, Narrative-Critical Reader Response', *NTS* 41: 546–86.

—— (1997) '"The Truth Will Make You Free" (John 8:32). The Power of the Personal Voice and Readings of/from the Gospel of John'. Paper presented at the Research Consultation on 'Ideology, Power, and Interpretation' at Selly Oak Colleges/Westhill College, University of Birmingham, 3 August 1997.

—— (1998, forthcoming) '"How Can This Be?" (John 3:9). A Feminist-Theological Re-reading of the Gospel of John', in Segovia (ed.) *Reading John.*

Long, T. (1996) 'A Real Reader Reading Revelation', in West and Dube (eds) *'Reading With'*, 79–107.

McKnight, E. V. (1985) *The Bible and the Reader. An Introduction to Literary Criticism*, Philadelphia, PA: Fortress.

—— (1988) *Postmodern Use of the Bible: The Emergence of Reader-Oriented Criticism*, Nashville, TN: Abingdon.

Miller, N. K. (1991) *Getting Personal: Feminist Occasions and Other Autobiographical Acts*, London and New York: Routledge.

Moore, S. D. (1989) *Literary Criticism and the Gospels: The Theoretical Challenge*, New Haven and London: Yale University Press.

—— (1995) 'True Confessions and Weird Obsessions: Autobiographical Interventions in Literary and Biblical Studies', in Anderson and Staley (eds) *Taking It Personally*, 19–50.

O'Brien, J. (1995) 'On Saying "No" to a Prophet', in Anderson and Staley (eds) *Taking It Personally*, 111–24.

Patte, D. (1995) *Ethics of Biblical Interpretation. A Reevaluation*, Louisville, KY: Westminster John Knox.

—— (1996) *Discipleship According to the Sermon on the Mount. Four Legitimate Readings, Four Plausible Views, and Their Relative Values*, Valley Forge, PA: Trinity International.

—— (1998, forthcoming) 'When Ethical Questions Transform Critical Biblical Studies', in Fewell and Phillips (eds) *Ethics, Bible, Reading as If.*

Plett, E. (ed.) (1991) *Intertextuality*, Research in Text Theory, 15, Berlin and New York: Walter de Gruyter.

The Postmodern Bible (1995) The Bible and Culture Collective, New Haven and London: Yale University Press.

Prior, M. (1997) *The Bible and Colonialism. A Moral Critique*, The Biblical Seminar, 48, Sheffield: Sheffield Academic.

Schüssler Fiorenza, E. (1988) 'The Ethics of Interpretation: Decentering Biblical Scholarship', *JBL* 107: 3–17.

Segovia, F. F. (1995a) '"And They Began to Speak in Other Tongues": Competing Modes of Discourse in Biblical Criticism', in Segovia and Tolbert (eds) *Reading from This Place. Vol. 1*, 1–32.

—— (1995b) 'Cultural Studies and Contemporary Biblical Criticism: Ideological Criticism as a Mode of Discourse', in Segovia and Tolbert (eds) *Reading from This Place, Vol. 2*, 1–17.

—— (ed.) (1996) *'What is John?' Readers and Readings of the Fourth Gospel*, SBL Symposium Series, 3, Atlanta, GA: Scholars.

—— (ed.) (1998, forthcoming) *Reading John. More Interpretations than the World Could Hold*, SBL Symposium Series, 4, Atlanta, GA: Scholars.

Segovia, F. F. and Tolbert, M. A. (eds) (1995a) *Reading from This Place. Volume 1: Social Location and Biblical Interpretation in the United States*, Minneapolis, MN: Fortress.

—— (eds) (1995b) *Reading from This Place. Volume 2: Social Location and Biblical Interpretation in Global Perspective*, Minneapolis, MN: Fortress.

Smith-Christopher, D. (1995) *Text and Experience. Towards a Cultural Exegesis of the Bible*, Sheffield: Sheffield Academic.

Spivak, G. Ch. (1990) *The Post-Colonial Critic. Interviews, Strategies, Dialogues*, ed. S. Harasym, London and New York: Routledge.

Staley, J. L. (1988) *The Print's First Kiss: A Rhetorical Investigation of the Implied Reader in the Fourth Gospel*, SBL Dissertation Series, 82, Atlanta, GA: Scholars.

—— (1995) *Reading with a Passion. Rhetoric, Autobiography, and the American West in the Gospel of John*, New York: Continuum.

—— (1996) 'Reading Myself, Reading the Text: The Johannine Passion Narrative in Postmodern Perspective', in Segovia (ed.) *'What is John?'*, 59–104.

Sugirtharajah, R. S. (ed.) (1991) *Voices from the Margin. Interpreting the Bible in the Third World*, London: SPCK.

Tompkins, J. P. (ed.) (1980) *Reader-Response Criticism: From Formalism to Post-Structuralism*, Baltimore, MD: Johns Hopkins University Press.

Veeser, H. A. (ed.) (1996) *Confessions of the Critics*, London and New York: Routledge.

Voelz, J. W. (1995) 'Multiple Signs, Aspects of Meaning, and Self as Text: Elements of Intertextuality', in Aichele and Phillips (eds) *Intertextuality and the Bible*, 149–64.

West, G. and Dube, M. W. (1996) *'Reading With': An Exploration of the Interface Between Critical and Ordinary Readings of the Bible. African Overtures*, Semeia 73, Atlanta, GA: Scholars.

Wiltshire, S. Ford (1997) 'The Authority of Experience', in Hallett and Van Nortwick (eds) *Compromising Traditions*, 168–81.

Woolf, V. (1945) *A Room of One's Own*, Harmondsworth: Penguin Books (first publ. 1928).

1

THE GUARDED PERSONAL VOICE OF A MALE EUROPEAN-AMERICAN BIBLICAL SCHOLAR

Daniel Patte

> 'Who am I? They mock me these lonely
> questions of mine. Whoever I am,
> Thou knowest, o God, I am Thine.'

Dietrich Bonhoeffer's poem, 'Who Am I?' (*Letters and Papers from Prison*, 347–8), underscores three essential characteristics of personal voices that are most significant for me as a male European-American biblical scholar.

The opening line of the first three quatrains – 'Who am I? They often tell me . . .' – expresses that a personal voice is always *a construct that took shape with the help of others*, and not some 'natural thing' that would exist in and of itself, even though it is very personal, 'what I know of myself'.

The second and third parts of the poem – which begin respectively with the questions 'Am I then really all that which others tell of?' and 'Who am I? This or the other?' – underscore the polyvalence of our personal voice and the necessary distrust we must have towards any formulation of it. Since any formulation of my personal voice is a construct shaped by an Other with whom I am in conversation, even if this Other is my self (as in the case of a soliloquy), in each case its relative trustworthiness and value must be carefully assessed. Which one of my personal voices should I call mine? Indeed, can I truly claim that any of them is 'my' personal voice?

In his concluding statement, 'Who am I? They mock me these lonely questions of mine. Whoever I am, Thou knowest, o God, I am Thine', Bonhoeffer stesses that, even though he cannot say with any certainty who he *is*, he can claim without any hesitation that he is known by God and that he belongs to God: 'O God, I am Thine.' Similarly, even though I cannot have any certainty regarding what characterizes my personal voice as I interpret biblical texts, I can speak of my interrelation with these texts. I can speak of those aspects of my experience I bring to them and of the ways these texts affect me in the concreteness of my life. I can say how 'I' who reads the text is read by the text. My personal voice is truly heard in interpretations of the Bible that are transformative encounters with an Other who transcends me, that is, in *pro me* (or *pro nobis*) biblical interpretations which reflect experiences of a mysterious Otherness that I cannot control and encompass in my interpretations. The encounter of this mysterious Otherness through the biblical text so deeply affects 'my' life, however I might have construed it, that it is no longer mine alone: 'Whoever I am, Thou knowest, o God, I am Thine.'

'Who am I?' What is my personal voice?

The question is no longer: Do personal voices play a role in critical interpretations of New Testament texts? Some (calling on Bultmann) denounce personal voices as preunderstandings and presuppositions to be overcome. Others (including feminist and other advocacy scholars) applaud them as manifestations of valuable interests and concerns. Yet, all biblical scholars agree that any interpretation is marked by the interpreter's personal voice, whether it is kept implicit, or made explicit, suppressed or affirmed. The question is: What is my personal voice? How can I identify it and its role in my interpretations? 'Who am I?'

My personal voice contributes to shape my interpretations of biblical texts, including my critical studies of them. Yet, my personal voice is also deeply shaped by the Bible, by my interpretations of it, and by the interpretive practices through which I approach these texts. My personal voice has been shaped by my ever-evolving practice of critical biblical studies. As a male European-American[1] biblical scholar I have been trained to mute my personal voice. This critical practice has marked my personal voice with the sign 'suspect', which clings to it even when I have learned from feminist and other advocacy scholars that I should not be ashamed of it and should make it explicit (Patte 1995). Thus, I cannot help being somewhat suspicious of my personal voice and/or of its role in my interpretations. Is not 'my' personal voice always a construct? Furthermore, isn't this construct often proposed to me by others? Can I trust them, even when I do recognize my face in the mirror they hold before me?

'Am I then really all that which others tell of? Or am I only what I know of myself?'

I must confess nostalgia for the personal voice I was trained to silence in my work as a critical biblical scholar. Shouldn't I seek to retrieve the personal voice I was asked to deny in my interpretation during my traumatic first encounter with critical biblical studies?

In 1958, most of my fellow students and I were bewildered by our apprenticeship in critical biblical studies at the Protestant Institute

(Montpellier, France). We were entering a programme supposed to prepare us for a ministry of the Word and sacraments. But, ironically, it demanded that we ignore and reject as sentimental, emotional, naive and childish the very *pro me* and *pro nobis* interpretations of the Bible that had convinced us to pursue theological studies, with, of course, a major focus on biblical studies. In my case, critical biblical studies demanded that I disregard the transforming religious power of the biblical text upon me, upon others and upon society! I was demanded to ignore how deeply this text affected me by offering to me the daily bread of its teachings-for-us-today (*pro nobis*) that I discovered in private and collective meditations of the Bible as well as in sermons. As an evangelical descendant of Huguenots, these powerful biblical teachings defined my identity as a member of my family and of my small Protestant community. But, they also defined my/our vocation in a secular society which in post-World War II was, at least in Europe, more than ever a society 'harassed and helpless, like sheep without a shepherd'. Reading the Bible in terms of secular contemporary issues (including those raised by the last French colonial wars and by writers such as Sartre, Camus and Malraux whom we read avidly and discussed passionately in the Federation of Christian Students) would allow us to discern the message of hope needed in our society at that time. How could I deny the legitimacy of my interpretations of the Bible developed in terms of these interests, concerns, and commitments? Should I not retrieve this personal voice of mine?

Despite my initial resistance, I was taught to make an essential distinction between critical exegesis and hermeneutics and convinced to engage in critical biblical studies. My interests, concerns and commitments raise the hermeneutical question of what the biblical texts *mean for us today*. As such they are legitimate, and can be critically explored and addressed in homiletics, pastoral theology, and systematic theology. Yet these hermeneutical critical studies should not be confused with critical biblical studies, which seek to address the prior question of 'what the biblical texts *meant*'. Thus, I was taught that disregarding my personal voice was only temporary; it is a part of the critical stance necessary for the descriptive exegetical task which prepares the hermeneutical task.

These views became mine. Even as I progressively moved away from historical criticism to develop the use of literary, semiotic, and structural methodologies, critical biblical studies remained for me a *descriptive* task (involving a description of the narrative, discursive/rhetorical, and/or mythical characteristics of the text) in preparation for hermeneutical appropriations. The latter were always my ultimate concern (see Patte 1965). However, these hermeneutical concerns were beyond the purview of critical biblical studies, in which I muted (but not quite silenced) my initial personal voice in order to be as 'critical' and 'objective' as possible. In this way I was to prepare the ground for an eventual appropriation of the biblical teachings for today that would be as legitimate and as relevant as possible.

Now I am convinced that hermeneutics and critical biblical studies are closely intertwined and that acknowledging my personal voice is a necessary part of the critical task. This is due to a paradigm shift brought about by advocacy critical interpreters (feminist, African-American, and Two-Thirds World scholars) and theoretical research (in hermeneutic, semiotics, poststructuralism and deconstructionism). From this new perspective, the distinction between objective exegesis and subjective hermeneutic is not only unwarranted and inappropriate but also ethically problematic (Patte 1995). It is now clear that I must allow my personal voice to play its positive and constructive role in my critical interpretations. Yet, my personal voice can no longer be the voice of my youth. Despite all my nostalgia, I cannot experience again the marvel of reading these texts for the first time. So, the question of the identity of my individual voice becomes even more confusing.

'They mock me these lonely questions of mine.' The guarded personal voice of a male European-American biblical scholar

Who am I? What is my personal voice? I know that I should acknowledge and affirm the role it plays in my interpretations of the Bible. Feminists as well as African, Asian, South American and North American advocacy readers of the Bible have convinced me that I should do so. And I try.

Ironically, just when I am convinced that acknowledging my personal voice is an integral part of my critical exegetical task, I find impossible to identify it with any certainty in my interpretations of the Bible. What is my personal voice in my interpretations if it is no longer the voice I was trained to denounce as the inappropriate intrusion of a subjective dimension in my exegetical description of the text? Is it my voice as a critical biblical scholar? After all, my trained voice is mine, isn't it? The face that I self-consciously present on the surface of my critical interpretations is my face. Why would it be a mask? Am I not this person who endeavoured to make sure that each comment be grounded on textual and contextual evidence through the use of appropriate critical methods?

Who am I? Distrust, suspicion are in order. The clearest characteristic of my personal voice appears to be its deep suspicion *vis-à-vis* personal voices in interpretations! Yes, I am convinced that I should stop silencing my personal voice. I strive to make it explicit. But the only personal voice I can utter is a cautious, guarded voice.

Is it, perhaps, because I am not used to expressing it? After so many years of impersonal interpretive discourses, it is hard to free myself from old habits. Am I so deeply shaped by my critical training that I cannot help but

15

be suspicious of uninhibited appeal to personal interests and concerns in readings of the Bible? At first, this seems to be an appropriate explanation of my reluctance to be fully autobiographical. As Stephen Moore noted, my attitude appears to be self-contradictory (Moore 1996). Even as I affirm that ethical accountability demands that I make explicit the personal, contextual character of my interpretations (Patte 1995, 1996), I remain cautious regarding the role of personal voices in interpretations, including my own. The voice that I do make explicit is cautious, self-conscious, hesitating. And so it is. Yet is it a self-contradicting practice?

Reflecting more specifically on the role of my personal voice in my biblical interpretations, thanks to the timely prompting of Dr Kitzberger, helped me recognize that it is not self-contradictory for me to make explicit my personal voice in a cautious, guarded manner. I have to be cautious in uttering my personal voice for the simple reason that it is unstable, fleeting. In each instance it is at least ambivalent, if not polyvalent. It has indeed been moulded by my initial interests and concerns as a young reader of the Bible. Yet, by now my personal voice has also been moulded by a quarter of a century of involvement in critical biblical studies envisioned as an exegetical descriptive task. I can disavow neither one nor the other, even though I believe my personal voice is, at the moment, also something else. But, how can the three be at the same time my personal voice? With Bonhoeffer, I have to wonder: 'Am I one person today, and tomorrow another? Am I both at once?' If so, how can I trust my personal voice?

More concretely, on the one hand I welcome postmodernism as a required critical response to the present multicultural, global world (see The Bible and Culture Collective 1995). Yet 'I' am and remain a male Protestant scholar with primary responsibilities toward readers of the Bible in the European-American context, and especially in Protestant churches.[2] As such, I cannot but share their suspicions *vis-à-vis* subjective readings and eisegeses. Reading into the text myself or reading what I want to hear too often ends up denying the Bible as Scriptures, because such interpretations are either trivial or dangerous; for example, don't people read their anti-Semitic, racist, sexist, or colonialist views in the Bible?

In part, my cautious personal voice reflects common concerns among European-Americans who are disorientated by the advent of postmodernism and multiculturalism. Even as I embrace postmodernism, my identity and voice remains marked by modernism, at least through the issues it raises for me. I cannot turn a deaf ear to my colleagues who vehemently object to any manifestation of postmodernism and its affirmation of personal voices in interpretations. From my perspective, their protestations against subjective readings and eisegeses cannot be ignored; to a large extent they are quite appropriate. While I remain convinced that my interpretations of biblical texts must make explicit their personal character in order to be both critical and ethically responsible, I am also convinced that my personal voice interpretations should be neither subjective readings nor eisegeses. Furthermore, I am convinced that acknowledging a plurality of personal voice interpretations of each given text should in no way undermine the authority of the Bible as Scriptures.

In a brief article, Elizabeth Achtemeier, a specialist of 'Bible and homiletics' in a Presbyterian seminary, conveniently summarizes these issues as she challenges a decision of what she calls 'a post-modernist assembly' of the Presbyterian Church (USA). Her personal voice can be heard clearly when she complains that according to postmodernists:

> There is now no objective truth out there beyond us. Rather, truth is entirely subjective and entirely relative to the individual. Whatever the individual thinks is true, is true. Whatever the individual thinks is false, is false . . . there is no objective standard of right and wrong . . . In such a view, the Bible too conveys no objective truth and no objective standards of right and wrong. The Bible means only what the reader brings to it.

I do hear echo of my personal voice in Achtemeier's. I too find wholly inappropriate interpretations that are 'subjective' and thus 'entirely relative to the individual'. While such interpretations might be fun – in the sense of very creative – their idiosyncratic character would make their conclusions regarding the teaching of a biblical text totally irrelevant for me. More important, such subjective interpretations can only be artificial, affected, fake, because a truly subjective, individual interpretation does not exist. No personal voice is truly individual. In a first person interpretation, consciously or not, I necessarily bring with me those who shaped my voice – all a community of interpreters. A personal voice is always a collective construct, as Bonhoeffer suggests by underscoring that our perception of who we are is always constructed on the basis of what other people tell about us. Thus, with Achtemeier, I readily denounce subjective interpretations. They can only be fanciful and frivolous. Whatever teaching I find as a result of 'my' interpretation of a text should not – and cannot – be grounded in my self; the truth of this teaching is grounded 'out there beyond' me as an individual.

Consequently, with Achtemeier, I have to insist that biblical interpretation cannot be a free for all in which anything goes. With her, I have to reject as fake those 'readings' that consist in finding in the text what one already thinks or knows. Yes, a grade F (or zero) is appropriate for those interpretations that some of my undergraduate students dare to propose without having read the biblical text. Similarly, I cannot accept that through such fake readings individuals pretend to establish each on their own what is 'right and wrong' and in the process, as Achtemeier says, pretend to be God-like, as the serpent suggested in Genesis 3. Thus, my appeal to my personal voice has to be guarded. I do not want to be trapped in the illusory world of subjective or fake interpretations.

On the other hand, my rejection of subjective readings and of eisegeses as fake interpretations is not a denial of the positive role personal voices play in interpretations, as it is for Achtemeier. Unlike her, I do not reject subjectivism and eisegesis in order to affirm 'that there is in fact objective truth and an objective standard of right and wrong given us through the Scriptures'. For me, her implicit claim that there is only one, universally true interpretation of a biblical text is a misguided response to actual problems, and she ends up denying the very authority of the Bible as Scriptures that she seeks to protect.

Claiming that there is only one true interpretation that I strive to uncover would amount to pretend that I am God-like. I would make an idol out of my interpretations by denying what is clearly visible (cf. Rom. 1:20ff.), namely, that I use my personal voice in each of them and that they have limitations brought about by my shaky, tentative personal perspective. Denying that there is a plurality of legitimate interpretations of any biblical text, as Achtemeier does, leads to a conception of a text as a dead letter, rather than as a living Word. To deny that as readers we need to bring to the Bible our life experience is to renounce the ability to approach it as Scriptures, in order to discover how a given biblical text addresses, confronts and transforms our perception of our specific experience and becomes Word of God for us – *pro nobis*. Wrestling with this Word in order to be blessed by it (as Jacob was at Jabbok following his wrestling match); acknowledging its mysterious (holy) character that we can never encompass and control; finding it 'awful'; rejecting its teaching in the name of higher convictions (as the Canaanite woman did with Jesus); re-reading this text; bringing to it a different experience; hearing a different Word of God from it, and so on. This is the ongoing process of reading the Bible as Christian Scriptures that nourish us as believers, warm our hearts, move us, open up new vistas before us, comfort us, put demands upon us, chasten us, put the fear of God in us and anger us. Isn't it appropriate for critical biblical studies to account for this great diversity of effects of the text as living Word upon diverse believers, as W. C. Smith urges us to do? And upon me as an interpreter? How do the texts have all these effects? Why did I choose one interpretation over another? Or, did I have any choice in the matter?

Then we have come full circle. Having a plurality of personal voices, and thus being unable to identify what is my personal voice (singular!), is most appropriate when dealing with critical interpretations of the Bible as Scriptures whose teaching is a living Word. So, whenever I express my personal voice (singular), I have to do so in a guarded way – indeed, tongue in cheek! I have to expect that as I re-read the text, my personal voice will change because I will bring a different (part of my) experience to the Scriptures.

'Who am I? Whoever I am . . .'

As I ponder these mocking questions of mine, it becomes clear that long before I became involved in critical biblical studies I did not trust my personal voice. And I had good reasons to be suspicious.

After all, I remain someone formed by my participation in a family and a church with Huguenot roots in an European society during and after World War II. Someone who, as a child in occupied France, learned to call strangers who stayed in our home for a few days 'Aunt', 'Uncle', or 'cousin'. Someone who later discovered that these were Jewish refugees on their way to the hoped-for safety of Switzerland. I am someone who was taught through biblical studies that treating Jewish people as family members, even if this meant putting at risk one's direct family, was not merely an expedient to avoid accidental betrayal by us children; it is an appropriate attitude for Christians towards members of the Chosen People who, as our elder brothers and sisters, needed to be treated as kin in a situation of need.[3] I am someone who also learned from family and church that the Bible teaches us to respond in similar ways to the plight of those who suffer from any kind of injustice and need. Bringing to the biblical texts the plight of other people by voicing my concerns for them is certainly appropriate. Should I not want to give a central role to my personal voice so as to make sure that my interpretations be driven by the commendable concerns and interests that it utters?

Yet, I am reluctant to do so, even in a book, *Ethics of Biblical Interpretation* (Patte 1995), which deliberately underscores that we need to assume responsibility and ownership for our interpretations. Moore is puzzled. He should not be. In this book I underscore that the moral dilemma we have to address as biblical scholars is rooted in a false self-consciousness, akin to Sartre's concept of 'bad faith'. Yes, I am someone who, because of my upbringing, has deep respect for Jewish people and for Judaism and has true concerns whenever I recognize anti-Semitism in any form. If it were necessary and useful, I could make a foolish list (cf. 2 Cor. 11–12) of concrete actions that demonstrate the sincerity of these claims. But, I do not trust this righteous voice of mine because I hear another voice, an ugly one which, I have to confess, is also mine.

As a child and young adult I was taught never to trust my personal voice and the views and concerns it utters, even when they seem most praise-worthy. For me this is a basic interpretive principle impressed upon me through biblical studies in my family and church. Why should I not trust my voice? Because in the same breath that expresses my commitment to respect Judaism, to honour Jews as elder brothers and sisters and to reject anything in which I perceive traces of anti-Semitism, I must confess that anti-Semitism 'dwells within me', as Paul said about sin. Is this an artificial confession of sin? Unfortunately, not. I must acknowledge and confess that again and again I need to be freed from the anti-Semitism (and by extension from all kinds of racism and of oppressive attitudes) that 'dwells within me' so much so that 'I do not do the good I want, but the evil I do not want is what I do' (Rom. 7:17, 19). Insidiously, my personal voice ('I') misleads me into thinking that it has value in and of itself and that it can help me discern between good and evil. It deceives me by calling me to be faithful to good and worthy commitments (for example, towards my nuclear family, towards the church, or even towards my study and teaching of the Bible), even though this faithfulness might demand that I ignore the plight of others and indirectly or directly to contribute to their oppression. This is the dreadful banality of evil (see Arendt) that ultimately engendered the Holocaust, genocides of all kinds, slavery, colonialist and imperialist oppression, sexism, patriarchalism, as well as all kinds of oppressive and/or self-destructive behaviour. Consequently, 'sorrow and pity'[4] are the only feelings I can have for the victims of oppression, without even recognizing that 'sorrow and pity' (if not anger) are the feelings that the victims themselves have when they look at me who cannot even imagine that I contribute to their oppression. The best-intentioned personal voice interpretation of the Christian Bible has become a devouring monster of oppression and of destruction, which we again and again turn loose against Jews and many other people.

Then, should I make explicit my personal voice in my biblical inter-pretations in order to denounce it and to reject the interpretations it has spoiled? 'By no means!' (Rom. 7:7). My personal voice and its interpreta-tions have this vicious and destructive effect only when I lose sight of their tentative, fleeting, constructed character and when I forget that I should never trust my personal voice, especially in matters of interpretations. Partial, biased personal interpretations are not spoiled; they are the only ones which, as *pro me* or *pro nobis* interpretations, can bring the teaching of the text to bear upon our lives. Yet these interpretations 'that promised life proved to be deadly to me' (Rom. 7:10) and became deadly weapons turned against others, because I was deceived and with a darkened mind suppressed or repressed their personal character.

Thus for me the task of critical biblical studies is not to mute or to silence personal voices in interpretations, but on the contrary to elucidate, high-light and preserve the personal voice character of each of the interpretations of the Bible. This involves acknowledging the tentative, fleeting, con-structed character of my attempts to formulate not only conclusions about the teaching of a text but also conclusions about what the text is and says (apparently a more descriptive task). This involves trying to say why 'I' chose this interpretation, rather than another one of the many possible interpretations. Yet when 'I' make explicit my personal voice in an inter-pretation, 'I' must present it in a guarded, tentative way. After all, whatever 'I' might say about 'my' personal voice is always partial and biased, because, as in this sentence, consciously or not, there are always several 'I's involved. My voice, like my face according to Levinas's analysis, is always a mystery, which by nature can never be grasped, controlled, encompassed. Presenting it in a guarded, tentative way is neither shyness nor refusal to reveal it. It is respecting its mystery. Who am I? At one moment, this one; at another moment, this other one, and often, both at the same time. Therefore, when 'I' read, I can only read with my personal voice of the moment.

'Whoever I am, Thou knowest, o God, I am Thine.' Constructing my voice as a male European-American critical biblical scholar

Making explicit my personal voice involves acknowledging that my interpretations are as constructed, partial, and selective as my personal voice is tentative, changing, and fleeting. How can I recognize my personal voice for the fleeting construct which it is? Bonhoeffer explains it: by listening to the voices of others – 'They tell me'; by recognizing that the voices of others reveal me to myself, and give me a voice of mine; by acknowledging the mystery of the voices of others, which I cannot fathom; by acknowledging that I can never really know who is right about me; by suspecting that all of them might be partially right or partially wrong, although I can never fully understand which. Similarly, I have to acknowledge the mystery of the diverse interpretations that others give of these texts. Whatever might be their sophistication, all are personal voice interpretations, all are constructed, partial, selective.

One could, of course, lament: 'Who am I?' What is *the* only true interpretation? I need to know for sure. 'They mock me these questions of mine.' With Bonhoeffer, the proper response to the uncertainty of our situation is: 'Whoever I am, Thou knowest, o God, I am Thine.' The question is no longer an ontological '*who* am I?' but an ethical '*for whom* am I?' Therefore, the critical task of choosing among interpretations of a biblical text is no longer conceived of as addressing an ontological issue – 'what is *the* true teaching of this text?' – but an ethical issue. It involves keeping in mind that each interpretation is marked by a personal voice that is a construct characterized by a certain pattern of relationships with Others and elucidating this personal voice by making clear *for whom* the interpretation is performed. For this, I must ask who benefits from this interpretation (*cui bono?*) or who is hurt by it, by weighing the different positive and negative ways in which people are affected by it. In short, I can assume personal responsibility for the choice of a specific interpretation of a text.

This does not mean that the other critical tasks are neglected. On the contrary. More than ever, critical biblical studies involve acknowledging that the process of interpretation is nothing but a string of choices and making explicit the ways in which these decisions were made. The difference is that by acknowledging the constructive role of the interpreter's personal voice as a construct, one can recognize that interpreters choose among equally legitimate and plausible interpretations. As I discuss elsewhere (Patte 1996: 1-57), the critical task includes making explicit how I, as an interpreter with a certain personal voice, choose to ground my interpretation on certain significant features of the text over others (a choice between alternative kinds of legitimate textual evidence, based upon particular legitimacy judgements) and how, in order to make sense of this evidence, I choose certain epistemological categories (from alternative kinds of plausible epistemological categories on the basis of epistemological judgements). Then, in order to be truly critical, I must also answer the question 'Why did I choose this interpretation rather than another one?' by making explicit the personal voice that presided over these choices, and by assessing its relative value. '*For whom* is this personal voice?' Do I want to be associated with such a voice? Or should I construct another one for myself? Choose another interpretation?

'I', whoever I am, cannot of course perform this critical task on my own. I need to be empowered by Others who, either as ordinary or as scholarly readers, make explicit the personal voices of their readings. As such they offer to 'read *with*' me and allow me to 'read *with*' them (see West and Dube 1996). In the polyphony of our different voices, I can recognize my own voice for what it is – a construct distinguished from other voices by certain characteristics that reflect certain ethical commitments. However, for this, I must be open to hear other voices and interpretations *in their otherness* as legitimate, plausible, and valuable. Passing over the differences in order to focus on the similarities among our respective readings amounts to denying the role of our respective personal voices. Furthermore, I cannot be content to read with people who read like me because they share social, economic, class, cultural, and religious perspectives; I must read with readers whose interpretations surprise me. Then will I be in a position to assess the relative value of the personal voice I adopted in my interpretations and of the ethical commitments they reflect. At last I can recognize that I really do have a choice between interpretations and that I do not need desperately to hold on to my personal voice interpretation of the moment.

Then, as I read with feminists who, each in her own way, deliberately emphasize the distinctiveness of their readings as women in given contexts, I can become aware of the androcentrism of my own interpretations as a male. The question is then: How is my voice as a male interpreter constructed? Does my interpretation address the issues of gender construction and of authority structures or does it ignore them? What is the relative value of this interpretation? Do I want to hold on to it? Or do I want to abandon it in order to adopt one that represents an androcritical perspective which is more appropriate, for instance, because it more directly reflects a 'discipleship of equals' (Schüssler Fiorenza 1993), though from the perspective of a male reader who has 'benefited' and continues to benefit from patriarchalism? Similarly, reading with people who are from cultural, social, economic, or class contexts different from mine provides me with the possibility to acknowledge the middle-class, educated, European-American character of my interpretations, and to assess how these aspects of my personal voice are constructed in my interpretations.

As I read with others and ponder critically a wide range of personal voice interpretations, I am free to ask: Which one of these is Word of God *for me/ us* today? My critical studies of biblical texts are no longer divorced from my/our meditations of Scriptures. As I read with others, my descriptive studies of the texts are also assessments of the ways in which I/we are transformed by these texts when I/we read them. Reading the biblical texts achieves what it should according to Foucault (1986: 48, 51), 'prevent[ing] me from always being the same', that is, constantly transforming my personal voice and the concerns and interests I brought to the text. Otherwise, I would betray my commitment to the incarnated Otherness I encounter in the mysterious faces of Others who confront me in the text and in the mysterious faces of the Others who read this text with me. 'Whoever I am, Thou knowest, o God, I am Thine.'

Notes

1 The phrase 'European-American' refers both to Europeans and to North Americans of European descent and culture.
2 It is this personal voice that I must make explicit in order to be accountable to readers of the Bible in other cultural, social and/or religious contexts (see Patte 1995).
3 My Protestant Huguenot community and my family were among those who during World War II received and hid thousands of Jewish people in the Cevennes mountains (in the South East of France). See Hallie, *Lest Innocent Blood Be Shed: The Story of the Village of Le Chambon and How Goodness Happened There* (1978) and the movie/documentary *Weapons of the Spirit* by Pierre Savage. The houses of my grandparents and my parents were safe-houses of the underground from Le Chambon toward Switzerland.
4 I allude to Marcel Ophuls's motion picture *Le chagrin et la pitié*.

References

Achtemeier, E. (1997) 'A Post-Modernist Assembly', *The Presbyterian Outlook*, 179/ 26, Aug. 4–11, 1997, 7.

Anderson, J. Capel and Staley, J. L. (eds) (1996) *Taking it Personally: Autobiographical Biblical Criticism, Semeia* 72, Atlanta, GA: Scholars.

Arendt, H. (1963) *Eichmann in Jerusalem: a Report on the Banality of Evil*, New York: Viking.

The Bible and Culture Collective (1995) *The Postmodern Bible*, New Haven and London: Yale University Press.

Bonhoeffer, D. (1971) *Letters and Papers from Prison: The Enlarged Edition*, ed. E. Bethge, New York: Macmillan.

Bultmann, R. (1960) 'Is Exegesis without Presuppositions Possible?' in S. Ogden, (ed.) *Existence and Faith: Shorter Writings by Rudolf Bultmann*, Cleveland and New York: World Publishing, 289–96.

Foucault, M. (1986) *The Care of the Self*, trans. R. Hurley, New York: Random House.

Hallie, P. (1979) *Lest Innocent Blood Be Shed: The Story of the Village of Le Chambon and How Goodness Happened There*, New York: Harper.

Levinas, E. (1969) *Totality and Infinity: An Essay on Exteriority*, trans. A. Lingis, Dusquesne Studies Philosophical Series, 24, Pittsburgh, PA: Dusquesne University Press.

Moore, S. D. (1996) 'True Confessions and Weird Obsessions: Autobiographical Interventions in Literary and Biblical Studies', in Anderson and Staley (eds) *Taking it Personally*, 19–50.

Patte, D. (1965) *L'athéisme d'un chrétien ou un chrétien à l'écoute de Sartre*, Paris: Nouvelles Editions Latines.

—— (1990) *The Religious Dimensions of Biblical Texts: Greimas's Structural Semiotics and Biblical Exegesis*, SBL Semeia Studies, Atlanta, GA: Scholars.

—— (1995) *Ethics of Biblical Interpretation: A Reevaluation*, Louisville, KY: Westminster John Knox.

—— (1996) *Discipleship According to the Sermon on the Mount: Four Legitimate Readings, Four Plausible Views of Discipleship, and Their Relative Values*, Valley Forge, PA: Trinity International.

Schüssler Fiorenza, E. (1993) *Discipleship of Equals: A Critical Feminist Ekklēsia-logy of Liberation*, New York: Crossroad.

Smith, W. Cantwell (1993) *What is Scripture? A Comparative Approach*, Minneapolis, MN: Fortress.

West, G. and Dube, M. W. (eds) (1996) *'Reading With': An Exploration of the Interface Between Critical and Ordinary Readings of the Bible, African Overtures, Semeia* 73, Atlanta, GA: Scholars.

2

MY PERSONAL VOICE: THE MAKING OF A POSTCOLONIAL CRITIC

Fernando F. Segovia

From the perspective of cultural studies, that umbrella model of interpretation within which I presently situate myself both outside and within the field of biblical studies, the question of the personal voice – the voice and role of the critic behind criticism, the historian behind historiography, the scholar behind scholarship – lies at the very heart of the critical enterprise. Thus, Fred Inglis, one of its major exponents and proponents, describes cultural studies as creative or imaginative thought with a focus on human values (Inglis 1993: 3–24, 227–48). To understand the centrality assigned to the personal voice within such a framework, one would do well to recall the origins, aims, and methods of cultural studies, and for this I draw on the fine work of Inglis himself. This review will serve, in turn, as the basis for my own reflections on the personal voice in biblical studies.

To begin with, cultural studies emerged as the result of a generational revolt – at the height of the Cold War and with the student demonstrations of 1968 as a symbolic point of departure – against the established beliefs and practices of the human sciences.[1] This was a reaction driven, *inter alia*, by a new generation's consciousness of a profoundly pluralistic world, concern for the entire spectrum and messiness of everyday life, commitment to all those human actors excluded from consideration, and a penchant for uncertainty in the face of metanarratives or grand theories. As such, cultural studies set out to restore a balance between spontaneity and seriousness to all the human sciences, with an emphasis on vitality and solidarity, bringing theory face to face with the actuality of experience and assuming responsibility for others as well as for oneself.

To do so, cultural studies would insist on such governing principles as honouring the plurality of perspectives, relishing the varieties of intellectual experience, and acknowledging the location and uncertainty of knowledge. They would insist as well on the interested character of all knowledge: on the one hand, because 'knowledge' itself was regarded as the product of the human interest that had made it so; on the other hand, because 'human interest' was regarded as broken and refracted by nature, given its emergence in different human groups (classes; nations; races; genders). Consequently, in the absence of a truly external stance or truly supernal view, cultural studies would turn such variables of knowledge into an object of study and proceed to study them from the inside.

For Inglis, in the end, cultural studies represent the critical study of human values. It is a study that takes into account the enormous diversity and refraction of such values, that looks upon such values as a mixture of fact (the way the world is) and commitment (the way human subjects see the world), and seeks to do good in so doing, as reflected in its own values as an academic subject. In their concern for diversity and pluralism, for the quotidian and the plebeian, for the excluded and the marginalized, and, above all, for the location and interested character of all knowledge, a fundamental concern for the personal voice is evident as well.

This concern comes across most tellingly perhaps in Inglis's own pre-ference for narrative in general and biography in particular as a way of doing cultural studies. Thus, he argues, one should always look for historical narrative wherever possible and should let such stories intertwine as theories, framing actions and making them intelligible. Further, he continues, there is no story more ready or more useful than a life-history that throws light on a historical moment and reveals its basic parameters on the historical map. For Inglis, therefore, biography and autobiography bring about an ideal combination of observer and observed, subject and object, the way of the world and the way of seeing the world, in so far as the human subject is thereby thrust as an actor into the world and the world is read in and through the life of this human actor.

In this study I should like to pursue the question of the personal voice in biblical studies, and, as a subscriber to cultural studies, I should like to do so by inserting myself, in autobiographical fashion, into the world of biblical studies. I shall weave a story about that world in terms of my own life and experience as a critic within it, tracing both the emergence of the personal voice as such in the recent history of the discipline and the emergence of my own personal voice as a postcolonial critic in that world. A preliminary comment is in order, however, with regard to this self-description of myself as a 'postcolonial critic'. A postcolonial critic such as I am is both born and made. In other words, the adoption of a postcolonial optic is not a given, even if the individual in question happens to be a child of imperialism and colonialism or of neocolonialism and postcolonialism, as I am, and in multi-layered fashion. It is an optic that requires a choice, and hence a process of conscientization and construction as well. In the story that follows I proceed to recount the emergence of such a voice and the decision for such an option by way of a personal journey in and with the discipline, a journey involving three major stages.

Historical criticism: Suppression of the personal voice

Personal anecdote

At the beginning of my academic and professional career in the late 1970s, I submitted an article for publication to one of the major journals of the discipline. At some point in this article, I wrote something to the effect that I discerned or perceived – I no longer recall the actual formulation – a particular structure in the passage under consideration. The article, which was accepted for publication, was returned with a request for a few minor changes, as suggested by the editorial readers. One of these changes, however, was phrased in a very different tone altogether, best described perhaps as a mixture of unbelief and exasperation. The reviewer thundered: The structure of a passage lies in the passage itself, not in the eyes of the exegete, and care should be taken to make sure that the language employed reflects such a critical given. This change I incorporated willingly and without hesitation, although the tone of the comment continued to strike me as most peculiar for years to come.

Little did I know at the time of the momentous implications and ramifications involved in such a directive. Indeed, it is only with the benefit of twenty years of critical hindsight that I am able to see such a seemingly minor disciplinary transaction as a significant cultural text in its own right. At the end of the 1970s, precisely as my own study was under evaluation, the discipline found itself in an incipient state of ferment and on the verge of fundamental change. The first voices of protest against the hegemony of historical criticism – the much-beloved scientific method that had held sway in academic circles since the early nineteenth century until the third quarter of the twentieth – had already been raised, with accompanying calls for reform along two divergent paths: re-direction, by way of literary criticism; and re-casting, by way of cultural criticism (Segovia 1995a: 1–32; 1995c: 1–17).

Now, it would make for a wonderful story were I to lay claim to the heroic mantle of the *avant-garde* visionary at that time, striking quixotically at the ever-spinning wheels of tradition. The truth of the matter, however, is much more prosaic. The study in question happened to be a quite traditional piece, deeply steeped in historical criticism. After all, that is how I, like so many others before me, had been trained, not only thoroughly ignorant of the broader tradition of criticism in the academy, its manifold movements and developments, but also quite oblivious to ongoing and profound changes within the field of historiography itself.

The last thing on my mind would have been to argue that structure should not be seen as residing in the text itself, for readers to uncover and expose, but rather in the interchange between text and reader, or that structure should not be approached as fixed and stable but rather as variable and dependent on readers. My ready compliance with the change requested in no way represented, therefore, a strategic move on my part with publication in mind but actually an honest attempt to sharpen the language as requested, so that it did come to reflect as accurately as possible this view of structure as inherent in the text – determinate and determining. That had been, after all, my intent all along; yet, there was something about the militant tone of the comment that bothered me.

Not that I think, even for a moment, that my reviewer was aware of the profound critical issues involved – not in that journal and not at that time. Rather, I tend to see his comment as a gut reaction on his part – I use the masculine advisedly, for there were no female associate editors at the time. It was but the perceived appearance or hint of a subjective dimension in interpretation, in the exercise of biblical exegesis, that had caused his academic persona to go into convulsion and provoked such a heartfelt eruption. This was no encounter, therefore, between the old and the new, no battle between the traditional and the *dernier cri* – not at the surface anyway. Yet, in retrospect, the episode can be seen as profoundly symptomatic of things to come, already well under way at the time.

To understand the power of the reaction, it is necessary to recall the world and ideology of traditional historical criticism. Within the framework of such criticism, to raise the issue of the personal voice in interpretation was to commit *the* unthinkable and unforgivable sin. It was the very point of historical criticism to submerge, to bypass, to transcend the personal, the subjective, the contextual – to engage in exegesis, not eisegesis, as it was incessantly recited. [2] In its struggle against the dark forces of tradition and dogmatism, subjectivism and emotionalism, historical criticism purportedly brought the modern light of reason and science to bear on the study of ancient texts and antiquity itself. This was a light at once highly rewarding and highly demanding.

It was a light firmly grounded in positivism: both the meaning of the ancient text and the path of history were regarded as objective and univocal. As such, it was a light that called for a scientific approach in the study of such realities: textual meaning and historical development were retrievable, to the extent made possible by the sources, through the proper exercise of the right methodological tools. Such a light further required a universal and informed type of reader; a reader who aimed at objectivity and impartiality in interpretation through the rigorous and patient acquisition of the scientific method under the trained and watchful eyes of a master scholar.

A first and sacred goal of historical criticism was, therefore, the divestiture – through a combination of self-conscious exposé and methodological expertise – of all presuppositions and preconceptions, mostly framed in theological terms but also extending in principle to all matters sociocultural or ideological. The purpose behind such de-contextualization was to lay open, for the first time in the history of interpretation, as it was claimed, the meaning of the ancient texts and the course of ancient history 'in their own terms'. Only then could such meaning and history serve as proper point of departure for any type of hermeneutical translation, reflection or application.

Nowhere is this agenda of historical criticism more evident than in an article that proved quite influential, certainly in US circles, for many years after its appearance. I am referring to the long entry on Biblical Theology authored by Krister Stendahl in the early 1960s for *The Interpreter's Dictionary of the Bible* (Stendahl 1962: 1.418–32). The classic programme of historical criticism at its very best was to be found here.

Biblical Theology, Stendahl argued, encompasses three distinct movements: at one end, the 'descriptive' task focused on the historical meaning of the biblical text – 'what it meant'; at the other end, the 'theological' task centred on the contemporary meaning of the biblical text – 'what it means'; in the middle, the task of 'translation', which presupposes extensive as well as intensive competence in the field of hermeneutics. The task of description, the realm of historical criticism, was sharply defined: the original meaning of the text – what the words meant when uttered or written – was to be spelled out 'with the highest degree of perception' in its *own terms*, with the material itself providing the means to check whether or not the interpretation was correct.[3] In retrospect, the enormous self-confidence of the whole enterprise proves as astounding as its blessed innocence.

Within such a framework, one can readily understand how any consideration of the personal voice, any possibility of admission of its role and influence in interpretation, was looked upon as an unpardonable transgression of the ultimate epistemic taboo – a reading of the past in terms of the present. I would contend that it was precisely from such a context and such a world that the gut reaction of that reviewer of mine emanated. He perceived in my choice of expression, though quite unintended, an unacceptable hint of subjectivism and proceeded to rebuke me accordingly. Little did we both know at the time how things would change in the years to come.

Cultural studies: irruption of the personal voice

Personal anecdote

In the mid-1990s, I had a chance encounter, at one or another of the annual meetings of the profession, with a colleague from the

United States, approximately my age, with whom I share an area of specialization and whom I have known for a number of years. We had both been trained in the 1970s and had witnessed the development of our respective academic careers through the 1980s. In the course of our exchange, as we touched casually upon our recent work in our mutual field of interest, this individual suddenly began to chide me for abandoning the path of historical criticism, engaging in a quite unfair critique of its foundations and goals, and turning to other approaches that were patently political in character. Growing increasingly agitated, he brought this unexpected tirade to an end by proclaiming *ex cathedra* that historical criticism, as a scientific method, possessed no ideology. When I retorted, quite ironically I confess, what a blessing it must be to have surmounted all values and agendas, the exchange, such as it was, came to a rather abrupt silence, finally interrupted only by the departure of my interlocutor in obvious displeasure.

By this time a good fifteen years had elapsed since the first anecdote (see page 27). The tone of the reaction no longer proved surprising or disconcerting, although its vehemence was certainly striking, especially coming as it did from a younger scholar who had presumably lived through the very same disciplinary developments I had. By then, of course, those early voices of protest from the mid-1970s had not only congealed into fullfledged critical movements, quite diverse as well as quite sophisticated, but had also displaced historical criticism from its position of pre-eminence, turning the discipline into a veritable arena for competing paradigms. Clearly, as I described the changes in question, what for me had meant the liberation and decolonization of the discipline, for him amounted to a decline in standards and the anarchy of partisanship. In the process, needless to say, such transformations also served to bring about a critical reconsideration of the personal voice in biblical scholarship.

In effect, with the flowering of literary criticism and cultural criticism, increasing attention began to be paid to the role of 'the reader' in interpretation. An initial focus on formal reader-constructs, along the lines of the universal reader type, eventually gave way to a concern for 'the real reader' as such, and with that came the inevitable realization that real or flesh-and-blood readers could only be approached and analysed in terms of the manifold and highly complex dimensions of human identity. As a result, a fourth critical movement, cultural studies, began to claim its voice and fight for space in the disciplinary arena. It was from out of this movement, after fruitful sojourns in both literary and social criticism, that I proceeded to formulate my own rationale for the introduction of the personal voice in biblical criticism (Segovia 1995b: 57–73; 1995d: 303–30).

First, I came to realize that there was no such thing as a neutral and disinterested reader and that the proposed de-contextualization aimed at the formation of the universal and informed reader was but the universalization of a bracketed identity. Readers, I argued, were always and inevitably positioned and interested, culturally and historically conditioned and engaged.

Second, I further realized that a text has no meaning and history has no path without an interpreter. I argued, therefore, that all reading strategies and theoretical models as well as all recuperations of meaning and re-constructions of history were constructs on the part of such real readers.

Third, I clearly realized that I had to incorporate such insights into my own critical apparatus and practice. I thus argued for a reading strategy, intercultural criticism, that would regard and analyse all texts, readings of texts, and readers of texts as literary or aesthetic, rhetorical or strategic, and ideological or political constructs in their own right. I further based this method on a theoretical model, a hermeneutics of otherness and engage-ment, that sought not only to acknowledge and respect these others as others but also to engage such others in critical dialogue.

Finally, I fully realized, as reflected in the pivotal role attached to contextualization and perspective within this approach, the profoundly political character of the interpretive task. I argued, therefore, that the fundamental mode of discourse within cultural studies as a whole, and thus within both intercultural criticism and the hermeneutics of otherness and engagement, was neither historical nor literary nor cultural but rather ideological in nature.

In the light of these critical wanderings of mine – which in the end led me to affirm that the long-standing and much-beloved distinction between exegesis and eisegesis had altogether collapsed and that all exegesis was ultimately eisegesis – the charges of my interlocutor were, to a large extent, quite to the point, even if the scolding itself was out of order. From the point of view of his adherence to and espousal of historical criticism, its model and agenda, he had correctly perceived that I had abandoned the parameters of historical criticism, that I had mounted a fundamental critique of it, and that I had turned to a variety of other methods in my critical practice.

In so doing, I had come to adopt a point of view radically opposed to that which had at one time united us: there is no objective and impartial reader; all views of the past are contemporary constructions; all interpretation is contextual and ideological. Only such an antinomian position, such an open violation of the epistemic taboo, could provoke such a chiding; I stood guilty, not only plainly so but self-admittedly so, of espousing subjectivism in interpretation. Of course, so did many others as well by that time, and the riposte involving charges of an unfair critique and affirmations of objectivity appeared ever more fragile and obsolete, especially when devoid of any substantial theoretical foundations. The personal voice was here to stay in biblical scholarship, and our own parting of the ways in silence and discord captured accurately, as another significant cultural text in its own right, the pulse of the discipline as a whole.

Postcolonial studies:
Entrenchment of the personal voice

Personal anecdote

Quite recently, at a dinner at a committee meeting of one of the various professional societies to which I belong, I happened to sit next to a well-known and established scholar. This was a gentleman many years my senior, perfectly cast in the social mould of the traditional learned scholar – the *homo eruditus* oblivious to and distrustful of matters theoretical, with a view of all theory as outside the realm of history; largely unaware of as well as unconcerned by any major shifts in either discipline or academy; and thoroughly self-absorbed in his own work. After speaking at length on his most recent accomplishments, he asked unexpectedly about my own research interests. When I explained my growing interest in the competing ideologies of the early Christian texts in the face of the Roman imperial situation which they faced and within which they had been produced, he asked politely whether I thought such a connection was really important. When I responded that I thought the connection was not only important for the ancient world but also for both the modern world and the contemporary world, since the development of criticism had paralleled the imperial expansion, contraction, and transformation of Europe and the United States, he discretely dropped any further inquires about my work and proceeded to outline at considerable length his own research agenda for the future.

Now, coming as it did a couple of years after the second anecdote (see pages 29–30), the nature of this brief exchange could hardly prove unexpected or baffling. Even its friendly tone, with no visible signs of exasperation or frustration, was fairly predictable. I had by then come to learn that in dealing with individuals committed to the more traditional methods and agendas of the discipline, especially the older erudite type, the best strategy to follow was that of polite give-and-take. In effect, harmless banter designed to pass the time in an amicable fashion, while skirting issues of a controversial or problematic nature having to do with the discipline or the academy, even though such a policy might lead, as it did in this case, to interminable c.v. recitations.

This is a strategy born of social grace and professional wisdom, a strategic realization that any type of serious critical exchange is not only bound to disrupt a culturally preferred ambience of *bonhomie* but also go absolutely nowhere, given the discursive and theoretical gulf involved. To be sure, on this particular occasion I did depart from such a strategy, but only as a result of questions addressed to me, and even then I proceeded to answer in as pithy and global a fashion as possible. Such brevity proved effective; my own interests were so remote from those of my interlocutor that he rapidly moved on to the much more familiar territory of his own work.

By then I had begun to move into postcolonial studies (Segovia 1998: 49–65). While turned to cultural studies, I had argued for the pre-eminence of the political or ideological element in biblical criticism. In my formulation of intercultural criticism and the hermeneutics of otherness and engagement, I had set out to introduce this element at all levels of the interpretive task – at the level of texts, readings of texts, and readers of texts. At the same time, I had continued to struggle with the question of how best to engage in ideological analysis – in effect, with the question of theory and method. By that time, there were others engaged in ideological criticism from a number of different perspectives, but I wanted to do so specifically at a geo-political level.

Certainly, I had already called upon key terms and concepts of postcolonial studies to describe developments in the discipline in terms of liberation and decolonization. I had also explained that such developments were due in large part to the infusion of outside voices heretofore absent from the study of religion, including voices from outside the West and voices from non-Western minorities residing in the West. I had further argued that the diversity now present in the discipline, methodological and theoretical as well as socio-cultural, was the inevitable result of a postcolonial world. What I still lacked was a more expansive and systematic conceptual framework and practice with which to pursue the ideological dimension from a geo-political perspective and at all levels of interpretation.

By the time of this conversation, I had come to realize that the phenomenon of imperial reality, of imperialism and colonialism, lay at the very heart of the discipline, across all levels of analysis: across the world of antiquity, the world of the Roman Empire, the world of the texts; across the world of modernity, the world of Western expansionism – the world of modern biblical criticism, its readers and readings; and across the world of postmodernity, the world of Western imperial contraction and transformation, of postcolonialism and neocolonialism – the world of contemporary biblical criticism, its readers and readings. I had also come to realize that it was proper, indeed imperative, to examine not only what the texts had to say about imperial reality but also how what they had to say had been interpreted in the modern Western tradition as well as in the contemporary Western and non-Western traditions. I looked upon such a multi-dimensional, interrelated, geo-political approach as an ideal way of coming to terms with the political and ideological dimension of the discipline at all of its various levels of analysis.

After 'subjectivism' there is perhaps no term more objectionable for any universal reader-construct, such as that behind the *homo eruditus*, than 'ideology'. To insist on the political character of the biblical texts, alongside or even over its religious or theological, literary or cultural, dimensions, by situating them within the geo-political context of Roman imperialism and colonialism is already a daring move. To insist on the political character of all biblical criticism, modern as well as contemporary, by situating interpretations and interpreters within the geo-political context of Western imperialism and colonialism goes beyond daring. While such linkage at the level of the ancient texts may come across as quizzical, the proposed connection at the level of interpretation is beyond comprehension – in effect, how can any universal-reader construct be construed as profoundly ideological, thoroughly enmeshed in matters political and geo-political, whether consciously or unconsciously so?

By arguing that the discourse and practices of the discipline had to be seen against the broader discourse and practices of modern imperialism and colonialism as well as postmodern neocolonialism and postcolonialism, I had politicized the discipline to an unacceptable level. The response could only have been wrathful indignation or silent dismissal. My interlocutor in this case opted for the latter alternative, in part because of my own conversational strategy and in part because of the seeming outlandishness of the claim. Yet, ideological criticism, in all of its various forms, was here to stay, as was my own geo-political approach to the personal voice; and thus, the silence of politeness and insouciance that greeted my remarks can readily be taken as yet another significant cultural text in its own right.

Concluding comments

This is by no means the first time that I deal with the question of the personal voice in my work. At a fundamental level, I have used my life-story as a foundation for my work as a critic in biblical studies, as a theologian in theological studies, and as a critic in cultural studies. In more specific studies, I have used that story as a point of departure for reflections on the life and role of racial and ethnic minorities in theological education and scholarship in general, as well as in biblical studies in particular (Segovia 1994; 1996: 469–92). In the present study I have had recourse to that story once again to trace both the emergence of the question itself within biblical studies and the development of my own option for postcolonial criticism. In so doing, I have relied on both the individual and the social dimensions of that story, depending on the context and aims of each writing in question, but always with a view of such dimensions not as binary opposites but as interrelated and interdependent.

In the present study I have concentrated on the social dimension, focused on the personal voice within the discipline as such. Thus, I proposed to show how the emergence of my own postcolonial voice within the academy paralleled the emergence of the question of the personal voice in the academy. It is a focus that could be described as socio-educational or socio-academic. Certainly, I could have underlined instead the personal dimension or highlighted both at the same time. I would have related then how the development of my postcolonial optic was also the result of struggle – the unceasing and unrelenting *lucha* (literally, 'fight') of a child of the colonized against the forces of imperialism and colonialism.

Here the option for a postcolonial optic went hand in hand with a process of conscientization and construction, of decolonization and liberation, as life in a variety of imperial and colonial contexts caused layers of ideology to fall one by one from my eyes. Climactic in this regard was my intense experience as an outsider, as 'the other', within that quintessential institution of the dominant culture, the Divinity School (Cherry 1995). It was within such a context – at the very heart of theological liberalism itself, with its much-vaunted message of openness and freedom – that I finally came to the marvellously energizing realization that the emperor had no clothes, just as I was beginning to deal with real readers and cultural studies in the discipline. Indeed, it should not go unsaid that all three interlocutors alluded to in my personal anecdotes were exemplary specimens of liberal culture and theology. However, the story of this *lucha*, this concomitant personal struggle, behind the making of this postcolonial critic must be left for now, alas, to another time and place.

Notes

1 In 1968 I found myself rather safely ensconced in a seminary, pursuing studies towards ordination in the Roman Catholic Church. Nevertheless, while we in no way resembled what was happening at Columbia University or the University of California at Berkeley, much less what was happening in the streets of Paris, in our own way we too felt and expressed this sense of generational frustration and revolt. After all, these were the years that followed the conclusion of the II Vatican Council, when its many reforms of *aggiornamento* were beginning to be implemented across the universal church. Such reforms touched the world of theological and ministerial education and occasioned many a battle between the old generation and the new generation.

2 The letter of invitation for the project (Ingrid Rosa Kitzberger, April 22 1996) made this point quite clearly, as it sought to define 'personal voice criticism': 'In contrast to the traditional historical–critical paradigm with its claim for objectivity and the strict separation of the critical task and the critic's person. . . .'

3 To be sure, Stendahl (1962: 422) was not unaware of the obstacles involved in the descriptive task: the subjectivity of the historian in the selection of

material; the paucity of sources, which does not allow for certainty in all areas; the appeal to some comparative material while neglecting other such material. In the end, however, such obstacles were not considered overwhelming; not only would the material itself serve as a proper corrective but also the task could be carried out by believer and agnostic alike, even in unison. All that was required, Stendahl argued, was 'description in the terms indicated by the texts themselves'.

References

Cherry, C. (1995) *Hurrying toward Zion: Universities, Divinity Schools, and American Protestantism*, Bloomington and Indianapolis, IN: Indiana University Press.

Inglis, F. (1993) *Cultural Studies*, Oxford and Cambridge, MA: Blackwell Publishers.

Segovia, F. F. (1994) 'Theological Education and Scholarship as Struggle: The Life of Racial/Ethnic Minorities in the Profession', *Journal of Hispanic/Latino Theology* 2: 5–25.

—— (1995a) '"And They Began to Speak in Other Tongues": Competing Modes of Discourse in Contemporary Biblical Criticism', in F. F. Segovia and M. A. Tolbert (eds) *Reading from This Place. Volume 1: Social Location and Biblical Interpretation in the United States*, Minneapolis, MN: Fortress.

—— (1995b) 'Toward a Hermeneutics of the Diaspora: A Hermeneutics of Otherness and Engagement', in F. F. Segovia and M. A. Tolbert (eds) *Reading from This Place. Volume 1: Social Location and Biblical Interpretation in the United States*, Minneapolis, MN: Fortress.

—— (1995c) 'Cultural Studies and Contemporary Biblical Criticism: Ideological Criticism as Mode of Discourse', in F. F. Segovia and M. A. Tolbert (eds) *Reading from This Place. Volume 2: Social Location and Biblical Interpretation in Global Perspective*, Minneapolis, MN: Fortress.

—— (1995d) 'Toward Intercultural Criticism: A Reading Strategy from the Diaspora', in F. F. Segovia and M. A. Tolbert (eds) *Reading from This Place. Volume 2: Social Location and Biblical Interpretation in Global Perspective*, Minneapolis, MN: Fortress.

—— (1996) 'Racial and Ethnic Minorities in Biblical Studies', in M. G. Brett (ed.) *Ethnicity and the Bible*, Biblical Interpretation Series, 19, Leiden, New York, Köln: Brill.

—— (1998) 'Biblical Criticism and Postcolonial Studies: Toward a Postcolonial Optic', in R. S. Sugirtharajah (ed.) *The Postcolonial Bible*, The Bible and Post-colonialism Series, 1, Sheffield: Sheffield Academic, 49–65.

Stendahl, K. (1962) 'Biblical Theology, Contemporary', in G. A. Buttrick (ed.) *The Interpreter's Dictionary of the Bible*, 4 vols, Nashville, TN: Abingdon, 1418–32.

3

THE FUNCTION OF THE NON-FULFILLED PROMISES

Reading the Pentateuch from the perspective of the Latin-American oppressed people

J. Severino Croatto

The subtitle of this essay is not difficult to understand, not so perhaps the title itself. Can we talk about promises that God does not fulfil? What are these 'non-fulfilled' promises? If we refer to their literary 'function', the issue in itself is important, but why? And what has this all got to do with my *personal* experience as an Argentinian, a Latin-American, and also a biblical exegete?

What I am about to express regarding the Pentateuch is the fruit of a long exegetical journey in which I have received so much from so many scholars I have read. It is also the result of having read *in* the text the experiences of the oppressed people of Latin America. It is a fact often observed by the socio-logical analysis of biblical texts that the situation of the subdued peoples of today is similar to that of the people who produced the great texts of the Bible. How do I read and what do I make of the Pentateuch in the situation I live in as a Latin-American, as an Argentinian, as 'Severino'? How can I join the usefulness – and the enjoyment – of all that modern biblical scholarship offers, with my service to a community of readers who regard the Bible as a relevant 'message'? In each line of what I am about to say – and within the technical language I will use – lies my personal (and social!) voice. My 'personal' voice is in fact 'social', because what I am and what I do are, in one way or another, determined by my social environment, and also because my exegetical work is undoubtedly influenced by the historical, social, and spiritual life of the people to which I belong.

Motivation for this reading

My growing interest in literary studies and in what some scholars call 'rhetorical criticism' led me to a deep concern about the unity of the great literary compositions, such as the prophetic books. This concern also prompted me to look at the Pentateuch as it is, and why it stands so and not as an 'Hexateuch', for example. What were the actual problems, what was the social and religious situation of the groups that wrote this monumental work? So I started to think that as long as an exegete remains focused on the question of the J, E, D and P traditions or that of their origin, she/he may discover many things, but not *what* the Pentateuch *actually says*.

The form of the Pentateuch

To begin with, it is essential to consider the Pentateuch as a *literary work*. With this in mind, every text is, in one way or another, significant. The meaning is generated not only by words or concepts, but also by the organization of the discourse, by the distribution of themes and motifs within the textual whole, and by other resources that have to do with the 'form' of the text. But what, in a literary sense, is closed – and must be read as such – is open *pragmatically*. What I mean by this distinction is that every text proposes something that the reader must 'fulfil' in some way. The text continues in the life of its addressee. Now, in what way do I perceive that the manner in which the Pentateuch closes is precisely its opening to the praxis of its addressees, whether those in the past or of ourselves as present readers?

I would like to point out some hints that the text of the Pentateuch itself offers us in order to understand its meaning and its message. My attention will be focused particularly on the literary and hermeneutical aspects. The first aspect is essential to the proper reading of every *text*; the latter is also essential, because such an important text as the Pentateuch must be read bearing in mind the questions that *reality* calls for. The questions that I ask myself are the following: What does the Pentateuch propose to me as its message? Does it want to narrate a 'past' history? Or rather, does it want to generate – through some fragments of historical memory and based on the actual situation in which the redactor writes – a great *utopia* of liberation and ensure a cultural and religious *identity* for a people that is disintegrating among other nations? For a long time I have suspected that the Pentateuch is *not* simply a set of laws in a historical context (a *tôrâ*); I believe it is also the presentation of a project through *models*.

This angle began to dominate my study of the Pentateuch as I paid attention to its structure as a literary composition and observed its deep syntony with the needs of the landless (or those invaded in their own land) and all those who are losing their personal, cultural, and even religious identity. This perspective became totally clear to me while I was writing my commentary on Genesis 4–11 (Croatto 1997).

The model of the 'itineraries'

A structuring element of the Pentateuch, which has not been given due attention, is the literary genre of 'itineraries'. These are well known in Assyriology (Goetze 1953; Weidner 1966; Hallo 1964). Itineraries consist of a list of the stages and stopping-points of meaningful journeys, generally of a king with his army, and have been studied for geographical purposes because of the sequence of toponyms and, in some cases, the indication of the travelling time.

My concern about itineraries started at the earliest stage of my exegetical work when I was fully involved in Orientalism. But only at my most recent hermeneutical stage was I able to see how helpful the itineraries were for understanding not simply the structure but also the metamessage of the Pentateuch. Those aspects will be explained in what follows.

The itinerary in the structure of the Pentateuch

A complete itinerary – more likely from the P source than from the final redactor of the Pentateuch (Davies 1983: 6) – has been kept in Num. 33:5–49. It has only one 'opening', in order to insert the death of Aaron (vv. 38–9). A similar itinerary is found in Exodus. The place (Rameses), which was the scene of the oppression, the introductory episodes of the liberation and the celebration of the Passover, marks the beginning of the stages of the itinerary. It is inaugurated in Exod. 12:37 ('the sons of Israel left from Rameses . . .'). From there on, we find a few interesting episodes.

The point is that the model of the itinerary is the spine which, on the literary level, structures and knits together the rest of the Pentateuch. The stopping-points may be different from those in Num. 33, but their function is the same: the organization of a sequence of events directed towards an ultimate aim. Obviously, many problems arise related to redactional criticism (Davies 1983: 9–11), but it is important to note the way in which the episodes are 'fitted' into the scheme of the itinerary and which events are emphasized.

The centrality of the Sinai tradition (from Exod. 19 to Num. 10:11, that is, one third of the Pentateuch!) must also be considered in the light of the itinerary, for the whole material appears as God's revelation to Moses at only one stage, but such a significant stage that the dates of its beginning and end are explicitly stated (Exod. 19:1 and Num. 10:11a: nearly one year). Such details are the work of a P hand, probably redactional. The Sinai stage divides the great journey of Israel into two main periods: from Egypt (but before the crossing of the sea) up to Sinai, and from there to the plains of Moab in front of Jericho. The first period starts, according to the old priestly calendar, on Wednesday 15 (month I, year 1), the day after the paradigmatic Passover (Num. 33:3); the second period starts on Wednesday 20 (month II, year 2), after the second Passover (Num. 9:1–5 and 10:11). We could analyse every stopping point in order to see what events take place at each one.[1] But we are going to focus on only one feature, because it appears in more than one stopping-point, and because of its impact on the understanding of the Pentateuch as a whole. It is the theme and literary figure of the desert 'complaints'.

There are up to a dozen episodes of complaint of the people against Yahweh or Moses, or those of Moses against Yahweh. In the redaction of the Pentateuch, the account of the complaint against Moses in Paran, after the exploration of the land of Canaan (Num. 14:2), proves to be significant. V. 30 relates explicitly the complaint to the *promise of the land*; the counter-oath of not granting the land to the generation that left Egypt, but only to their children follows (v. 31). The accumulation of episodes of lament and complaint reaches a critical expression at this point, in which the promises of Gen. 17, affirmed in a new context of oppression (Exod. 6:3, 8), enter into a critical phase. The language of Num. 14:30a is particularly akin to that of Exod. 6:8 (the motif of the oath with a lifted hand, related to the gift of the land).

This is just one example of the way I read the biblical texts as intratextual totalities,[2] not simply as a sum of literary fragments. I interpret the episode of Num. 14:20–45 as the negative expression (a warning to the readers) of the positive message of the text as a whole: the promise of the land remains, but the promised land will not be reached by all.

Where does the itinerary of Israel end?

Nevertheless, a noteworthy fact is indicated by the scheme of the itinerary itself that links Exod.–Num. to Deut.; in Num. 22:1 the last stopping-point is reached: 'The sons of Israel left and camped in the plains of Moab, on the other side of the Jordan, across from Jericho.' The journey comes to an end; there are no more stages or stopping-points.

The account, however, does not come to an end. There are still new episodes and revelations from Yahweh, but everything occurs in the same place, which is mentioned with insistence (26:3; 31:12; 33:49, 50; 35:1, and the conclusion of 36:13). When we proceed to Deut. we find the same thing. From the beginning, we realize that Moses' subsequent discourses were pronounced 'on the other side of the Jordan . . . in Moab' (Deut. 1:1a, 5). The book closes with the people still in the same place. Deut. 34:8 points out that the sons of Israel are 'in the plains of Moab'. It is the same location as in Num. 22:1.

Some reflections regarding the redaction and structure of the Pentateuch seem fitting at this point. The geographical reference in nearly one-third of this composition is the country of Moab, 'across from Jericho', which means within sight of the promised land. The promise of the land,[3] the central theme of Genesis, which appears again in the two versions of the 'liberation project' of Exod. 3 (v. 8) and 6 (vv. 4, 8), has *not* been *fulfilled* when the Pentateuch – the fundamental and archetypal text for Israel – comes to its end. Why is this so?

The theory of an Hexateuch blocks the meaning of the Pentateuch

The attempts to seek a prolongation of the traditions of the Pentateuch in the historical books that follow it are very well known, but these apparent prolongations are in fact re-readings (and not necessarily literary 'sources') that were submerged into the historical texts. In any case, this hypothesis makes the question of the abrupt ending of the Pentateuch even more crucial. Who made the separation that we have now? And under what conditions?

Another explanation imagines the existence of an Hexateuch that includes the book of Joshua. If there is to be any coherence between the 'creeds' that recite Yahweh's deeds, from the promise to the gift of the land (Deut. 6:20–5; 26:5–10a) and the formation of the Pentateuch, the fulfilment of the promise should be also narrated in the text. An Hexateuch would explain this dilemma. However, no one has ever seen an Hexateuch; no ancient tradition and no version attest it. The 'creeds' mentioned do include the gift of the land because they were composed later, but, in the redactional context of the Pentateuch in which they are placed, the gift of the land is assumed as something that belongs to the future. The exclusion of this gift, then, expresses the real coherence between the 'creeds' and the composition of the Pentateuch as a whole.

It is striking that in the great display of information on issues regarding the origin of the Pentateuch, or its literary conclusion, little or nothing is said about the context of the production of the text. Sometimes the most simple things – such as life – are forgotten. An emphasis on the socio-analytical reading of the texts would greatly enliven the exegetical task. A socio-analytical approach is essential, from my point of view. I have indeed experienced the usefulness of a synchronic reading of the texts but while also seeing them in their diachronic dimension – especially as far as the time of their production is concerned. The threefold convergence on the synchronic and diachronic levels – the 'Sitz im Leben' of the original community; the redactional stages of the text; and its final literary and structural form – has helped me enormously in the interpretation of the Pentateuch as a pragmatic message as well as a set of laws.

A simple but nevertheless necessary question is the following: What, in Persian times, motivated the construction of such a formidable masterpiece as the Pentateuch with a truncated, unexpected ending that obviously frustrates the expectations that run through the whole work? This question leads to a second one: Is the Pentateuch just a historical (and legal) composition, only a memory of the past? Or is it a *kerygma*, proclaimed with existential intensity, in a situation of crisis but also of trust in the God of the promises? Only the second alternative makes sense. How could the scribes who composed such a fundamental work include the possession of the land, which at the time was under Persian rule, and when most of the people were in the 'diaspora', far from their own land?

The promise of the land, which stands out in the course of the Pentateuch, is precisely the *kerygma* that is proclaimed on the literary level. *The land is still a promise.* The work, composed to be read as it is (neither as an Hexateuch nor as an Enneateuch), seeks to generate hope in the addressees and to move them toward a new liberation process. The perspective is the same as that of the book of Isaiah (Croatto 1994). The province of 'Yehud', extremely reduced in size (Crüsemann 1989: 360), and a people disintegrated and dispersed among foreign countries, were crying out, on a purely historical level, that the promises had had a transitory fulfilment in the past, but had ended in frustration; history was denying them flagrantly. Now, the key to activate these promises as a seed of hope was precisely to show that they had not been fulfilled yet. In this way the utopia – at least the utopia! – could nurture a project of future liberation.

The Pentateuch, as a new 'unfinished' literary symphony bears a vital message, precisely because it is *unfinished*. In trying to 'finish it', with an imaginary Hexateuch or anything else, its key message gets lost. In any case, the hypothesis of a previous Tetrateuch (Gen.–Num.), whose kerygmatic perspective does not change with the addition of Deut., is much more coherent. The unfinished journey is, in fact, already indicated in the book of Numbers (22:1).

The 'periodization' of history

We are now going to follow another conductive thread through the whole composition of the Pentateuch in order to converge with the previous outlook, but this time referring more specifically to the promise of an offspring.

It is clear that genealogies have a prominent literary and theological function in the book of Genesis (1–11 and 12–50) and in the Pentateuch as a whole (Robinson 1986; Renaud 1990).[4] As shown in Table 3.1, narrative and genealogies alternate throughout the whole composition:

On the one hand, genealogies indicate the continuation of the 'blessing' or simply the divine plan in history; on the other, they indicate the 'selections' of the particular within the universal: each genealogy reduces the visual scope of the subsequent account. For example, in the genealogy of Gen. 5 the 'sons and daughters' of each character are left aside, in order to concentrate on one of them. The genealogies of Ishmael and Esau obviate

Table 3.1

	Narrative	Genealogy
Origins:	Gen. 1–4 (world, man)	5 (Adam)
	6–9 (flood)	10 (nations)
	11:1–9 (city/tower)	11:10–32 (Semites)
Canaan:	12:1–25:11 (Abraham)	25:12–18 (Ishmael)
	25:19–35:29 (Isaac)	36:1–37:1 (Esau)
	37:2–46:7 (Jacob)	46:8–27 (offspring)
Egypt:	46:28–Exod. 6:13 (in Egypt)	6:14–27 (Levi)
	6:28–Num. 2:24 (exodus)	3:1–3 (Aaron)
	3:4–36:13 (desert)	

the need to relate special facts about both characters, so that the account about the three patriarchs (Abraham, Isaac, Jacob) comes to the fore. When Jacob's family is in Egypt, the long accounts (left column) are interrupted by the genealogies of Levi and Aaron, who are outstanding characters but by no means the only ones. Why is this so? The last two genealogies are specially relevant, as they seem to legitimate the role of the priestly class.

The formula *'elle toledot* appears ten times in the book of Genesis, followed by a name that defines the contents of what is described as 'history/generations'. Possibly on purpose, there are five *toledot* in Gen. 1–11 and another five in Gen. 12–50, which is a literary indication that does not allow us to separate the history of the origins from that of the patriarchs. It is worth indicating, as it has not been observed yet, that such a formula, followed by the name of the character, does not overlap with the above-mentioned 'narrative/genealogy' model, but goes through it indistinctly. Is it the mark of a later redactional hand, perhaps? It is important to visualize the new resulting scheme (the quotations indicate where the formula appears): see Table 3.2.

Table 3.2 shows that the *'elle toledot* formula, in spite of its reference to the generation (lexem *yld*), is equally distributed between accounts and genealogies. The fact that the genealogical pattern is also found within the accounts suggests that the accounts are actually inserted into the pattern, and not the other way round.

The redactors of the Pentateuch actually wanted to divide the history of the world into characteristic sections. In Genesis there are ten periods from the origins to the entrance of the sons of Israel into Egypt. Why precisely ten? We must remember that in Gen. 5 there is also an equivalent scheme of ten pre-flood characters (Adam, Seth, Enosh, Kenan, Mahalalel, Jared, *Enoch*, Methusela, Lamech, *Noah*), that might have been inspired – as a counter-cultural form of resistance in the ideological instance – by the Mesopotamian list of ten kings prior to the flood. In a socio-political reading of the Pentateuch this ideological 'confrontation' with imperial

Table 3.2

	Narrative	*Genealogy*
Origins:	Gen. 2:4 (heavens/earth)	5:1 (Adam)
	6:9 (Noah)	10:1 (sons of Noah)
	–	11:10 (Shem)
Canaan:	11:27 (Terah–Abraham)	25:12 (Ishmael)
	25:19 (Isaac)	36:1.9 (Esau)
	37:2 (Jacob)	–
Egypt:	–	–
	–	Num. 3:1 (Aaron/Moses)

traditions appears to be an affirmation of the identity of the exiled or emigrated people in an adverse context.

In the prophetic and wisdom books, and especially in the Pentateuch, I have discovered a great number of passages like Gen. 5 in which the oppressed re-create, as a form of resistance, the traditions imposed on them from outside. A similar phenomenon can be perceived in the cultures of the Third World when seen from the perspective of Liberation Theology; this perspective has enabled me to do a completely new exegesis of texts I had read hundreds of times. This approach is not purely academic; my cultural and theological 'belonging' is a hermeneutical key for the use of semiotics and the historical–critical methods.

The use of the 'elle toledot *formula*

A thorough look at the introductory formula of the periods of history is very instructive.

1   I have come to realize that the genealogies are not placed at random. They introduce significant periods of history in which materials from different strata, not just 'priestly' ones, are combined. Such periods are marked by the first character mentioned (Adam, Noah, sons of Noah, Shem, Terah, and so on). Finally, each time the formula appears and names the main character, we find he has already been introduced in the text of the previous stage (see Table 3.3). This phenomenon has not been sufficiently observed. The redactor distinguishes the background of a character from his main history that is about to be narrated.

The first thing that we notice is the position of the formula: in the previous source/tradition P it is used to introduce the characters with their genealogical lines, but in the present text of Genesis (and Num. 3) it is placed in the middle. The character is already known by then. Whoever remains at the P-level is not reading Genesis as 'text' but as archaeological fragments that, in fact, only make sense in the present

Table 3.3

Period	Formula	Theme	Background	Main history
I	(2:4)	heavens/earth	1:1–2:3	2:4–4:26
II	(5:1)	Adam	1–4	5:1–6:8
III	(6:9)	Noah	5:28–32	6:9–9:29
IV	(10:1)	Noah's sons	6:9–10	10:1–11:9
V	(11:10)	Shem	6:10; 9:18–27; 10:1, 22–31	11:10–26
VI	(11:27)	Terah	11:24–6	11:27–25:11
VII	(25:12)	Ishmael	26:1–16; 21:8–21	25:12–18
VIII	(25:19)	Isaac	21–22; 24; 25:5, 11	25:19–35:29
IX	(36:1, 9)	Esau	25:25–34; 27; 28:6–9; 32:4–22; 33:1–17	36:1–37:1
X	(37:2)	Jacob	25:26–34; 27–35	37:2–50:26 (Exod. 1–Num. 2)
I'	(Num. 3:1)	Aaron/Moses	Exod. 2:1	Num. 3:1–Deut. 34:12

literary context. The position of the formula is a redactional creation. The final editorial work, although later, is also 'priestly'. This is an evident fact for me, as it has already been indicated.

2 At the same time, it is likely that the formula, original in the genealogies as such (II, IV, V, VII, IX), is only an imitation in the narrative sections of I, III, VI, VIII, X. That is why the 'genealogical' elements are scattered (Renaud 1990: 12–13) or non-existent (Gen. 2:4–3:24). The literary function of the *'elle toledot* formula, therefore, is mainly to introduce the different periods of history according to the scheme of the final redactors, and also to organize the events.

3 The variations in the genealogical scheme are more significant than the rigid model. Differences make the meaning. The birth of the son, who will be the main character of the following period, is the central fact of each one of the main *toledot*, and what makes the separation between a 'before' and an 'after'. But in III (Noah's *toledot*), what divides Noah's age between a 'before' and an 'after' is not the birth of his three sons (6:10) but the event of the flood (7:6, 11 = 600 years); the other 350 years are measured again starting from the flood in 9:28.

In the X period there is also a variation. The birth of Jacob's sons has already been narrated within the history of Isaac (VIII = 21:1–35:29); and so the most prominent event in Jacob's history is his migration to Egypt, which marks a 'before' (130 years according to 47:9) and an 'after' (17 years in Egypt, 47:28a, making a total of 147 in v. 28b). Even so, the period is neither closed with the arrival in Egypt nor (in a literary sense) with Gen. 50:26 but continues up to the following section (the *'elle toledot* formula) which we find in Num. 3:1. This indicates, at a literary level, that the stay in Egypt is assumed as part of the history of Jacob and his sons. It is also worth observing that in Num. 1–2 the history of the sons of Jacob is somehow closed by means of their census and organization for the great journey towards the land (cf. 2:34b).

One could expect the 'history of Jacob' (Gen. 37:2–50:26) to be followed by a 'history of the sons of Jacob' (starting from Exod. 1), just as the history of Noah is followed by that of his sons. It is possible that the redactor of the Pentateuch wanted to condense Jacob's history and that of his sons in only one period in order to maintain the 'ten' pattern. The oppression and the liberation from Egypt, and also the Sinai event, take place within the X period.

4 The I' period (preferable to XI) is in fact the most relevant, kerygmatically speaking, as it contains the ritual preparations for the great journey towards the land that started in the second Passover (Num. 9:1–5), which is parallel to the first one in Exod. 12. This final stage is the one that remains open in the literary structure of the Pentateuch, as we have seen.

5 It is striking that such an important character as Abraham is inscribed within the history (*toledot*) of Terah. But this is in accordance with the normal scheme: the main event in the account about Terah is the birth of his son Abram. The history of Abraham, on the other hand, begins in Ur of the Chaldees, a fact that is very relevant in the production of the message of the Pentateuch. The addressees of the text are invited to imitate Abraham's itinerary towards the promised land. Thus, he becomes the model for those in the 'diaspora', especially for those who are still in Babylon (the Ur of their time).

6 In this historical scheme, there is no history of Joseph. The beginning of Gen. 37:2 is taxonomical: 'this is the history (*'elle toledot*) of Jacob'. The episodes of Joseph's life, although important, are now part of the history of Jacob, whose migration to Egypt they prepare. The last days of Jacob are much more important (47:28–50:14) than the death of Joseph (50:24–6). Within the coherence of the account, the Jacob of chap. 27–35 belongs to the 'history of Isaac' (cf. 27:1; 28:1; 35:27–9). On the contrary, Jacob's own period is marked by the providential events that take him to Egypt, where he becomes a numerous people (Gen. 47:27–Exod. 1:7, 9–10), although far away from the land of the promise. This detail is important, even more so as it marks the end of the book of Genesis.

The meaning of the 'periodization' of history

It seems fitting at this point to ask about the theological intention that motivates the division of history into ten periods. The parallel seems to be the same Mesopotamian tradition about the ten pre-flood kings that governed prominent cities (Eridu, Suruppak) during very long periods of time (up to 36 000 years). This is known as the 'Sumerian King List'. It was composed at the beginning of the III dynasty of Ur, around 2100 BCE, but was widely-known as it has been found on tablets that span from the Sumerian up to the Seleucid times. The Judeans, who were exiled in the Chaldean empire in the VI century, created a parallel counter-tradition, now incorporated into Gen. 5 (the period from Adam to Noah). Thereby, the exiles were able to maintain their cultural identity within the dominating cultural context.

Likewise, but in a 'macro' dimension, the redactor of the Pentateuch divided the primeval history of humankind into ten periods, only that in this case, instead of finishing it with the flood (as in Mesopotamia and Gen. 5) he finishes with the sons of Jacob residing in Egypt. The flood is a significant event but not the 'end of history'. The main feature for the 'Sumerian King List' as well as for the Israelite re-readings of it, is the 'after the flood' (an expression that appears in Gen. 9:28; 10:1, 32; 11:10). Actually, after the flood 'kingship was brought down (once again) from heaven' to the city of Kish, then to Uruk, and later to Ur, and so on.[5] The list does not remain in prehistory but in the political history of the Sumerian city-states.

I have always been impressed by the ability of the biblical authors to 're-create' that great Mesopotamian tradition, but only in recent years have I been able to value its counter-cultural implications, by seeing how oppressed peoples react when they are confronted with cultural impositions from outside. This brought about the suspicion that the transposition of the scheme of the 'Sumerian King List' in biblical historiography may not be reduced to Genesis. The ten periods registered there (five before and five after the flood) must be only one side of the history; the other side is the 'after'. In Exod. 1–15, in effect, there is a turn of the history. The promises made to the patriarchs, authenticated from one to another, have had their risks (Abraham and Jacob had to leave Canaan temporarily, and Isaac had to confront problems with the Philistines). Jacob leaves for the second time when he goes to Egypt, and does not return in his lifetime. His sons, who multiply there, suffer oppression and, after their liberation, a new search for the promised land through the desert begins. It is as if history began once again, starting with the liberation.

Now, if the 'periodization' of history was indicated in Genesis by genealogies starting with the *'elle toledot* formula, we may ask whether this formula is used at some other time to indicate the period that introduces the new and definite history. And so it is. We find it in Num. 3:1–4, which begins in this striking way:

> '*elle toledot* (this is the history) of Aaron and Moses *the day that Yahweh spoke to Moses on Mount Sinai.*
>
> (v. 1)

What follows in vv. 2–4 is the genealogy of Aaron; that of Moses is not really of interest, as the intention, through this genealogical recourse, is to underline the continuation of the priesthood of Aaron in Eleazar and Itamar, even before the rights of the Levites (3:5–4:49) are affirmed. Why then is Moses introduced, together with Aaron, in this recurrence of the '*elle toledot* formula? I believe the explanation is very simple. After Egypt (equivalent to 'after the flood') the present history begins. It is marked by the Sinaitic institutions based on Yahweh's word to Moses on Mount Sinai. Aaron is associated to Moses through the genealogical scheme in order to legitimize the high priesthood of his line, but the main figure of Sinai is Moses, as the sentence of v. 1b, which excludes Aaron, explicitly states.

It has been noticed and is clear at first sight that the inclusion of Moses in Num. 3:1 is unexpected (his lineage is not registered). It has been qualified as 'less significant' (Weimar 1974a: 187–8), or as 'secondary' (Tengström 1981: 55). From the point of view of literary criticism it overlaps the genealogical model (regarding Aaron), but that in itself is the proof of its greater importance in the construction of the text. The redactor is calling attention precisely to Moses as co-initiator (with Aaron) of the last stage of the history of Israel, regulated by Sinai norms. The expression 'the day that Yahweh spoke to Moses on Mount Sinai', as strange as it may seem, is no less significant. Its similarity to Gen. 2:4b and 5:2 is striking. The journey from Egypt to the promised land is only one 'historical period', not yet ended for those who read the Pentateuch 'properly'. When I explain this reading key in my classes, or in biblical workshops, all the participants give evidence of an immediate 'reception' of the biblical message as addressed to them/us.

Programmatic centrality of Exod. 1–15.
Oppression and liberation

The dividing line is in Exod. 1–15. The history has a 'before Egypt' (as it had a 'before the flood') and an 'after Egypt'. Therefore, Exod. 1–15 is equivalent to the flood period, with the same duality of meaning (destruction and salvation) and with the equivalence between Noah and Moses as leading characters. Recalling the use of overlapping one period in the previous one, the stage of Aaron–Moses (I') is related to that of Jacob (X) through the 'sons of Jacob/Israel' (Exod. 1–15 is full of actions performed by both characters).

From the perspective of the redactor of the Pentateuch, however, the Egypt stage is not enough; the revelation of laws at Sinai must be added.

On the other hand, the liberation process is dramatized, in an almost cyclical way by the repetition of the 'project in march/delayed realization' scheme, in each of the units of Exod. 1–15. Such a dramatization is a generator of meaning at the level of the total *kerygma* of the Pentateuch. From a post-exilic perspective, what occurs in the account of Exod. 1–15 is quite significant. Israel is far away from its own land and oppressed by a foreign empire, but Yahweh manifests his liberating project, which begins with the flight from Egypt and the journey through the desert. The flight is a sign that it is possible to be liberated, but the hardships and 'fears' show the risks of the process. The unfinished journey, however, indicates the 'not yet' of the promises. They must be fulfilled *now*.

The message of the Pentateuch

1   The recourse to foreign traditions, especially those of Mesopotamia, is a way of expressing counter-messages and generating hope in a context of assimilation and cultural as well as religious '*dis*-identification' with its socially, politically, and economically (= domination) harmful effects. This counter-cultural orientation of the Pentateuch seems clear to me now especially after writing a commentary on Gen. 4–11 (Croatto 1997) in the context of the 'inculturation' of Latin America. The social context in which I do exegesis is at the same time my personal context; hence my engagement to this kind of hermeneutical exegetical/eisegetical work.

2   The Pentateuch is an *open text*, a generator of hope. The journeys of the patriarchs and the sons and daughters of Israel through the desert, with their crises, their risks, and their suffering, indicate that the land is an objective that is to be achieved. It is there that they will become a strong, innumerable nation.

3   Concerning the name of Yahweh, Exod. 3:13–14 does not narrate the revelation of a new divine name. And that name does not mean 'I am who I am' – in any case, according to the literary context, the meaning would be 'I am who is (with you)'. Whatever its origin, Exod. 3:13–14 is a sort of midrash about the (already known!) name of Yahweh (assonance with the verb *hayah*). This midrash is narratively connected to the *experience of liberation*. Just like the Passover (Exod. 12), every celebration of the name of Yahweh arouses the 'exodus memory'. We should note that Exod. 6:2–9 develops the same motif: through the experience of liberation 'you shall know that I am Yahweh, your God' (v. 7) (Croatto 1991). It is, therefore, within Exod. 1–15 where we find the formulation of the theology of the name of Yahweh, the God of the promises which, even if not yet fulfilled, are nevertheless guaranteed in such a way that they ensure hope and preserve the utopia.

Hope and utopia constitute the message that the Pentateuch, as a literary, theological and kerygmatic work, continues to proclaim to each generation of readers.

Notes

1 The stages are indicated in Exod. 12:37; 13:20; (14:1); 15:22, 23, 27; Num. 22:1.
2 'Intratextuality' refers to the meaning of a text in itself, taken as a structured totality; distinguished from 'intertextuality', i.e. the meaning of one text in the light of others within the same worldview (for more details, see Croatto 1995: 43–4, 54–5).
3 To Abraham, 12:1–3; 13:14–17; to Isaac, 26:2–3; to Jacob, 28:13; 35:12.
4 With objections to Tengström (1981) and Weimar (1974b).
5 *ANET* (1969: 265f.); for other aspects, cf. Hess (1989: 244ff.).

References

Ancient Near Eastern Texts Relating to the Old Testament (1969), ed. J. B. Pritchard, Princeton, NJ: Princeton University Press.

Croatto, J. S. (1991) 'Die Relectüre des Jahwe-Namens. Hermeneutische Überlegungen zu Exod. 3, 1–15 und 6, 2–13': *EvTh* 51 (1991) 39–49.

—— (1994) *Isaías. El profeta y sus relecturas hermenéuticas II: 40–55: La liberación es posible*, Buenos Aires: Lumen.

—— (1995) *Biblical Hermeneutics. Toward a Theory of Reading as the Production of Meaning*, Maryknoll, NY: Orbis Books, 1987, 3rd edn 1995.

—— (1997) *Exilio y sobrevivencia. Tradiciones contraculturales en el Pentateuco*, Buenos Aires: Lumen.

Crüsemann, F. (1989) 'Le Pentateuque, une tora. Prolegomènes à l'interprétation de sa forme finale', in A. de Pury (ed.) *Le Pentateuque en question*, Geneva: Labor et Fides, 339–60.

Davies, G. I. (1983) 'The wilderness itineraries and the composition of the Pentateuch', *VT* 33: 1–13.

de Pury, A. (ed.) (1989) *Le Pentateuque en question*, Geneva: Labor et Fides.

Goetze, A. (1953) 'An Old Babylonian itinerary', *JCS* 7: 51–72.

Hallo, W. W. (1964) 'The road to Emar', *JCS* 18: 57–88.

Hess, R. S. (1989) 'The genealogies of Genesis 1–11 and comparative literature', *Biblica* 70: 241–54.

Renaud, B. (1990) 'Les généalogies et la structure de l'histoire sacerdotale dans le livre de la Genèse', *RB* 97: 5–30.

Robinson, R. B. (1986) 'Literary functions of the genealogies of Genesis', *CBQ* 48: 595–608.

Tengström, S. (1981) *Die Toledotformel und die literarische Struktur der priesterlichen Erweiterungsschicht im Pentateuch*, Uppsala: Gleerup.

von Rad, G. (1938) *Das formgeschichtliche Problem des Hexateuch*, Stuttgart: Kohlhammer.

Weidner, E. (1966) 'Assyrische Itinerare', *Archiv für Orientforschung* 21: 42–6.

Weimar, P. (1974a) 'Aufbau und Struktur der priesterschriftlichen Jakobsgeschichtsdarstellung', *ZAW* 86: 174–203.

—— (1974b) 'Die Toledotformel in der priesterschriftlichen Geschichtsdarstellung', *BZ* 48: 65–73.

4

MARK'S OPEN ENDING AND FOLLOWING JESUS ON THE WAY

An autobiographical interpretation of the Gospel of Mark

Maria Gemma Victorino, PDDM

Introduction

This might not be the right thing to say for a beginning but I need to say it just the same: I hesitated to write this article for a long time, even up to the last moment. I feared that my voice was too small and my story so trivial as to be not worth sharing at all. Such fears grew stronger as I came to realize that what I'm doing here – exposing myself – is exhibitionistic. For that is what autobiographical or personal criticism is all about; it is a form of self-disclosure, of self-exposure, though of wildly-varying degrees (Moore 1996: 21). And, at the same time, this self-exposure is interpreted as a performance, 'an explicitly autobiographical performance within the act of criticism' (Miller 1991: 1). I can't help but picture myself as a real ecdysiast at this point!

On second thought, I must say I am enthused that there is such an approach as this for biblical critics. Since the time I began to study the Scriptures, I have been asking, and been asked, if there is any way we can make the text speak more personally, render it closer to the lives of actual people living in the contemporary setting. Reader-response criticism caters to this need, and with personal criticism as one of its daughters, things become even more intimate. A new relationship, a new bonding is created between the reader and the text.

Personal criticism dares to say that there is interdependence between the text read and the person doing the reading. Intertextuality comes to the fore here as it too asserts that a dialogue goes on between written texts and the reader as text.[1] As a person, the critic approaches biblical texts with his or her life-experience and particular story. We cannot take for granted the 'text

53

written on the person's soul' (Kitzberger 1994: 192), and its effect on his or her way of reading. I know how challenging this sounds to many biblical critics, for instance, to my former mentors in Scriptures. I imagine them saying that such an approach is not exegesis but eisegesis. They would prefer to maintain the distance between the text and the reader (or author or anybody/anything extratextual, for that matter). But is not the process of critical reading essentially an open venture? In a recent article, Aichele and Phillips affirm its essential openness to the different systemic forces at work that bind texts to one another, readers included. Thus, Phillips even had to propose what he calls 'intergesis' in place of the binary opposition of exegesis/eisegesis. Meaning does not lie 'inside' texts but rather in the space 'between' texts, arising from the subjective, or ideological, juxtaposition of text with text *on behalf of* specific readers in specific historical/material situations in order to produce new constellations of texts/readers/readings (1995: 14–15).

In this particular study, I attempt such an 'intergetical' reading and re-reading of particular texts, namely Mark 16:1–8 (as focus text), some other relevant Markan texts and, finally, my life texts as touched by the focus text. The meaning of Mark's ending came to me at various points in my life, periods which correspond to the three parts of this paper: the initial experience of being personally disturbed by Mark's ending and finding meaning out of such disturbance; the need to find answers to the subsequent questions evoked by the said text, leading me to a re-reading of the Gospel and discovering other insights in the course of my reading; and an attempt to re-read and re-write two significant life-experiences in the light of the meanings I discovered.

In the end, I realize that the dialogue that ensued between Mark 16:1–8 and me changed not so much the text as me. Perhaps, this is the main reason why, in the end, I decided to share what I have written – despite all the hesitations; or perhaps, my option to write this is already a manifestation of how the book of Mark is affecting my life. There is so much fear to be conquered and so much silence to be overcome, both in that text and in my own life.

Reading Mark's ending

In May 1990 I made a 30-day Ignatian Retreat in one of the Jesuit Retreat Centres in Manila. During that retreat, I heeded the spiritual director's recommendation to use the Gospel of Mark for my reflection and prayer. As I came to the end of the Gospel I had an inkling that something is amiss in the way Mark ends his story. I am speaking here of Mark 16:1–8, which scholars believe to be the authentic ending. Reading Mark's ending made me wonder and ask: What kind of good news is this that ends with no announcement because of fear? Indeed, how can a Gospel end this way? The question remained with me for some time. Later, however, I had to set it aside as I needed to attend to more urgent matters, including, among other things, my impending departure for Rome for further studies.

Two years passed. I finished my Licentiate in Biblical Theology at the Gregorian University in Rome and immediately returned to the Philippines. Back home, before taking on any work, I decided to make an 8-day retreat again using the Gospel of Mark. This time I started with the passion–resurrection narratives, applying what I had learned, namely, that the Gospels were written in the light of the Paschal Mystery and must therefore be read in that light. Now, when I reached the all too brief resurrection story, I was again struck by the ending. This time I had the stronger intuition that such an ending was really intentional. I allowed the insight to illuminate me and became convinced that it was done for a certain effect; this effect, at least to me, was one of 'suspended animation' or even 'animated suspension'. No wonder early readers of Mark could simply not tolerate this 'state' and had to write other endings. We have at least three included in the canon.

What about me? How was I taken down from a state of 'suspended animation'? I remember, while searching for a way out and looking back at the text, I was caught by 16:7 –

> Go, tell his disciples and Peter that he is going before you to Galilee; there you will see him as he told you.[2]

The impact of this line on me was immediate. Shifting my attention from the frightened women, I, as a present reader disciple, suddenly recognized the strong possibility that the story was not yet meant to be over. Rather, it begins again as it apparently comes to a close. The message to me was: The disciple who wants to meet the risen Jesus is enjoined to move, to go back to the beginning: Go to Galilee and there meet him where he walks anew.

I realized then that Mark's Gospel was not meant to be read once, not twice, not even three times but must be read over and over again if it is to make sense. The surprise ending, much like a modulation note in musical terms, is there to transpose it to another key. The invitation to me was one and the same: 'Continue to listen to the music, read on. The story is not over yet.' It continues to the present moment, to the time of the reader (Tannehill 1985: 152; Boring 1991: 69; Myers 1988: 399). The fact is that the future the storyteller is most concerned about is the future of the reader. How the reader responds to the end of Mark's Gospel is what the end of Mark's Gospel is about (Fowler 1991: 248).

Going back to the beginning

I am one of those who decides that the story continues in my own life. First of all, when I read Mark's ending now, I ask what does 'for they were afraid' say to me? How much does it say to me? Second, how do I make sense of the command 'Go and tell the disciples'?

The disciples' fear

In the first place, the women's reaction could very well be a natural human response to a supernatural phenomenon. To be told that a dead person is not dead anymore, who would not be afraid? Yet there seems to be more to the women's fear. To my mind it serves as a poignant reminder of the male disciples' fear. Going back to the first part of the Gospel, such fear is alluded to in the episode of calming the storm, which elicited a rebuke from Jesus about the disciples' lack of faith (cf. 4:40–1). Then again in another episode, Jesus walking on the water (6:48), when, in the light of their lack of understanding and hardness of heart, their fear consequently takes on a negative connotation (6:50–2). Two related instances are also given in Mark 9: one in the transfiguration of Jesus to which Peter reacts in confused chatter because of fear (9:5–6), and the second, towards the end of the chapter. Here, Jesus talks of the fate awaiting him in Jerusalem but the disciples do not understand what he is saying and do not ask for clarification because 'they were afraid' (9:32). Finally, in the last part of their journey, as they are going to Jerusalem, it is observed that 'those who followed were afraid' (10:32). All these instances reach their inevitable climax in the passion narrative where such an attitude is translated into actions of betrayal, desertion and denial (cf. 14:43–5, 50–2, 66–72). The desertion of the disciples is dramatically displayed in the figure of the young man who follows him with nothing but a linen cloth about his body. When Jesus's enemies try to seize him, he leaves the linen cloth and runs away naked (14:51–2). Most poignant of all is the case of Peter, who tries to cling to the Master and even follows him in the High Priest's courtyard only to end up denying that he ever knew him when confronted with the direct challenge to confess being a disciple.

Given this disappointing sequence of events, I realize how much value there is in the figure and the actions of the women mentioned towards the end of the Gospel (cf. 15:40–1; 15:47 and 16:1). These women serve as the lifeline of discipleship (Myers 1988: 396). When everybody else leaves, they remain. Furthermore, they are clearly introduced as disciples, the model ones who 'followed and served' (Kinukawa 1994: 96; Myers 1988: 396) hence, raising the reader's expectation that they, at least, will not fail the Master. That is why their final reaction of 'silence because of fear' is most disheartening. It is climactic in the sense that it reinforces and completes the desertion of the male disciples. In short, such an ending tells me that Jesus's disciples – both men and women – failed him. There are no perfect disciples in Mark, no example of perfect discipleship. Yet the mandate remains; it hangs in the air. What do I make of it now?

The command: 'Go and tell'

The Gospel ends in silence because the women disobeyed the charge to proclaim the resurrection message. There is a very interesting irony here, as noted by one scholar:

> Now that the resurrection has taken place, the silence can be broken and the women are given the commission to begin the process of telling . . . The reader cannot resist the thought that in the women's response of telling nobody anything, it is as if, perversely and at precisely the wrong time, Jesus' women followers have become the ones who do carry out the pre-resurrection injunction to silence.
>
> (Lincoln 1989: 291)

But careful reading of the text shows that the women were not the only ones enjoined to tell the good news and that, in fact, the process of telling has begun even before the resurrection. I refer here to the man from Gerasa (Mark 5:1–20), who after being freed of the legion of demons possessing him, expressed his desire to follow Jesus but was advised instead to go and tell his friends how much the Lord has done for him.[3] Incidentally (or could this be deliberate?), this is also a tomb scene (5:2–5) involving a man freed from spirit-possession sitting fully clothed and in his right mind (5:15). Note here the striking parallel to the tomb scene in 16:1–8, which also portrays a young man sitting dressed in a white robe. The similarity between these two characters is mystifying. Thought-provoking, too, is the seeming continuation of their vocation. The first was ordered to 'Go and tell his friends . . .', while the other in the resurrection account orders the women to 'Go and tell his disciples . . .'

The 'healed' Gerasene is one of the few people in the Gospel who was transformed by Jesus to the point of being an evangelizer himself. Compared to the women, we can say he even fared better. The women fled in fear and said nothing to anyone; the man, on the other hand, went away and began to proclaim in the Decapolis how much Jesus had done for him. His immediate response was to move in accordance to the command. The women's response, on the other hand, was one of disobedience. Instead of going to the community and telling the disciples the message received, they turned back on themselves. The response of the man was to 'move out', that of the women was to 'move in'.

At this point I am led to consider the importance of moving back to the community as an initial step in overcoming fear and in completing another aspect of discipleship, that is, proclaiming the good news. The women may really be faithful servant-disciples who followed and served but are still enclosed in themselves and in need of liberation in order to carry out the mission of proclamation. They need to get out of the spiral of self, go back to the community, go to Galilee, there see Jesus and, together with the rest of the disciples, proclaim what he has done for them.

Fear. Silence. Self-absorption. Could this possibly say something about the community of Mark? For one thing, Juel thinks that the surprise ending of the Gospel involving the women is intended for an implied audience composed of insiders whose problem is indifference and a tired lack of perception about the way things are (1994: 145). It serves as some kind of a shock therapy that jolts them out of apathy and challenges them to action. This situation is not very different from the condition of many Christians today who are weary of waiting, increasingly comfortable in a world capable of hiding from the truth (ibid: 146).

Going back to the comparison between the Gerasene and the women, I suspect that the disciples also need some form of healing or exorcism to be freed from entanglements with the self and be empowered to follow Jesus and proclaim the good news. Whether it be in Mark's time or in ours, we all run the risk of being content with ourselves, failing to remain ever open to the God of surprises. The importance of the community enters here, since it is only in the community that all other Gospel values can be tested: denial of self for the sake of the other, servant-leadership, courageous proclamation of the good news, fearless following of Jesus to the point of death, and so on.

Thus, to shake off one's fear and indifference and return to the community to proclaim the good news becomes the immediate and urgent invitation to me in reading and re-reading Mark's Gospel. Challenged by such provocation, I examine my own following of Jesus and what do I see? I recognize my own fear-infected discipleship that reinforces my silence and hinders me from contributing my share in proclaiming the Gospel.

Following Jesus

Two personal life-experiences come to mind as I read Mark's story now. I shall now attempt to do a re-reading of these two life texts in the context of the insights gathered from my study of Mark 16:1–8. The first happened almost ten years ago when I fell into some kind of depression. The second concerns my involvement in recent events that rocked the local political scene in the Philippines.

Overcoming fear and going back to the community

Immediately after I finished my Master's studies in theology in 1988, I was given an assignment that I subconsciously perceived as stifling my creative energies. However, I found myself helpless in expressing what was in my mind openly to my superiors. As the new porter of the community, I opened doors, welcomed people, attended to the needs of the community and outsiders.[4] But as I opened the gates to others, something in me seemed to shut, namely the flow of my creative intellectual energies. I didn't mind it in the beginning. I tried to convince myself, 'This is the service the community wants from you; be generous'. After all, isn't this true to Jesus's call to his disciples: Seek to serve and not to be served? But the involuntary reactions came: low blood pressure, lack of enthusiasm in everything, isolation from the community, and the like. Even now, I find it embarrassing to accept the inconsistency between my belief system and my actual life, something not very far from the experience of Jesus's disciples who followed and listened to him and yet were unable to do as he did. Consequently, in a matter of 9 months or so, I contemplated asking for a leave of absence since I could see no other way out. It was then that a vivid dream came to me.

> I was in the rooftop of the convent. On the other side of the place I could see and hear my sisters laughing as they were having recreation. I asked myself sadly, 'How can I move from here to join them?' Then I noticed a child beside me. He said, 'Come, I will show you'.
> I followed him as he reached out for an opening on the floor and slowly entered it. He moved down slowly into what I imagined to be a spiral staircase. Curiously, I peeped into the opening and what did I see? It wasn't a spiral staircase but a grinding machine! I was overcome with fear and I shouted, 'Oh no, I can't follow you there!' I heard him shout back, 'Sure, you can!'

As I re-read this experience in the light of the story of the women disciples in Mark, I note two important similarities. For one thing, just as the women were enjoined to go back to the disciples, I too was given the revelation that the way out of my dilemma was to leave my isolation and go back to the community. I believe it was my healthy and positive self using my subconscious to rescue me from the tomb of self-absorption. I cannot stay this way and say I am 'alive'. Life is expressed (at least, symbolically in my dream) in laughter, in joy, in union with others, with the community. So far as I stay enclosed in myself, I am in the tomb; I am not alive. The second similarity concerns my response to the invitation to enter the process of going back to the community as pointed out to me by the child in my dream. Before that, I must say something about the child. This child is, for me, the symbol of 'finding greatness through littleness', the lesson of Mark 9:36–7, probably the most important lesson I have to learn in my life. I need to be humble and recognize that insignificant and menial tasks (for example, doing the work of a porter) could really be my 'door' to understanding and practising Jesus's real values, such as service, gift of self, not in the way I choose but as the community asks of me. The child, personifying littleness, guides me to the 'kingdom' (10:15). In fact, the child is Jesus himself leading me into his paschal mystery – the going down into the depth and darkness (of death) in order to come out into light and laughter (or life). Now, my reaction: Faced with the suggestion that I, too, need to be ground (like wheat? like meat?) in this process of following Jesus, I found myself responding in the same way as the women in the Gospel: I was overcome with fear. It was a concrete fear, fear to lose myself in the process, lose everything I had worked for, everything I valued. I never realized how much my studies and the development of my mind mean to me. My dream, replete with Gospel images, revealed to me what was going on in my actual life. I resisted following the servant Christ. I had other ideas, other aspirations. My dream was as open-ended as the Gospel story because at that point I was still 'in the struggle'. Yet I heard a reassuring voice and I held on to that.

There is no need to narrate what happened next. The fact that I'm still here re-reading Mark time and again and re-telling this story indicates that something good has turned out. Or perhaps, at least up to this point, I can safely say that I eventually managed to overcome my fear (just as I believe that the women consequently overcame theirs) and went back to the community with renewed zeal and commitment.

Facing fear with the community

This second story is still ongoing even at the moment of writing. A few months earlier, my country, the Philippines, was in turmoil, faced with many urgent crises such as a dwindling economy that is affecting the entire Asian region, full-scale globalization that further marginalizes the poor and greatly benefits a chosen few, threats of drought and other natural calamities, inefficient and insufficient delivery of basic services, and so on. But we were still relatively peaceful until politics came onto the scene. The lawmakers whose terms are ending and who cannot seek re-election next year (as provided for in our Constitution) plotted to amend the law of the land. Ambition for power and honour is very evident here, once more reminding me of the male disciples in Mark, whose preoccupation was to be the greatest, to sit at the right and the left of the Master in his glory (Mark 9:33–7; 10:35–44). The President of the Republic was not strong enough to stop these men for the obvious reason that he too would be among the beneficiaries if such a move should succeed. In the Philippine Constitution, the incumbent head of state cannot seek a second term; this is to protect the country from repeating the painful experience of dictatorship, the wounds of which we still suffer, albeit to a lesser degree. [5]

For us mid-September was like being in the tomb. There was no light, no truth. There was a crisis of credibility on the part of our leaders. Finally, the church leaders, namely the Catholic Bishops Conference of the Philippines, dared to speak, backed up by some concerned citizens. Following this, two leaders rose up. One is a woman, former President Corazon Aquino, the other a man, Jaime Cardinal Sin, Archbishop of Manila. Their invitation was unique: 'Let us go out as one people for a prayer rally on 21 September. Let us pray for truth, courage and peace in our country. Let us tell the President and our lawmakers: We want democracy, truth, justice!' The united voices of these two leaders were to me like that of the young man at the tomb 'Go and tell his disciples . . .'

The response of the majority was similar to that of the frightened women. Different expressions of fear were felt, but fear camouflaged in various forms. Criticism came from many fronts of society, including the President himself. A psychological war ensued. 'Do not go out! Something will happen to you,' said the military. Politicians clamoured, 'There is separation of Church and state here; why is the church meddling in our affairs?' Bomb scares were everywhere but especially the day before the announced rally. Two bombs were discovered in large churches of Manila.

Fear was all over the land. There were rumours of martial law or a possible military take-over. At this point, my conscience struggled with the profound question: Must I go out and join the rally or not? My fellow sisters asked themselves the same question: Must we go out and join the people and the church that cry out for support, accompaniment and guidance or should we stay home and pray? Are we convinced that this is part of our duty as Christians? Are we being too politically involved? Is the street a proper place for us considering that a big part of our life is contemplative and our Founder said, 'You are never as efficacious as when you bring the needs of humanity in prayer before Jesus in the Blessed Sacrament?' How should we interpret such statement in this specific condition? Above all, given the different threats of violence around us, are we ready to die?

The few days that followed was a time of intense prayer and discernment. In the context of the Gospel, it was a period of being with Jesus on the way to Jerusalem calling me to assess my faith and courage to follow him wherever he leads. At some point in my discernment, I cannot say exactly when, I felt strong enough to decide to go and join my people. It was not important anymore whether I would be suffering from the violent plots of the lawless elements of the society. I knew deep within that I would not be alone. Perhaps that is also where I found that strength – in believing that Jesus is walking before us and that there are many other disciples out there who also want those true values of truth, justice and peace to reign. They too, like their Master, are ready to fight, even to die, for such values. When I went out with a number of my sisters that fateful day, I was still a little apprehensive, especially as there were threats of assassination hurled at the two leaders, but such fear was not enough to extinguish the light that guided us.

21 September 1997 was a day full of irony just as the good news preached by Mark is a Gospel of irony. Former President Cory Aquino, who spoke to

the crowd after the ecumenical prayer and the Eucharist that afternoon, asked pensively, 'What should the mood of this rally be considering that this is the anniversary of the imposition of martial law years ago? Should the mood be sad for the day democracy died 25 years ago?[6] Or should the mood be happy because we are free to commemorate that tragic event in freedom again?' (Aquino 1997: 17) She herself answered the question, expressing completely what everyone was feeling despite all the turmoil:

> Here we celebrate the unity that makes people power. We are many, we are free, we are committed and we are strong. We are people power once more. We triumphed over tyranny before; tyranny cannot triumph over us again – not while we are many, vigilant and united.
>
> (ibid.)

I was glassy-eyed as I joined my people, 600 000 of them present in Luneta Park in Manila (simultaneously joined by tens of thousands in separate prayer rallies in key cities of the country), in applauding this woman who pledged her whole life to fight any attempt to destroy democracy, a woman, so soft-spoken, peace-loving, devout in her religiosity and yet as tenacious as steel in her love for country and people. I know that this goes beyond the story of the women-disciples in Mark for here, even for a brief moment, I behold the personification of perfect discipleship: fearless following of Christ, selfless servant-leadership also in the socio-political arena. And I know that fear cannot have the last word for as long as such disciples as these are present in our midst.

Epilogue

I return to where I began. The ending of Mark's Gospel remains as open-ended as when I first read it. But now, I am even more convinced that it makes sense as it is. Mark leaves no marks of the risen Jesus, no resurrection appearances similar to those in the other Gospels; only an empty tomb, a group of frightened disciples and a command that hangs in the air. In deciding to end his Gospel this way, he opens a way for me to re-think my following of Jesus in the various dimensions of life.

What kind of response we give to the Gospel command 'Go and tell his disciples' will determine the quality of our following. Fear and silence may be the disciples' response, making them the last words in Mark's Gospel, but that was only meant to awaken those who might be 'slumbering' in their faith in and following of Jesus. My experience (together with my people) proves that there is a way to offset this fear and silence, and continue re-telling the never-ending story of Jesus.

Notes

1 Voelz (1995: 154) says, 'Matrixing for interpretation *is not restricted to the same type of text* . . . One must also consider what might be called "experiential texts." *A reader must be seen as a text.* Or perhaps more accurately, the states, actions, hopes, fears and knowledge of a reader's life-experience comprise a "text"' (emphases his).

2 The highly important relationship between vv. 7 and 8 is affirmed by Petersen (1980: 162–3) who says, 'The ironic equivocation of the meaning of 16:8 redirects the reader's attention back to the immediately preceding words of the young man. These words restore the continuity interrupted by 16:8 and begin the reader's experience of the second effect of the irony.' Cf. Lincoln (1989).

3 I am indebted here to another Markan reader, Fr. Charles Wolf, S.J. who pointed out to me such an interesting parallel. I am aware, though, that my reading here is still insufficient and needs a more thorough investigation.

4 Ours is a twentieth-century foundation engaged in evangelization through the Eucharistic–Priestly–Liturgical apostolate; expressions of such mission vary widely ranging from teaching to doing manual and domestic services.

5 The Philippines were under the regime of Marcos' dictatorship for more than twenty years (1965–86) until the world famous People Power Revolution led by Former President Corazon Aquino deposed him in February 1986.

6 Martial law was imposed in the country on 21 September 1972, the year before Marcos was about to end his term as President of the Republic.

References

Aichele, G. and Phillips, G. A. (1995) 'Introduction: Exegesis, Eisegesis, Intergesis', in G. Aichele and G. A. Phillips (eds) *Intertextuality and the Bible, Semeia* 69/70, Atlanta: GA, Scholars, 7–18.

Aquino, C. (1997) 'Trust the Filipino'. Speech delivered to the Filipino People in the 21 September Prayer Rally, published in *Philippine Daily Star*, Manila, 17.

Boring, M. E. (1991) 'Mark 1:1–15 and the Beginning of the Gospel', in D. E. Smith (ed.) *How Gospels Begin, Semeia* 52, Atlanta: GA, Scholars, 43–81.

Fowler, R. M. (1991) *Let the Reader Understand. Reader-Response Criticism and the Gospel of Mark*, Minneapolis, MN: Fortress.

Juel, D. (1994) *A Master of Surprises. Mark Interpreted*, Minneapolis, MN: Fortress.

Kinukawa, H. (1994) *Women and Jesus in Mark. A Japanese Feminist Perspective*, Maryknoll, NY: Orbis Books.

Kitzberger, I. R. (1994) 'Love and Footwashing: John 13:1–20 and Luke 7:36–50 Read Intertextually', *Biblical Interpretation* 2: 190–206.

Lincoln, A. (1989) 'The Promise and the Failure: Mark 16:7–8', *JBL* 108: 283–300.

Miller, N. (1991) *Getting Personal. Feminist Occasions and Other Autobiographical Acts*, New York and London: Routledge.

Moore, S. D. (1996) 'True Confessions and Weird Obsessions: Autobiographical Interventions in Literary and Biblical Studies', in J. Capel Anderson and J. L. Staley (eds) *Taking It Personally: Autobiographical Criticism, Semeia* 72, Atlanta, GA: Scholars, 19–50.

Myers, C. (1988) *Binding the Strong Man. A Political Reading of Mark's Story about Jesus*, Maryknoll, NY: Orbis Books.

Petersen, N. (1980) 'When is the End not the End? Literary Reflections on the Ending of Mark's Narrative', *Interpretation* 34: 151–66.

Tannehill, R. (1985) 'The Disciples in Mark: The Function of a Narrative Role', in W. R. Telford (ed.) *The Interpretation of Mark*, Philadelphia, PA: Fortress, 134–57.

Voelz, J. (1995) 'Multiple Signs, Levels of Meaning and Self as Text: Elements of Intertextuality', in G. Aichele and G. A. Phillips (eds) *Intertextuality and the Bible, Semeia* 69/70, Atlanta, GA: Scholars: 149–64.

5

FATHERS AND SONS

Fragments from an autobiographical midrash on John's Gospel

Jeffrey L. Staley

Fragment one

'They answered him, "Abraham is our father".' John 8:39

And Abraham knew his wife, and she conceived and bore a son, and they named him Isaac. And Abraham lifted up his eyes and looked west. And he saw that the land of Indiana was good land, and he journeyed westward and settled there. Abraham Staley and Mary had two sons and two daughters. Abraham lived seventy-seven years, and he died and was buried beside his wife beneath a grove of hickory trees near Cumberland, Indiana.

And Isaac knew his wife, and she conceived and bore a son. And they named him Abraham. Isaac and Lavinia had five sons and four daughters. Issac lived seventy-five years and he died and was buried beside his mother and father, beneath the grove of hickory trees near Cumberland, Indiana.

And Abraham knew his wife, and she conceived and bore a son. And she named him Arlonzo. For she said, 'There have been far too many biblical names in this family.' And Abraham lifted up his eyes and looked west, and he saw that the land of Kansas was good land, and he journeyed westward and settled there. Abraham and Eliza had nine sons. Abraham lived eighty-two years and he died and was buried beside his wife in Ottawa, Kansas.

And Arlonzo knew his wife, and she conceived and bore a son. And they named him Lloyd. Arlonzo and May Belle had five sons. Arlonzo lived ninety-one years and he died and was buried beside his wife in Wellsville, Kansas.

And Lloyd knew his wife, and she conceived and bore a son. And they named him Robert. And there was a famine in the land, so Lloyd and Mary moved to the city. Lloyd and Mary had six sons and three daughters. And when they were old, lo, they lifted up their eyes and looked west. And they saw that the land of California was good land, and they journeyed westward and settled there. Lloyd lived eighty-eight years and he died and was buried beside his wife in Atascadero, California.

And Robert knew his wife, and she conceived and bore a son. And they named him Jeffrey. And Robert lifted up his eyes and looked east, and he saw that the land of Arizona was good land, and he journeyed eastward and settled there. Bob and Betty had four sons and two daughters. And Betty died and was buried at Immanuel Mission, on the Navajo Reservation. Then Robert took Esther for his wife, and they moved to Phoenix, a royal city, a miracle of glass and steel rising like a gigantic bird from hot desert ashes. And there they live, even until this day.

And Jeffrey knew his wife . . .

Fragment two

'Very truly, I tell you, unless you eat the flesh of the Son of Man and drink his blood, you have no life in you.' John 6:53

And he said,
'This is my body;
take, eat ye all of it.
Run your tongue
over its soft round smoothness.
Breathe deep its heavenly scent.
Gaze long at its fragile opaqueness.
Cup it in your hands, caress it tenderly.
Nibble its outer edges
slowly, slowly.
Then swallow me whole.
Eat me up, up, up;
sup on me, one long,
everlastingly long sip –
dip in,
dine, thine.
Come to me,
oh come.
Come unto me,
on to me
now, now,
and I will give you rest.'
And it was so.
And he said,
'Here is my life blood
poured out for you;

drink deeply of it.
Remember me
in the rhythmic passages
of your life.
Wash your body
in my heavenly flow.
Find in its tingling flush
yourself
unearthed,
rebirthed.
A wriggling mass
of unumbilicled joy.'
And it was so.

And so she conceived and bore a son, and they named him Benjamin, for they said, 'It is a good name, a family name.'

Jeffrey and Barbara had one son and one daughter. And they are alive, even until this day.

Fragment three

'In the beginning was the Word, and the Word was with God, and the Word was God.' John 1:1

I have always wanted to be a father, just like in the beginning. But I wanted to be the father of a daughter first. A son could come later. Just give me the daughter first. My mother promised I would have the daughter first. Moments before she died I saw my daughter in her eyes – a translucent embryo in her last, silent tear that said, 'I'm sorry I will never get a chance to hold your baby girl in my arms.'

Now I have two children. A son and a daughter. But my mother was wrong. The son came first.

En arche en ho logos, kai ho logos en pros ton theon, kai theos en ho logos

En can mean 'in, with, or by' says Arndt and Gingrich's *A Greek–English Lexicon of the New Testament and Other Early Christian Literature*. And it can mean a host of other things too. It's like the Hebrew preposition *be*. The rabbis speculated about the meaning of the prepositon *be* together with the noun *reshith* in Gen. 1:1. Does the expression mean 'in the beginning' or 'with the first thing'? And if it means 'with the first thing', then what is that first thing to which it refers? Maybe it refers to *hokmah*, said the rabbis. God made wisdom first, a female creature, and then everything else followed from her and was imprinted with her image. Perhaps John 1:1–18 is a fragment of a hymn to wisdom in which the feminine, Hellenistic *sophia* or the feminine, Semitic *hokmah* has metamorphosed into the masculine *logos*.

Some say that Christians, like those Jewish rabbis of old, also have a theology of prepositions. In argument with Calvinists and Roman Catholics Lutherans say the real body and blood of Jesus are given 'in, with, and under' the bread and wine. You are baptized '*en pneumati hagio*' says the author of Luke–Acts (Acts 11:16). But does the writer mean 'in the Holy Spirit', 'with the Holy Spirit', or 'by the Holy Spirit'? Entire Pentecostal denominations have been founded upon fine-line distinctions such as these. It's the difference, for instance, between telling my son, 'Go play by yourself for a while' and telling him, 'Go play with yourself for a while'. The distinction is crucial, but he doesn't seem to do much of either. Most often he is outside in the neighbourhood, organizing games among his friends. My daughter, on the other hand, is more apt to play by herself and with herself.

'See dad, I have a little penis,' she announces proudly as she sits in the bathtub and spreads her labia apart.

'Well, kind of,' I say. I try to explain to her the difference between boys and girls. But she has already lost interest. She is busy blowing bubbles and trying to catch them in the palms of her hands.

I want to be right up front about this issue of gender in John, just as I have been with my children. Gender matters.

'*En arche en ho logos, kai ho logos en pros ton theon, kai theos en ho logos*', writes the author of the Fourth Gospel. One feminine noun and two masculine nouns. And the two masculines, hiding behind the one feminine, have overpowered (*katelaben*) the feminine *sophia* and *hokmah* in the history of exegesis.

But if you take the masculine ending '*os*' from *theos* you simply have '*the*'. 'In the beginning was the *The*.' I like that. The terminal sigma, shaped like a slithering snake, is absent, and in its absence *theos* loses its masculine power.

In the beginning was the word – defrocked, emasculated, skinned, undone. And the word was with *the* . . . *the* . . . whatever – and the word was – whatever. Whatever the *os* will make it be. And mark my words, the *os* will make itself into something.

Fragment four

'*All things came into being through him, and without him, not one thing came into being.*' John 1:3

That sneaky, sibilant sigma, shaped like a snake, is the one sound I could not say as a lisping boy of four. And not only at four. It would be twenty more years before my future wife finally taught me where to place my tongue.

'Like this,' she said, smiling encouragingly. And she opened her mouth into a wide *O*. So esses came spewing out of my mouth, just as if I were the Gihon Spring or the Euphrates River. And from that day forward the esses have not stopped coming.

Then one day a son came out. Right out of a wide, pulsating *O*. The unique child of his father. Half Chinese. The first non-Caucasian Staley child that I have been able to find in my family genealogy; the first non-Asian child in my wife's family. A wrong-headed child from the Staley–Wong family. His mixed up genetics are a metaphor for my own mixed up life.

The Father is in me and I am in the Father.[1]

In the beginning there was my son. And then three years later a daughter came along.

I always wanted the girl to come first. Just like in John 1:1, where the feminine *arche* precedes the masculine *logos* and *theos*. But for five generations in the Staley family boys have come first. I am not as different as my mother thought I would be, nor as different as I had hoped.

I watch my firstborn slowly poke a head through the widening *O*, into the great unknown. Before the child is waist deep in the world I hear the strong cry of life. Regardless of gender, the child will be strong and healthy. I helped make this child. I will teach this child – born, borne, bone of my bone and flesh of my flesh – about truth, about love, about the ways of the world.

Oh.

Boy.

It's a boy.

Fragment five

'Look, here is the Lamb of God!' John 1:36

My newborn son's penis is huge. And it is not circumcised. He is not like me. What do I do now? I don't know anything about foreskins. This is America. American boys aren't supposed to be born with them. Snakes shed their skins. Baby boys shed their foreskins. Take him out behind the woodshed and have him skinned.

What do you do with a foreskin?
My son's is the first I've seen. Maybe we should cut it off.
'Do you want to make the first cut?' the doctor asks.
'*What*!'
'You know, do you want to cut the umbilical cord? Lots of fathers do nowadays. It's kind of a ritual.'
'Oh. No, not really. You can cut it. I'll just watch.'
Clip.

My daughter is different. We know she is a girl almost from the beginning. We saw her *in utero*, in a frontal position on the ultrasound. A head, two arms, trunk, two legs. No penis.

'Really?'
'Really. See?' says the doctor. 'Looks like a girl, all right!'

But just to be safe we pick two names: Allison Jean, if the sonogram is right; Stephen Isaac, if it has somehow missed an important part of human anatomy.

I was sicker than a dog when my daughter was conceived. My wife and I had been trying for months to have another child. The child should be born in summer, we decided, just like the first one, because I am a professor and will have the summer off to help with the new baby. So in September 1987 we begin baby making in earnest. But no baby. Now it is February, and I have a horrible cold.

'It's that time,' Barbara nudges me in the dark.
'Are you sure?'
'Yeah, I'm sure. I just took my temperature.'
'It can't be,' I groan, 'Not tonight. I can't even breathe!'
'But you've got to!' She whispers fiercely. And then she touches me.
I know it's going to be hard, but I give it a try.

Much to our surprise a child is conceived that night. Our daughter will be born in October, mid-semester, just in time for midterms. Oh well, I don't sleep much then anyway.

Allison's umbilical cord is wrapped around her neck. It stretches taut, her heartbeat quickens. Her face begins to turn blue. With a quiet, urgent tone that sends chills down my spine, the doctor commands my wife, 'Stop pushing'. Then she slips a knife blade between my half-born daughter's neck and my wife's vagina. Carefully, slowly she cuts the cord. I am surprised at the rush of air that escapes my throat. I feel lightheaded and look for a chair.

The boy is red and smooth; soft, like crushed velvet. He nestles in my arms as I try awkwardly to hold his huge, swaying head. He is perfect, not one blemish or mole on his entire body. A spotless lamb of God.

My daughter is different. She is born with a wine-stain birthmark in the middle of her forehead. It is a special sign. A bright pink star.

A nurse, noticing my intense gaze, says encouragingly, 'It will fade with time.' But she misunderstands my staring. I want the star to stay.

Star light, star bright,
first star I see tonight;
I wish I may, I wish I might,
have the wish I wish tonight.

I inspect the rest of her body. Ten fingers, ten toes. An engorged vulva. She waits three minutes before she utters a sound.

> She has a beautiful round mole on her left buttock.
> *– All things counter, original, spare, strange;*
> *Whatever is fickle, freckled (who knows how) –*
> 'That mole will make some man happy one day', I say, and my wife smiles.

His eyes try hard to focus on my face as I speak to him. I have talked to him many times in the past few months, as I nuzzled my wife's bulging belly. For seven months I have been calling him Katie, to help him become the girl I wanted first. But now I hold a boy in my arms and devise for him an impromptu oath as his eyes move around crazily in different directions.

'I know I will make many mistakes as a father,' I whisper in his tiny ear. 'I've never been one before now. But I promise that I will always love you.'

I silently pray that it will be true, for I have never been a father, and I had not been expecting a boy.

I carry him to the Alta Bates Hospital nursery, wrapped in a warm towel, where a nurse washes him off and lays him under a heat lamp, as though he were an entree to be served up from a cafeteria steam table.

This is my son. Hear him cry. A bleating little lamb.

I return to my wife's side, give her a kiss goodnight, and walk home alone to our two-room apartment on College Avenue in Berkeley. It is 7 June 1985. It is 2 o'clock in the morning. Even though I know that this will be my last chance in many months to get a good night's sleep, I lie awake for hours.

I am the father of a son: Benjamin (named for my favourite uncle, who was named for Benjamin Lamb, my paternal grandfather's maternal grandfather) Walter (named for my wife's father). A family name. Also a playful inversion of Walter Benjamin, a famous Jewish philosopher and literary critic whose writings I have recently read. My son's name is a subtle joke that no one in my family or my wife's family will ever catch. The son's father likes to pretend he is a famous New Testament literary critic. So the father gives his firstborn a famous name, turned upside down, just like the way he came into the world.

I have just finished writing a dissertation on the Gospel of John, and I will begin teaching that autumn in a tenure-track position at the University of Portland, in Oregon. I have a wonderful wife, a new son, and a new career. I know I will be a good provider, just like God was a good provider for his Son. I want to be like God. Tonight I feel like a god.

The world is a beautiful place. It is *my* place, *my* world. I have made it one person more beautiful than it was yesterday.

Fragment six

'Moses gave you circumcision' (it is, of course, not from Moses
but from the patriarchs). . . *John 7:22*

Okay. We've had some time to think about it. Should we have our son circumcised? I am vacillating. Just a few hours ago he was a girl. I was sure of it. Now he is Benjamin, my son. And he has a foreskin.

My wife and I weigh the pros and cons of circumcision for seven days. Finally, her brother calls. 'Look, I had to be circumcised when I was twelve, because of an infection. It was pure hell. Junior high and all that. You should do it now, so he won't be forced to have it done later.'

How do you clean a foreskin? I don't know how to do it. If we don't have him circumcised he will be different from me, and I will be unable to help him.

On the eighth day we decide to have Benjamin circumcised. Just like a little Jewish boy.

> He will look like me.
> He will be like me.

I hold him down while the doctor straps his tiny arms and legs to a pad.

> He will look like me.
> He will be like me.

My son begins to cry. He doesn't like being tied down, naked and spread-eagled, like the Greek letter

X^2

> Caught in the surgeon's finely woven web,
> He fights to free himself.
> In just a few moments it will be over, my son. Trust me.
> You will be free. Free indeed.
> I hear the bleating of a lamb.

> Abraham is my father.
> Abraham is my father.

'It won't really hurt, you know,' the doctor says reassuringly. 'I've done hundreds of these before. He won't remember a thing. Trust me. I'm a father too.'

> 'After properly cleansing the penis and pubis, the dorsal aspect of
> the prepuce is put on a stretch by grasping it on either side of the
> median line with a pair of hemostats.'[3]

This boy should have been named Isaac, like his great, great, great, great grandfather.

Isaac, my son, I want to hear you laugh.
Laugh, boy! Laugh!

But the joke's on me. I have helped bind you to an altar of plastic and steel. You will be altered, and no divine voice will tell the doctor to put down his knife.

You are my son, but you don't look like me.
I want you to look like me. I want you to be like me. I want you to fit in.
I don't want other American boys to laugh and stare at you in the gym or the bathroom when they see you naked, with a foreskin in your hands.

My eyes are on the doctor.
Steady, steady.

'A flat probe, anointed with vaseline, is then inserted between the prepuce and the glans to separate adherent mucous membrane. The prepuce is then gently drawn backwards exposing the entire glans penis . . . In cases where the prepuce is drawn tightly over the glans, a partial dorsal slit will facilitate applying the cone of draw stud [the bell] over the glans. After anointing the inside of the cone, it is placed over the glans penis allowing enough of the mucous membrane to fit below the cone so that too much is not removed. The prepuce is then pulled through and above the bevel hole in the platform and clamped in place. In this way the prepuce is crushed against the cone causing hemostasis. We allow this pressure to remain five minutes, and in older children slightly longer. The excess of the prepuce is then cut with a sharp knife without any danger of cutting the glans, which is always protected by the cone portion of the instrument, leaving a very fine 1/32 of an inch ribbon-like membrane formed between the new union of the skin and mucous membrane. The pressure is then released.'[4]

No anaesthesia is used.
It is finished.

Fragment seven

'The Father loves the Son and has placed all things in his hands.' John 3:35

Watch my son writhe.
He is purple with rage and pain.

'The application of two hemostats to the edges of the sensitive, unanesthetized prepuce, the application of a third crushing hemostat to the prepuce before cutting the dorsal slit, and the crushing of the entire circumference of the prepuce by turning a screw on the Gomco Clamp produces excruciating pain. Since Anand and Hickey's article in the *New England Journal of Medicine* (K. J. S. Anaud and P. R. Hickey, 'Pain and Its Effects in the Human Neonate and Fetus,' 317 [1987]: 1321, 1324, 1325), it can no longer be denied that pain is felt by the male infant during circumcision. Although the Gomco Clamp may have been designed to reduce the risk of bleeding, it has produced excruciating pain in every infant on which it is used. Even if anesthesia is used, the post-operative pain originating in a pleasure center can be expected to have serious untoward consequences.'[5]

My son screams. He screams and he screams.
I cannot console him.

The Father is in me and I am in the Father.
The father loves the son and has placed all things in his hands.
In his hands.
In his tiny pink hands.
I am the father.
The son of far too many Abrahams.
But I am worse than them.
I pay someone else to take knife in hand and do what I cannot do.

'During the biblical period (*c.* 1700 BCE – 140 CE), the operator, or mohel placed a metal shield with a slit in it near the tip of the foreskin, so only the tip was removed. Often the mohel . . . pulled up on the outside of the foreskin before placing the shield. The result was that virtually all of the inner lining of the prepuce was preserved. This was known as Bris Milah.

'The wonderful statue of David by Michelangelo appears intact but is in fact correctly represented because the future King David has been circumcised by the accepted procedure of the biblical era. Only the tip of his foreskin has been removed, fulfilling the covenant with Abraham (Genesis 17).'[6]

Hours later I am still clasping my son's doll-like fingers.

Benjamin!
Benjamin!
I will always love you.

Jesus!
Sweet, sweet Jesus!
I'm sorry.
I am sorry.

Look at me! I'm wet with your sweat and tears.
You look like me.
You will be like me.
You will like me.

Fragment eight

'Put your sword back in its sheath. Am I not to drink the cup that the Father has given me?' John 18:11

'Are you sure you want to go through with this?' my doctor asks as he enters the room where I lie, half-naked, on an examining table.

My legs are spread apart, and my feet are in webbed stirrups, as though I am about to give birth. A sheet covers the lower part of my body.

A nurse comes in and cleanses my crotch with some orange, purifying liquid. Does she find my penis tiny? How does it compare with other penises she has seen? Does she ever take notes? I watch her eyes. She gives nothing away.

Do I want to go through with this?

Of course I do. I have two healthy children, one girl and one boy. And I have to put them through college someday. I can't afford to have any more children.

Through with this.

Hmmm. . . *Dia* with the genitaliave? Expression of agency? (With a note of urgency.) Or is it an ablative of accompaniment? Perhaps it should be *eis* with the accusative. The idea of limit, extent, direction toward, is important in this case.

'Yes, I want to go through with it.'
'Ouch!'
The doctor's needle pricks my skin at a very sensitive point.
'Did you feel that?'
'Yeah, whaddyya *think*?'

The doctor removes the sheet covering the lower half of my body, and I lean forward, propping myself up on my elbows. I watch as the doctor makes an incision in my scrotum and pulls out two tiny threads that connect my testicles to their ejaculatory ducts.

Ah, the vas deferens.

Truly, truly, I am a vine, and my *Doktorvater* is a vinedresser. He is removing every living branch from me so that I can no longer bear fruit.

I am thinking of Derrida and one of his many books – was it in *Dissemination* that he talked about the vastness of différance? I can't remember. I'm having problems concentrating on Derrida. I have a weird sensation in my anus, my derrière –

da . . . yes, right there –

as though someone is pulling an enormously long stringnified from it.

The doctor explains the surgery's aftereffects in response to my unvoiced anxieties.

'You'll be sore for a few days.'
'Don't do any lifting.'
'Take pain pills.'
'Oh, and be sure to wear an athletic cup – you know, a Jacquestrap – for at least 48 hours.'

I am a vine.
Clip.
I will never be the same. I am forever différant.
Clip.
The penis . . . is . . . is . . . mightier than the sword.

Fragment nine

'Those who drink of the water that I will give them will never be thirsty.' John 4:14

I imagine a milky white, life-giving liquid seeping out onto the doctor's fingers.

From my side are flowing rivers of living water.

For ages, fathers and sons have drunk from wells like this. Jacob and his sons, for example. This liquid is a man's identity, the proof of his virility, masculinity, and power. I have been cut off from the land of the living.

Come, all you who are thirsty. Drink of me before I disappear.
A final drink.
To death, then.
Bottoms up. Derrière-da.
I go home and my wife makes a careful inspection of my body.
'Oh, my goodness, it has shrunk!'
She is worried.
'Is it supposed to look like that?'
I look down. It's true. My scrotum is black-and-blue and my penis is no larger than that of my 4-year-old son.

76

Within a few days, however, I'm a little kid, playing with myself again.
Every few weeks I masturbate and ejaculate into a little plastic cup.
I put the top on the cup and take it to the hospital.
See what I can do?

'Am I dead yet?'
'No, not yet.'

The well is deeper than I thought.
Four months later the harvest comes, and I finally hear the response I have
been waiting for.

'It is finished. You are dead.'
'Now you can go out and live again.'

Fragment ten

*'Very truly I tell you, the Son can do nothing on his own, but
only what he sees the Father doing; for what the Father does,
the Son does likewise.' John 5:19*

A poem for my son, at 5 years old.

Jigsaw Puzzles
So like the father is the son,
matching color to color,
shape to shape,
with quickness and precision;
with flashes of intuition.
Surprises are interlocked
with carefully crafted solutions:
Sometimes he follows shadows to light,
or bright hues to near whites.
At other times, the mere
slippery force of gravity
pulls pairs together.
But, curiously, he does not begin with borders.
He leaves
without speaking,
those straight edges
which protect the slow-forming picture
from the chaos creeping
across the dining room table,
for another to shape and fit.

Fragment eleven

*'You search the writings because you think that in them
you have eternal life; and it is they that testify
on my behalf.' John 5:39*

My son has decided to read my recent book, *Reading with a Passion*, for his
sixth-grade book report. The class assignment is to read an autobiography,
and since part of my book is autobiographical, he wants to write about me. I
am not crazy about his idea, since it is difficult reading and he won't
understand much of anything he reads. I think he thinks the assignment
will be made easier if he reads about someone he knows. Still, I am pleased
that he wants to read the book. After all, I gave him and my daughter
Allison autographed copies when it first came out. I was hoping he would
read the book sometime before I died. I just didn't expect him to try it
when he was 11.

Ben Staley
3/5/97
Reading
Book Report

Reading with a Passion

I   Introduction.

Have you ever dreamed of doing an autobiography book report on
your own father? Well, I did. My father's name is Jeffrey L. Staley.
He comes from an immense family that consists of one father,
Robert, two mothers, Betty, and the step-mother is Esther. My
dad also has two sisters, Brenda and Beth, and three brothers,
Rob, David, and Greg. Some of his famous ancestors are: George
Johnson, who rode horse-back in 'Buffalo Bill's Wild West Show.'
William Brewster is another famous ancestor of his, William was
the founder of the Plymouth colony.

On December 22, 1951, my dad's body met the world. Surprisingly, December 22 is the same day that the Mayflower unloaded
its cargo at Plymouth Rock. When my dad was born, doctors
found nothing wrong with him. But when his older, stronger
brothers found out he was born without peripheral vision in his
right eye, they would constantly try to coax him into playing
baseball. My dad has lived in many places in his life, these places
are: Ramona, Kansas, Immanuel Mission, Arizona, and Berkeley,
California. Jeff is currently living in Bothell, Washington. Before
coming to Bothell, he was living in Portland, Oregon.

II

Can an ordinary dad be famous? Although my dad is not really famous, he is to me. Famous to me is not always being the fastest in the world, or being the best known in the world. My dad is famous to me because he is responsible, loving, and caring to his family members. He is also cooperative. You would have to be if you had two older brothers. My dad has become 'famous' by accomplishing what he has done. He has taught at over four different colleges, been a father, a younger brother, an older brother, a McDonald's employee, and a son! If you ask me, that's a lot to be respected for. My dad has also been through peer pressure, and pressure in general. Just those two are some of the big things people have to overcome in a lifetime. Jeff has also come over many hardships too. His brother has given him drugs before, and he did not know what to do with them. So, being the good companion he was, he passed them out after school.

III

Although Jeff's accomplishments do not affect *us* today (us not being the world or country), they have affected many. For example, his accomplishment of becoming a teacher has affected his students. They are probably now more 'equipped' to go out in the world to teach others about Jesus Christ. Also, he has experienced being a younger and older sibling. This accomplishment lets him be a better father in a way. That experience helped him because it let him appreciate both sides of an argument. It also let him be a younger child with his younger brother and sisters, but I also think it let him be an older child with his more mature brothers. That is why I think my dad has made a difference to some people, but not necessarily everyone.

IV

Now you may think that just because a dad looks old, he is old. Well, my dad is an old guy, but not too old. At heart he is still twelve years old. Now, at the age of about nine and ten, my dad liked two weird things. He liked his brothers' 'girlfriends' and he liked butter, ketchup, and bologna sandwiches. Pretty strange, don't you think? By now you probably think my dad is pretty crazy. Well, he did some unusual things too, like in the summer, he liked to burn up ants with a magnifying glass. He also liked to pull the legs off of crickets or grasshoppers, then he would feed them to a nearby black widow spider, and watch it slowly devour them. [7] In the dark of night though, he and his brothers would pull the 'flashlights' off of harmless little fireflies, stick the lights on their fingers, and wiggle their fingers around!

Jeff tells the story of his most embarrassing moment when his family was not so very wealthy. In fact, they couldn't even afford to buy jelly for their toast. When they finally could buy a jar, they did. The next morning my dad was having a 'ceremony' in celebration of having jam. He was holding the jar above his head, then, he dropped it!

V

What I really admire about my dad is how, as long as he has lived, he really only remembers the good times and not his bad times. I hope one day I will be like him, in some ways. I also admire how he has stuck to teaching, even though he has been turned down, and been 'fired' by many colleges. Some day, I hope my dream will come true. My dad's accomplishments have changed my life because they have made me a better person. They have made me a better person because I have someone I can look to when I have problems, someone with experience.

Benjamin asked me to proofread his essay when he was done, and I did. I wrote at the top, 'Good work! You've done an excellent job!' in big round letters.

Now he is at my side, trying to get my attention.

'Dad, do you have any clothes I can borrow?'

'Why do you want my clothes?' I ask suspiciously.

'Well, tomorrow I have to do a class presentation about the auto-biography I read, so I thought I would dress up like you.'

I go upstairs and rummage through my closet, finding a hat and shirt that he can wear. I discover an old transistor radio that I bought when I was 12 years old, and show that to him, too.

'I used to listen to "Yours truly, KOMA, Oklahoma City!" on this little radio.' I pat it and sing their signature ditty from 1964.

'That's where I heard the Beatles for the first time, you know. Out there on the reservation, thirty miles from the closest post office, Navajo girls used to come running over to listen to my Montgomery Ward radio whenever I yelled, "It's the Beatles!"'

'KOMA was the only rock 'n roll station we could pick up there in northern Arizona. I would fall asleep with the earphone stuck in my ear, and wake up in the morning to static.'

'Cool, Dad. Does it still work?'

'I don't know, let's try it. I haven't used it in about twenty years.'

We find a 9-volt battery, put it in the radio, and turn it on.

Static.

I turn the dial.

Music. Maybe it's KOMA.

'She loves you, yeah, yeah, yeah!'

'Come on, Dad! That's a song by Alice in Chains!'
'Oh.'
'Hey, can I take this radio to school too?'
'Sure! Just don't lose it. It's one of the only things I have left from my childhood.'
'I'll take good care of it. Thanks, Dad!'

And he gives me a kiss.

Fragment twelve

*'While I was with them, I protected them in your name
that you have given me, so that they may be one,
as we are one.' John 17:12*

He is my son. I am his father. I am in him and he is in me.

But my daughter is different. She is the intruder, the one that upsets the natural equilibrium. I am in her too, and she in me. But it cannot be the same. Even though we occasionally still sleep together, it cannot be the same as with my son. And I worry about that. I am hot and I sleep in boxer shorts. It's the niacin. I take it to control my cholesterol. But it sometimes gives me hot flashes, and I have felt overly warm ever since I started taking it more than two years ago. So I sleep half naked.

My wife is out of town, and my daughter sneaks into our bed at two o'clock in the morning.

'Daddy, I hear scary noises.'

I mumble some incoherent words and turn over.

Will she remember this night and other nights like it when she is 20, and will she accuse me of unspeakable acts?

I have never touched her that way. But there were times before she was born that I thought I might. And I was afraid. And so God gave me a son first.

I will not hold you, daughter of Abraham, for I might ascend. Even though I am old and you are my daughter, I might ascend. So I turn my back to you and hide the shame of my nocturnal ascensions. I feel safe with my back to you, my daughter. And so I will show you only my backside, fleetingly, as I glide by in the night. Only our toes will touch. For no one has ever seen the father. But the only son, who is close on the father's other side, has made him known.

Fragment thirteen

*'Unless a grain of wheat falls into the earth and dies,
it remains just a single grain; but if it dies,
it bears much fruit.' John 12:24–5*

My daughter is 8 years old and we have just moved to Seattle. We have to find new doctors for our children, and now we are in the process of interviewing pediatricians for Allison. This is one my wife likes, and she wants me to meet her.

My wife and I are also somewhat concerned about the mole on Allison's bottom, the one that she was born with. It is no longer round and smooth as it was when she was a baby. It has grown larger. Now it is bumpy and asymmetrical.

'Allison is 49 inches tall, and weighs 48 pounds. Her blood pressure is 98 over 68. She's a healthy girl!' The pediatrician smiles reassuringly. 'Now, where's that mole?'

'Right – or is it her left buttock?' My wife looks at me with a question in her eyes. 'I can't remember.'

'It's on her left buttock,' I say without thinking. I know where it is. It has been mine for eight years.

– *All things counter, original, spare, strange;*
Whatever is fickle, freckled (who knows how). –

The new pediatrician does a careful inspection. 'We should really have it removed. The sooner the better, just to be on the safe side. Strange things can happen to moles like this when girls hit puberty.'

The doctor doesn't know that I have been saving this mark, this grain of wheat, and I am not ready to give it up.

'Will it hurt to take it off?' Allison asks. A worried frown crosses her face. 'Just a little. But not for long.'

I want to tell the doctor, 'You can't have it. It's not yours to take.' But the seed may not be dead, and I want my girl to live forever.

On 7 July 1997 the mole is removed. I squeeze my daughter's hand tightly as the doctor makes an incision, cuts out the mole, and sews up the remaining flaps of skin. My daughter is brave, she hardly cries.

The doctor saves the mole and sends it to the laboratory for testing.

'Just a precautionary measure,' she says cheerily.

The tests come back from the lab, and the doctor calls us to tell us the good news: the mole-seed is indeed dead.

In 4 months even my daughter's scar is gone. But she will always be to me a grain of wheat, sown and harvested before her time.

Fragment fourteen

'In a little while the world will no longer see me,
but you will see me; because I live, you will also live.
On that day you will know that I am in my Father,
and you in me, and I in you.' John 14:19-20

He still kisses me on the lips occasionally, this son of mine. And now he is nearly 12 years old. I thought the ritual would have ended long ago.

More and more often he just kisses me on the cheek. But there are times when only a kiss on the lips will do.

He started kissing me on the lips when he was about a year old. He would watch my wife and me kiss. Then he would mimic us, and we would laugh. Now I wonder when it will stop, when he will kiss me like this for the last time. He has no idea where and when the kissing began. And when it stops, he will probably forget that he ever did it. But I am his father, and I will not forget.

I don't want this kissing to stop, but I am afraid. What if someone sees us kissing like this, at our ages? What will they think?

He still sleeps with a night light on. Wrapped in San Francisco 49er blankets, he prays passionately each evening that God will keep him from bad dreams, and that God will keep his parents safe and alive until they are both one hundred.

When I am one hundred and praying on my deathbed, I want my son at my side. I want to hold his head on my chest. I want to feel his warm lips on mine. I want to smell his sweet breath tickling my moustache.

I want my daughter to slip into the room and ask, 'Dad, can I crawl into bed with you?'

And I will say 'Yes, you may – just this once.'

I will not turn away from her, and she will hold me as close as I held her when we were both young. Then she will sing to me softly an old Beatles' lullaby–[8]

> swift, slow; sweet, sour; adazzle, dim . . .
> He fathers-forth whose beauty is past change. . . .

I smile and drift off to sleep with no fear of bad dreams.

Even as the night light dims, I fear no evil, for thou art with me my daughter, my only begotten son.

Notes

1 Since I was unable to obtain permission to reprint the lyrics of the John Lennon and Paul McCartney song 'I Am The Walrus' (Northern Songs Ltd., 1967) – a song which shares certain theological motifs with the Fourth Gospel – I ask the reader to begin humming the tune at this point in my essay (the lyrics to the song may be found at http://www.public.iastate.edu/trents/beatles/imwalrus.html; see also http://kiwi.imgen.bcm.tmc.edu:8088/public/rmb.html). Or better yet, put the song on your stereo and play it as background music while you read the remainder of the essay.

2 'According to the χ (the chiasmus) (which can be considered a quick thematic diagram of dissemination), the preface, as semen, is just as likely to be left out [as it is in my essay], to well up and get lost as a seminal différance, as it is to be reappropriated into the sublimity of the father. As the preface to a book, [the χ] is the word of a father assisting and admiring his work, answering for

his son, losing his breath in sustaining, retaining, idealizing, reinternalizing, and mastering his seed. The scene would be acted out, if such were possible, between father and son alone: autoinsemination, homoinsemination, reinsemination' (Derrida, *Dissemination*, 44–5).

3 H. S. Yellen, 'Bloodless circumcision of the newborn', 147.

4 Ibid.

5 G. C. Denniston, '"Modern" Circumcision'.

6 Ibid. Cf. D. Gairdner, 'The Fate of the Foreskin', 1433.

7 'A spider emerging "from the depths of its nest", a headstrong dot that transcribes no dictated exclamation but rather intransitively performs its own writing (later on, you will read in this the inverted figure of castration), the text comes out of its hole and lays its menace bare: it passes, in one fell swoop, to the "real" text and to the "extratextual" reality' (Derrida, *Dissemination*, 42).

8 Replay 'I Am The Walrus'.

References

Anand, K. J. S. and Hickey, P. R. (1987) 'Pain and Its Effects in the Human Neonate and Fetus', *New England Journal of Medicine* 317: 1321–9.

Denniston, G. C. (1996) '"Modern" Circumcision: The Escalation of a Ritual', *Circumcision* 1,1: http://weber.u.washington.edu/~gcd/CIRCUMCISION/

Derrida, J. (1981) *Dissemination*. Translated, with an Introduction and Additional Notes, by Barbara Johnson, Chicago: University of Chicago Press.

Gairdner, D. (1949) 'The Fate of the Foreskin: A Study of Circumcision', *BMJ* 2: 1433–7.

Hopkins, G. M. (1967) 'Glory Be to God for Dappled Things', in *The Poems of Gerard Manley Hopkins*, New York: Oxford University Press (4th edn).

Staley, J. L. and Rebecca, G. (1997) 'Staley Family History'. http://www.u.arizona.edu/~rstaley/personal.htm

Yellen, H. S. (1935) 'Bloodless circumcision of the newborn', *Am. J. Obstet. Gynecol.* 30: 146–7.

6

READING AND
SENSE-EXPERIENCING
THE GOSPEL OF JOHN

Maria Anicia Co, RVM

Following the voice

I am happy to have the opportunity to share my personal reading of the Gospel of John in this volume. I believe that allowing personal voices to be heard in an academic context is a breakthrough in contemporary scholarship. It involves, however, a lot of risk-taking (Henking 1995: 243). I thank the risk-takers among whom are authors and scholars whose autobiographical readings inspire me with courage to take the same risk. I especially thank Ingrid Kitzberger for inviting me to contribute to this enterprise.

Ten years ago I used the image of entering a tunnel to describe my initial experience of doctoral studies. I did not know then that the image would be appropriate for the whole period of research. As I was finishing, I experienced being at the other end of the tunnel, seeing some light and feeling relieved that I was finally getting out of a very dark tunnel. There were many reasons why I experienced it that way. I was aware of why I was struggling inside even as I followed the voice of rigorous scholarship. I enjoyed being lured into the past to discover the background of the biblical texts. I cherished the knowledge offered by the historical–critical method, but somewhere deep within me was a voice demanding to be heard. It was the desire to be engaged fully in the interpretation of the texts as the thinking, feeling, believing person that I am. I agree with Tim Long that a real reader is several readers at the same time (Long 1996: 79–107).

My desire is conditioned by my background and experience as an Asian (Filipino) religious woman steeped in the tradition of St Ignatius of Loyola. My first exposure to biblical texts was in the context of faith, prayer and contemplation. In my exegetical studies, I felt that I had to bracket together this experience and perspective in order to be objective. It was profitable to distance myself from the text and listen to what the text as 'other' was saying. I tried to understand commentators of the text from within their perspectives. I learned how to listen to them. It was a gain, but at the same time something was neglected in the process. I began to consider my emotions and faith irrelevant to interpreting the text. Somewhere deep inside me was a cry of protest, a cry for integration. That voice demanded a hearing.

Teaching the Gospel of John was a stage in this process of integration. I have always had a fascination for this Gospel. Its language is appealing to me. I enjoy reading and re-reading it even without fully understanding it. Since I entered the convent, I have used it often for prayer and reflection. The Fourth Gospel provided the material of my one retreat 15 years ago. The director expounded the different episodes of the Gospel in conferences. My fascination for John did not diminish even as studies in the New Testament and exegetical research exposed me to the complexity of the problem of intepretation. In teaching the Gospel of John I attempted an integrative approach. I wanted to balance the historical–critical method with a narrative and aesthetic approach. I was well aware of the risks but I thought it was worth a try.

My first attempt at this approach was like following an elusive voice in the wilderness. I plodded through the Gospel of John hoping to find the basic thought that runs through it. Once I thought I detected a thread of continuity. I kept my focus on that idea. I realized, however, that it was but the lure of a voice that suddenly disappeared when I thought I found its source. I decided to go back to the beginning. Instead of approaching the text as a detective or an outside observer, I entered deeply into the world of the story by becoming aware of what the story invites me to feel, see, hear, touch and smell. I started to engage the text in contemplation, using the application of the senses suggested by St Ignatius of Loyola in the Spiritual Exercises (SE 102–19).

Episodic reading

It was not possible for me to undertake this sense-experiencing of the Gospel of John in one sitting. I did the reading by episodes. Originally I thought that I would share my reading of the entire Gospel of John. I realize as I write this article that that is practically impossible. Due to the limitation of space, I am sharing only the first two chapters of John and my reflection on the reading process. I choose the form of a journal to present my reading.

Day 1: Beginning with the Prologue (1:1–18)

'In the beginning was the Word, and the Word was with God and the Word was God' (1:1). I read silently and slowly. I hear with my inner sense of hearing. I take note of my feeling. Groundless, without a context, in the middle of nowhere. I see nothing, but I learn that the Word Is, God Is. The opening line of the Gospel of John has the power to detach my attention from my present location, my temporal existence. Without losing consciousness of myself as a reader, I am brought to the intersection of distance and nearness. There is something familiar and unfamiliar in the story world I am invited to enter.

Concern for beginnings and endings is built-in in our cultural script as Filipinos. Whenever we meet people on the road, we ask 'Where have you come from?' and 'Where are you going?' We are conscious that life is a continuous journey. Death is a voyage to the other side of life. We have a saying that 'those who do not look back to their point of origin cannot reach their destination'. In a cyclical view of life, the ending is the same as the beginning. Looking back to the point of origin guides me to my destination. I think this is the same with reading the Gospel of John. I need to keep looking back to the point of origin in order to understand the whole story. I mean this in two senses. First, to understand the deeper meaning of the different episodes in the Gospel, I need to be reminded continually of the story of the Word in the prologue. Second, I need to bear in mind that the origin of the Word is God in order to make sense of the details in the story, namely, the plot that can be read on two levels, and the irony and misunderstanding that permeate the narrative (Duke 1985).

For a moment I feel I am there at the beginning. Then, all of a sudden as if awakening from an illusion, I realize the distance of my present existence from the beginning. Having had a glimpse of the point of origin, I become keenly aware of the distance between the Word and me. I become conscious of myself as a female reader. I hear about the activity of the Word in the creation of all things and of humanity (1:3–4). I see oneness and separation coming about. It is difficult to keep my mind focused on the Word and creation at the same time. As I begin to see created realities, the Word recedes into the background. The distance between the Word and me seems greater. Yet, paradoxically, I realize my belongingness – to creation and humanity, and to the Word. I feel interconnected with other beings as I see the broader context of my individual existence. A new and wider horizon of meaning is offered to me.

The Word disappears but emerges as Life and Light (1:4). I feel life and light within and without me. A wonderful experience of harmony! Soon afterward, I perceive the struggle of light with darkness (1:5a). The harsh realities of Philippine society unfold before my eyes – mass poverty, a dwindling economy and the widening gap between the rich and the poor, violence against women and children, crimes against the human person and property, kidnapping, drug abuse and trafficking, graft and corruption, abuse of power by political leaders, environmental pollution, destruction of local cultures. I am angered and pained by these realities, and by my own helplessness to do something concrete to overcome the darkness.

To lose hope is to succumb to darkness. To keep on hoping and believing is the least I can do to witness to the light.

John was sent from God as a witness to testify to the light (1:6). I have no concrete image of him. I see him against the background of the light. I learn that bringing people to faith is the reason for his testimony (1:7–8). I need to continue believing that light will eventually triumph over the dark forces that assail our society.

Barely have I given my full attention to John when I am told of the coming of the true light (1:9) into the world. I fix my gaze beyond the world to see the light coming. As I look at the light, I see my focus changing. I find myself looking at the world. The coming of the light was not welcomed by those expected to accept it (1:11). I begin to see people in a dimly-lit room. I notice a figure in the distance. He illuminates the surroundings as he approaches. The room gets brighter and brighter with every step of his coming. The people, however, react with fear to this 'invasion' of light. They shut the door and the windows, any opening through which light may enter the room. The room, thus, gets darker and darker! Is the approach of light an alien invasion? Yes, it is to those who are alien to the light!

I notice another group of people inside the room. They decide to accept the light. Because of their acceptance, light cannot be shut off completely. What ensues is a struggle between them and those who refuse the light. They struggle for the light because they believe. They are given the power to become children of God. The birthing comes from God, not from the will of human beings, nor of physical union of life in sexual intimacy. To accept the light is to acquire a new existence. It is to become a child of God! To be a child of God in my present context is to continue witnessing to the light in the midst of the dark and harsh realities of existence.

Ho logos sarx egeneto. Something unexpected dawns on me. Against the backdrop of light, rejection and acceptance, the promise of birth and life, the Word emerges in the scene as flesh, becomes visible as human. I am invited to look at bodiliness. The body is not to be identified with darkness. The Word shows its glory in the flesh. There is solidity in its existence. '[the Word] dwelt among us; we have seen his glory, glory as of the only Son of the Father' (1:14). The light that formed the background converged into a human being. I recall the burning bush Moses saw (Exod. 3:2). I do not see a burning bush but a human being suffused with and emanating light, a human body of light!

I hear John's voice testifying to the mystery of this person, 'This was he of whom I said, "He who comes after me ranks before me, for he was before me"' (1:15). As I look at this person, I feel drawn into his circle of light and experience the warmth of his presence. 'And from his fulness we have all received, grace upon grace' (1:16). I see another figure in the background as I hear 'the law was given through Moses'. I recall the great role Moses played in the history of his people. As the voice continues, 'grace and truth came through Jesus Christ', I see how Moses recedes more and more into the background and with him the scroll of the Law. I hear the name of the Word – Jesus Christ (1:17).

'No one has ever seen God, the only Son who is in the bosom of the Father, he has made him known.' I see myself being drawn back to the reality of God. Yes, I am brought back to the beginning but with a difference. The Word now has a name! A new understanding of God is offered to me. Jesus reveals the identity of God as Father. I am invited to look closely at Jesus to see the reality of God. Jesus is in the bosom of the Father. He knows the very depths of God and I am invited to share in that experience of being at home in God.

Day 2: In Bethany (1:19–28)

I witness a scene where John is confronted by Levites and priests from Jerusalem. They ask about John's identity. There is no hesitation in John's answer, 'I am not the Christ.' The representatives of the Jews are not satisfied. They ask further. It seems like a guessing game – 'Are you Elijah?' 'Are you the prophet?' John answers 'No!' Finally, John identifies himself as the voice of one crying aloud in the wilderness, 'Make straight the way of the Lord.' John announces not himself but the dawning of a new era, the coming of the Lord.

I sense conflict in the story. The prologue has prepared me to identify with John and to look at his interrogators as his opponents. They come from the Pharisees (1:24). Their question seems to challenge his authority to baptize. I hear the splash of water as I listen to John saying, 'I baptize with water but among you stands one whom you do not know, even he who comes after me, the thong of whose sandal I am not worthy to untie' (1:26–7). My eyes are now fixed on the ground, looking for the feet of one whose sandal John feels unworthy to untie. As I look, I see the feet of someone girded with a towel, washing the feet . . . of his disciples (13:5). The image disappears as I follow the voice that invites me to look at the whole surrounding, Bethany beyond the Jordan. I watch and see water and wilderness, dusty feet, people moving to and from the water. I look at the man baptizing and the question 'Who are you?' reverberates in my ear.

Day 3: The Lamb of God (1:29–34)

I watch John's eyes as he exclaims, 'Behold, the Lamb of God who takes away the sin of the world.' I expect to see a lamb but John is talking of a man, 'This is he of whom I said, "After me comes a man who ranks before me, for he was before me."' I get the impression that John knows this man. As if reading my mind, John immediately adds that he does not really know this man. He says he baptizes with water in order for him to be revealed to Israel. John explains how he comes to know him. I see the vast expanse of the sky and watch the descent of a dove. I hear John's words amid the sound of the waters and the dove's fluttering wings, 'He on whom you see the Spirit descend and remain, this is he who baptizes with the Holy Spirit.' John calls him the Son of God.

Day 4: Come and see (1:35–42)

I see three people in the scene, John and two of his disciples. I watch his eyes follow Jesus as he walks. He repeats the words he said yesterday, 'Behold, the Lamb of God!' This time two of his disciples follow Jesus. I decide to walk with them toward Jesus. I see Jesus's back from a distance. I see him now turning to us. He realizes that we are following him. His first words are, 'What do you seek?' I pose the question to myself, 'What do I seek?' The answer can be varied, as varied as the contexts I imagine myself to be! They answer, 'Rabbi, where are you staying?' Jesus invites them (us), 'Come and see.' Yes, I can call him, 'Rabbi!' and I want to see where he stays. So I join them. We reach the place where Jesus is staying at about 4 o'clock. We remain with him that day. As I imagine the place, I find that I am not the only woman in the company. Jesus's mother welcomes us and makes us feel at home.

I learn that one disciple is named Andrew. I watch him look for his brother, Simon Peter, and introduce Jesus as the Messiah. He brings Simon to Jesus. I watch Jesus look at Simon and hear, 'So, you are Simon son of John? You shall be called Cephas' (1:42). I find something amusing. Simon appears so surprised at the experience. They meet for the first time and Jesus appears to know him. He even gives him a new identity. I am left with the image of Simon's surprised look! I wonder how Jesus reacted to that!

Day 5: In Galilee (1:43–51)

Jesus decides to go to Galilee. I see him looking for and finding Philip. His words to him are few, 'Follow me.' I learn that Philip is from Bethsaida, the city of Andrew and Peter. Philip goes to find Nathanael. He introduces Jesus as 'the one of whom Moses in the Law and also the prophets wrote, Jesus of Nazareth, the son of Joseph'. From Philip, I learn about Jesus's origin. He is from Nazareth and his father is Joseph. Nathanael is sceptical, 'Can anything good come out of Nazareth?' Philip uses the same words of invitation Jesus used, 'Come and see.' I watch Jesus as he looks at Nathanael coming to him. He identifies him, 'an Israelite indeed, in whom is no guile!' Is this Jesus's reply to Nathanael's remark to Philip?

I observe Nathanael's surprise, 'How do you know me?' Jesus's answer is even more surprising, 'Before Philip called you, when you were under the fig tree, I saw you.' Did Philip introduce Jesus to Nathanael the way he did because he found Nathanael meditating on the Law? Nathanael's response seems too sudden for me. 'Rabbi, you are the Son of God! You are the King of Israel!' I feel hope and expectation echoing from Nathanael's voice. Jesus seems to challenge this expectation, 'Because I said to you, I saw you under the fig tree, do you believe? You shall see greater things than these.' He affirms Nathanael's faith but challenges its basis. There is a promise of greater things – 'Truly, truly, I say to you, you will see heaven opened, and the angels of God ascending and descending upon the Son of Man' (1:51).

Looking at the heavens, I wonder how the distance between heaven and earth is bridged by the Son of Man. I imagine Jacob's ladder (Gen. 28:12) with the angels of God ascending and descending upon it. I am left with an image of Jacob's ladder being transformed into a human being, the Son of Man – Jesus.

Day 6: In Cana and Capernaum (2:1–12)

I hear the sound of a wedding celebration. I hear joyful music at Cana in Galilee. Jesus, his mother and the disciples are at the wedding. Jesus's mother is not named in the story. I wonder why. I observe how Jesus's mother notices the lack of wine. She does not delay in telling Jesus, 'They have no wine!' I feel the concern in her voice and see the anxiety in her face. She seems to have identified herself with the concern of the hosts and wants to save them from embarrassment (Collins 1995: 104). Jesus replies, 'Woman, what have you to do with me? My hour has not yet come.' I cannot figure out their faces. Is there bewilderment in the woman's face because of her son's retort? Or is there a smile beginning to form on her lips as she turns to the servants?

I imagine her looking at Jesus as she tells the servants, 'Do whatever he tells you.' Is Jesus trapped at this moment? Can he not escape the situation? Or did his mother turn to the servants only after seeing Jesus's desire to do something about the situation? Is there a secret understanding between Jesus and his mother? Did Jesus see through her heart and realize that it is time for him to begin moving towards the fulfilment of the hour?

Jesus begins to take action. Does he identify now with his mother's concern? I now see the six stone jars, each holding twenty or thirty gallons. They are for the Jewish rites of purification. I see a flurry of activity as the servants fulfil Jesus's command to fill the jars with water. I hear the sound of water being poured into the jars. It takes time to fill the jars to the brim. Do the other guests notice the stir? Do they think that some more guests are expected? Jesus tells the servants, 'Now draw some out, and take it to the steward of the feast.' I see them bring the water to the steward of the feast who knows nothing about what has happened. I watch the steward taste the water. I wonder how it tastes. Water? No! It has turned to wine! I imagine the face of the steward lighting up with glee. He calls the bridegroom and says to him, 'Everyone serves the good wine first; and after the guests have drunk freely, then the poor wine; but you have kept the good wine until now.'

I wonder what the bridegroom's reaction was. Wouldn't he say 'Fine, but I know nothing about what you say!' Then it is the steward who will be surprised. Will they look around to see what has happened? Will the servants tell the story, perhaps after Jesus, his mother and his disciples have left the scene?

I appreciate the steward's words that affirm the power of Jesus's action. They betray, however, his complete ignorance of the situation. The problem has come and gone. He knows nothing about it, but isn't he supposed to take responsibility for the situation? His competence is, nonetheless, affirmed. He can distinguish between good wine and poor wine. He confirms the superior quality of the wine given by Jesus. I try to imagine how it tastes and all my thoughts about the steward vanish. I recall, however, the final words, 'You have kept the good wine until now.' I see the images of the bridegroom and Jesus converge into one. I hear the voice interpreting the event and its effect. This is the first sign that manifested Jesus's glory and led the disciples to believe in him.

I follow Jesus, his mother, his brothers and the disciples to Capernaum. I am still thinking of the whole incident and the wine. Did Jesus's mother suggest that Jesus and his disciples leave because they have drunk a lot of wine? Is the reference to the hour occasioned by this suggestion? Is the hour to be understood on two levels of meaning – the hour to depart from the feast pointing to the hour to depart to go to the Father (13:1)? I think of the wine and its source and recall the discourse on the vine (15:1–11). Isn't wine produced from crushed grapes? Is Jesus's act of turning water into wine but a symbol pointing to his being crushed by suffering and death?

Whether or not his mother believed in Jesus is not mentioned. Is it because it is superfluous to do so? Her actions speak louder than words. She interprets Jesus's response positively for she tells the servants to obey Jesus. In that way, she prepares the way for Jesus to act. She believes even before Jesus performs the sign!

I put myself in his mother's place and wonder if I would take Jesus's words as a rebuff. In the first place, would I be sensitive enough to observe what is missing in the celebration? Would I be concerned enough to bring the situation to Jesus's attention? Would I grasp the true meaning of Jesus's response and cooperate in responding to the situation? Or, would I be like the steward? I see the images of the mother of Jesus and the steward converge. The mother of Jesus has fulfilled the role of the steward!

Day 7: In Jerusalem (2:13–22)

In Jerusalem, a festive mood is in the air. The Passover feast is approaching. I observe people moving about to prepare for the feast. I see Jesus going to the temple. He disrupts the normal order of the day. He causes a stir. He makes a whip of cords and drives the sellers and the money-changers out of the temple. I hear so much noise, the sound of the oxen and bleating sheep being driven out of the temple. I hear the clatter of coins and the shattering sound of the overturned tables of the money-changers. I observe the angry and pained face of Jesus as he speaks to the sellers of pigeons, 'Take these things away; you shall not make my Father's house a house of trade.' The Jews react with a challenge, 'What sign have you to show us for doing this?' Jesus answers, 'Destroy this temple and in three days I will raise it up.' I perceive that the Jews think he is silly. They say, 'It has taken forty-six years to build this temple, and you will raise it up in three days?' They want to make him appear a fool. Does Jesus know what he is talking about?

Jesus's first act in the temple sets the mood of his ministry in Jerusalem. It will be full of tension, conflict and opposition. Jesus goes to the seat of power and confronts the authorities with his prophetic claim to speak and act in God's name. Jesus's claim will be continuously challenged and opposed. The religious authorities of his day who refuse to give him a hearing reveal themselves to be resisting God himself. The consequence is fatal: they no longer deserve to act as God's representatives before the people.

I watch the disciples and find myself in another time. The disciples are looking back to the whole story of Jesus. They remember his action in the temple and his earnestness that reminds them of Ps. 69:10: 'Zeal for thy house consumes me.' By this time, they understand the meaning of Jesus's words as they look back to their experience of his death and resurrection. In faith, they comprehend that Jesus was referring to his body when he spoke of the temple. They believe the Scriptures and the words spoken by Jesus. The resurrection vindicates Jesus's claim. The disciples attest that Jesus truly is speaking and acting in the name of God.

I go back to the scene of the temple and Jesus's confrontation with the authorities. I see the shadow of the cross. It is a preview of the end. I sense and fear the tragedy even if I know the end will be full of hope. The story will end in triumph, a painful triumph, a triumph of love. Right now, I am only at the beginning of the story. The story is unfinished. The story of Jesus goes on . . .

Yes, the story of Jesus goes on not only in the text of John but in the text of my life. I cannot forget Jesus's passionate action and his face displaying anger, grief and compassion. I have the same feelings as I look at the realities affecting the lives of the majority of our people. I hear the call to move from mystic contemplation of Jesus to prophetic action. It is not easy to discern the proper action to challenge the new temples of our society that discriminate against the poor. How are we to fight against the detrimental effects on the poor of the devalued peso, the oil price hike, the dreams of powerful nations to forge one worldwide economy? The struggle between light and dark goes on inside me. The story of my discipleship is in the making as I listen to the voice that beckons me to follow Jesus, 'Come and see!'

Reflection on a sense-experience reading of the Gospel of John

The first step in my reading strategy is to read the whole Gospel of John and immerse myself in the details of the story. This enables me to re-create the scenes in my imagination. The second is to re-create an episode imaginatively and enter into the scene as if I were truly present there. The third involves reflection on the experience. I realize the limitation of my words to convey the feelings engendered in my reading experience. More significant than the thoughts that occurred to me in the process is the whole sense-experience. I find myself living in the world of the text and feel the text alive in my being. In recalling my experience of reading, I realize that I keep on moving in the axis of distance and proximity, in the dynamics of inner and outer realities. This prevents my reading from being an exercise divorced from the realities of the present. Immersing myself in the world of the text enables me to come back to my present world with a new sense of meaning. This sense-experience reading opens me up to a vision of what following Jesus means today in our troubled society. As I immerse myself in John's story of Jesus, I find myself growing in my sense of commitment.

I made no attempt to answer all the questions the text provokes. Posing questions is part of the whole process of reading. Finding answers is a different matter. My stance is to wait for light to dawn on me in the process of sense-experiencing the story. I have no desire to explain everything. For me, this is a refreshing way of engaging the text. It is rather different from the method I used to employ in finding meaning in the text. I realize that my present reading is an act of waiting, listening. There is no attempt to control the text. I think my approach to the text is very much influenced by my Asian background (my father is Chinese, my mother is a Filipina) and my natural gift of contemplation as a woman. The way our present society affects me also influences the feelings and thoughts evoked by the story. I try as much as possible to stay within the limits of the text. At some point, however, I fill in the gaps. In the case of 1:39, I note the presence of women in the scene. This is an imaginative reconstruction. At this point, I realize that a sense-experience reading of the text naturally leads to the recovery of what is forgotten in the text – the presence of women in the story. I also notice that it is easy to be drawn into the world of the story if I keep myself open to the signals in the text that call for imaginative sense-experience. At the end of the reading, I find myself wanting to go back to the text to relish and savour its meaning more deeply.

References

Brown, R. (1966) *The Gospel According to John.* Vol. 1, New York: Doubleday.
—— (1970) *The Gospel According to John.* Vol. 2, New York: Doubleday.
Blount, B. (1995) *Cultural Interpretation. Reorienting New Testament Criticism*, Minneapolis, MN: Fortress.
Carson, D. A. (1991) *The Gospel According to John*, Grand Rapids, MI: Eerdmans.
Collins, M. (1995) 'The Question of Doxa: A Socioliterary Reading of the Wedding at Cana', *BTB* 25: 100–9.
Culpepper, R. A. (1984) *Anatomy of the Fourth Gospel*, Philadelphia, PA: Fortress.
—— (1993) 'The Gospel of John as a Document of Faith in a Pluralistic Culture', SBLSP, Alpharetta, GA: Scholars.
Duke, P. (1985) *Irony in the Fourth Gospel*, Atlanta, GA: John Knox.
Grassi, J. A. (1986) 'The Role of Jesus' Mother in John's Gospel: A Reappraisal', *CBQ* 48: 67–80.
Henking, S. (1995) 'Who Better to Indulge? (Self) Indulgent Theorizing and the Stuff of Ambivalence'. In J. Capel Anderson and J. L. Staley (eds) *Taking It Personally: Autobiographical Biblical Criticism, Semeia* 72, Atlanta, GA: Scholars, *Semeia* 72: 239–46.
Howard-Brook, W. (1994) *Becoming Children of God. John's Gospel and Radical Discipleship*, Maryknoll, NY: Orbis Books.
Koester, C. (1994) *Symbolism in the Gospel of John: Meaning, Mystery, and Community*, Minneapolis, MN: Fortress.
Lee, D. A. (1994) 'The Symbolic Narratives of the Fourth Gospel', JSNTS Supplement Series, 95, Sheffield: JSOT.
Long, T. (1996) 'A Real Reader Reading Revelation'. In J. Capel Anderson and J. L. Staley (eds) *Taking It Personally: Autobiographical Biblical Criticism, Semeia* 72, Atlanta, GA: Scholars: 79–107.
Moore, S. (1995) 'True Confessions and Weird Obsessions: Autobiographical Interventions in Literary and Biblical Studies'. In J. Capel Anderson and J. L. Staley (eds) *Taking It Personally: Autobiographical Biblical Criticism, Semeia* 72, Atlanta, GA: Scholars: 19–50.
Patte, D. (1996) 'Biblical Scholars at the Interface Between Critical and Ordinary Readings: A Response'. In G. West and M. W. Dube (eds) *'Reading With': An Exploration of the Interface Between Critical and Ordinary Readings of the Bible. African Overtures, Semeia* 73, Atlanta, GA: Scholars, 263–76.
Saint Ignatius, *The Spiritual Exercises*, English transl. L. J. Phil, Allahabad: St Paul Publications (1975).
Staley, J. L. (1995) *Reading with a Passion: Rhetoric, Autobiography, and the American West in the Gospel of John*, New York: Continuum.

7

AN ADVENTURE WITH NICODEMUS

Francis J. Moloney, SDB

After a hard day at the office, caught up in the never-ending complications of academic administration, I went home to the pleasure of some finishing work on two reviews, one a doctoral thesis on the christological use of Scripture in the Fourth Gospel (Obermann 1996), and the other the major work of a long-standing friend (Byrne 1996). At about 9 pm I settled into an armchair to continue my reading of the recent volume of *Semeia*, dedicated to autobiographical biblical criticism. I discovered that Stephen Moore spent a couple of pages of his reflection on autobiographical criticism *writing my biography* (Moore 1995: 30–1). On the basis of one fleeting encounter and my review of his book *Poststructuralism and the New Testament* (Moore 1994; cf. Moloney 1994: 360–2), Moore was able to conclude that I am of Irish Roman Catholic stock (there is French blood in my veins), that we should be golf buddies (I don't play), that I am a Roman Catholic Priest (correct), and that my commitment to biblical scholarship might be a means to validate 'his original decision to become, his daily decision to remain, a priest'. I went to bed excited because I had a starting point for my adventure with Nicodemus.

Moore and many others who approach the Bible from an increasingly postmodern perspective are right in claiming that the so-called implied reader that narrative critics (like myself) find in texts is the *ego* that the interpreter puts into the text (Moore 1994: 65–81; 1995: 36–8; The Bible and Culture Collective 1995: 20–118). The introduction of my autobiography into the role of Nicodemus in the Fourth Gospel only slightly modifies my more objective (scholarly?) readings of John 3 (Moloney 1993: 104–31), John 7 (Moloney 1996a: 65–93), and John 19 (Moloney 1998; forthcoming). This means one of two things: either my earlier work on John 3, 7 and 19 has always been autobiographical, or the present essay is not genuine autobiographical criticism. But why should that be such a problem? In postmodern readings very little escapes devastating and subtle criticism. [1] In an agenda that subverts established interpretations, there is little space for the truth that each one of us – perhaps for autobiographical reasons – comes up with different answers to the same questions, and that this is acceptable. For example, Stephen Moore once asked: 'Is it my own strict Roman Catholic upbringing that renders these austere ideas so attractive to me?' (Moore 1994: 81). I am well known for affirming that it is the joy of belonging to the sinful but rich, seemingly unified but in fact immensely multifaceted, Roman Catholic tradition which renders *all* ideas attractive to me. It is healthy to say *vive la différence*, but not when this really means *à mort* any reading of a text within a tradition. A text might mean *many things*, it cannot mean *anything for me*, because of the limitations imposed upon me by my own story. I read the Bible from within a faith community that looks to the Bible for its inspiration, however flawed the biblical text, I the interpreter, and my tradition, might be. I am not asking you, my reader, to accept this reading of my adventure with Nicodemus as *the* reading, but it is *a* reading that focuses upon my story from the first shock of my introduction to the Bible down to the present time. My close association with the Nicodemus episode was part of this shock (cf. Moloney 1978: 42–67), but critical biblical scholarship as a whole was the broader context for the adventure which I share below. Familiarity with the text and historical criticism has not bred the contempt that I sense in some contemporary readings.

Are you the teacher of Israel? (John 3:10)

My first love was teaching, and I went to the University to do an undergraduate degree, followed by a postgraduate diploma in education that I might become a secondary school teacher. There was chalk in my blood, and the urge to be a first-rate teacher was strong. I had been brought up as a practising Catholic, and the social and cultural setting of my life, the 1950s and 1960s in Australia, was steady as a rock. There was no need for the Bible as I had the Pope, the Bishop, the Priest, and weekly Mass. My belief system came from the family and a Catholic schooling, reinforced by the weekly sermon, the Sacraments of the Catholic Church, and various devotions. They were happy days, weeks, months and years, full of as little study as possible, great friends, sport, movies, and dancing to rock-and-roll music.

At the University, however, my majors in Literature and History, and my minor in French Language and Literature, touched me in a way that generated a passion for books, and an insatiable desire to know more. But it also made me aware of my privileges, and I looked beyond myself to other young people. The passion to read and know more was gradually matched by a passion to share this experience with others. The Bible played no part in my 'original decision' to become a priest. In fact, it was the Catholic culture of the 1950s that made me move in that direction.

But the Bible was soon to become *a problem*, and the Johannine account of Jesus's meeting with a man who came from the darkness into the light in John 3:1–21, a living example of the many who 'believed in his name when they saw the signs which he did' (2:23), was one passage among many that generated an ongoing crisis (cf. Moloney 1993: 106–21). I was a Catholic, a leader of young people (cf. 3:1), and I knew who Jesus was: a teacher from God who had given the Catholic Church an authoritative teaching and a divinely-appointed hierarchical structure, substantiated by the fact that Jesus had God with him, as proved by his miracles (cf. v.2). The use of the miracles of Jesus and the historicity of his resurrection, the greatest of all miracles, as proof of the right-headedness of traditional Catholic theology had been re-inforced for me by the very first course that I undertook as an undergraduate theological student: 'Fundamental Theology', taught by the brilliant Professor (now Cardinal) Antonio M. Javierre Ortas. I was baptized, and I *knew* all that there was to be known, and I did my best to live accordingly. But the Jesus of the Fourth Gospel used a double-meaning word to insist that I, a reader of the Fourth Gospel, be born again from above (v. 3: ἄνωθεν) if I wished to see the Kingdom of God. I was, like Nicodemus, satisfied with only one of the two possible meanings of ἄνωθεν. I had been born again (v. 4: δεύτερον) in the waters of Baptism (cf. v. 5: ἐξ ὕδατος), and the Catholic community was the Kingdom of God. I had full sight of the Kingdom within the structures and the sacramental system of the one true Church. But the Johannine Jesus insisted that this was insufficient: I must be born of water *and also of the Spirit* (v. 5: καὶ πνεύματος), if I wished to enter the Kingdom. The double-meaning of ἄνωθεν (v. 3) had been unpacked in v. 5. To 'see' (v. 3) and to 'enter' (v. 5) the Kingdom of God, I had to leave my established ways and my closed system of truth (cf. v. 2), certainly through the external rite of Baptism (ἐξ ὕδατος), but also through some form of more radical transformation which reaches beyond the formality of a water ritual (καὶ πνεύματος). I was alright on the former (v. 3), but had I really 'entered' (εἰσελθεῖν) the Kingdom (v. 5)?

The 'water' rebirth had been part of my experience – although I had no recollection of it. It was something I accepted on the basis of the Roman Catholic and my family traditions; something that had been handed down to me by people who, in their own time, had received it from other generations who believed that it had come from the Lord (cf. 1 Cor. 11:23; 15:3). But this same tradition had said little to me about the Spirit, except some vague notions concerning the third person of the Trinity, in those days called the Holy Ghost. It had been taught that he (male, like everything else associated with God) was a part of the Mystery of the Trinity, and that it would be both arrogant and foolish to wonder further about a Mystery of Religion. I was happy to leave 'mystery' alone. '(Un)'fortunately, I was able to read on into the Johannine text to find

Jesus's clarification of what was meant by being born of the Spirit (cf. vv. 6–8), and I found especially '(un)'helpful the little parable in John 3:8:

The wind (τὸ πνεῦμα) blows where it wills, and you hear the sound of it, but you do not know whence it comes (πόθεν ἔρχεται) or whither it goes (ποῦ ὑπάγει); so it is with every one who is born of the Spirit (ὁ γεγεννεμένος ἐκ τοῦ πνεύματος).

But why the '(un)', qualifying what one would expect to be quite positive reading experiences? Because my convictions of the 1950s and 1960s began to crumble when I discovered that to be born of the Spirit meant to be caught up in an experience of life – in all its dimensions – that matched the experience of standing in the wind.

I know when the wind is swirling around me (v. 8a), and I can have the physical experience of its power to penetrate even the warmest of clothing. But, as Jesus's parable so rightly remarks, I have no idea where this wind has its origins, nor do I know where it is going (v. 8b). But it is a deeply disturbing comment that Jesus adds to the end of the parable: so it is with everyone who is born of the Spirit (v. 8c). My origin and my destiny were two things about which I was *absolutely certain*. I had been born of Mary and Dennis Moloney in 1940, baptized by water into the Catholic Church only a matter of weeks after that event, and assured a place in heaven as long as I lived as a good Catholic, loving God, my Church and my neighbour, and the many other obligations that these major headings involved in the 1950 and 1960s. The Bible was now telling me that this was a complete mis-understanding of being born in the Spirit. I had to experience the Spirit swirling around me in the confusion of *not knowing* where I had come from and where I was going. My true origins and my true destiny, both in terms of my future history and my final resting place, here and on the other side of death, were something shrouded in mystery, and living in this mystery was a fundamental aspect of life in the Kingdom of God. Here was the word that had been used to describe something that I should not bother my head about: mystery! I could only join with Nicodemus and ask 'How can this be?' (v. 9).

But it was Jesus's response to my question that hurt most: 'Are you the teacher of Israel, and yet you do not understand this?' (v. 10). Not only were all my former certainties questioned by the Johannine Jesus, but my very status in the community of faith was at stake. Jesus seemed to suggest that I should have known all that he was telling me about rebirth in water and the Spirit, and that my sight of and entry into the Kingdom of God depended upon my preparedness to let go of all that my traditional Catholic culture had given me. I was 'the teacher of Israel': an ordained Catholic priest, belonging to a prestigious Religious Congregation with 21 000 members spread across all the continents of the world. Despite my original desire to share the great passion for learning which had touched me as a younger man, I now found myself one of the privileged few within a highly-structured and hierarchical Church. As well as this, I was involved in scholarly, scientific reflection upon the Christian tradition, under the supervision of a fine scholar from the Methodist tradition (Professor Morna D. Hooker) in no less a centre than the University of Oxford. To return to Australia, one of the last bastions of the British Commonwealth, with a D.Phil. (Oxon) behind my name, gained in a hitherto unknown ecumenical setting, would put several notches in my belt. My youthful passion to be a teacher had not been dissipated; it had changed its focus and its context. But the Johannine Jesus was telling me that I was a fake, that my understanding of life in the Kingdom had little to do with the swirling winds of the Spirit leading me from I know not where into a destiny beyond my knowledge and control (v. 8).

I laid claim to be a 'the teacher of Israel' but I was only at the half-way house, having been born again of water. I was discovering that without the second half of the equation, rebirth in the Spirit, my many achievements were irrelevant in the Kingdom! My obvious identification with Nicodemus lined me up with the 'many who believed in his name when they saw the signs which he did' (2:23). This meant that 'Jesus did not trust himself to them (me), because he knew everyone and needed no one to bear witness of man (περὶ τοῦ ἀνθρώπου: me); for he himself knew what was in man (ἐν τῷ ἀνθρώπῳ: me). Now there was a man (ἄνθρωπος: me) named Nicodemus' (2:24–5; 3:1) (Moloney 1993: 104–6). I will never forget the anxiety that my initial encounters with critical Gospel criticism generated. The product of a community of faith and a culture which articulated that faith in a very clear fashion, I had taken all the right steps to become 'the teacher of Israel'. But now all of that had been undermined as I gasped, 'How can this be?' (3:9). I had to cope with the now obvious fact that the Gospels do not provide a record of the events from the life and teaching, death and resurrection of Jesus, but the Gospels are narrative proclamations of the belief of the early Church.

This only led to a further problem, as the last sentence is only partially correct. The more I acquainted myself with the Gospels and scholarly reflection upon it, I found they did not record the *belief* of the early Church, but the *beliefs* of the early Church. Not only did the early Christian churches produce a four-fold Gospel tradition (and many others that did not make the final selection to the team), but the Gospels told the story of Jesus in ways which demonstrated that different Christian communities proclaimed *different versions* of the significance of the person and message of Jesus. There was hardly a page in the Gospels that did not profoundly question everything that had brought me to my early thirties. It was then that I began to come to grips with an idea expressed by the Fathers of the Desert: to go forward it is necessary, momentarily, to lose the balance one had in the previously acquired situation. It is necessary to keep putting one's foot forward and in this way to regain the balance that was briefly lost (cf. Moloney 1997: xv).

Earthly things – heavenly things (John 3:12)

But my struggle to walk in this way was only beginning. The Johannine Jesus continued to address my arrogance. He made it clear that my difficulty arose from my having been content with those traditions which came to me from the culturally-conditioned understandings of God, the Christ, the Church and the Spirit that had produced the Frank Moloney of 1966. I should have transformed these understandings – so he said – in the light of the authentic Christian traditions that had been handed on to me. Indeed, maybe if the original desire to lose myself in self-gift to the underprivileged had not over the years been subtly re-directed towards the priesthood and an academic life as a theologian and a biblical scholar, I may have been caught up by those traditions. By this stage of my story they were again being laid bare in the Catholic Church by the heady years that immediately followed the remarkable event and subsequent documents of the Second Vatican Council (1962–5). But I had taken a different track, and the Johannine Jesus warned me: 'If I have told you earthly things and you do not believe, how can you believe if I tell you heavenly things?' (v. 11). I found it hard to accept that I should have done better up to that stage, accepting all that Jesus had told Nicodemus in vv. 1–10 as 'earthly things' (ἐπίγεια). I thought (and so did many others) that I had done rather well, but I had never even understood the best and the most significant truths of my own Christian tradition.

I began to see that I had unwittingly worked from the assumption (belief?) that a number of agents in the Catholic Church's hierarchy had access to the secrets of heaven, and I had been prepared to accept uncritically what these agents 'revealed' to me. But the Johannine Jesus declares that no one has ever gone up to heaven. There is only one person in the human story who can lay claim to having unveiled the mystery of God: Jesus, the Son of Man, who, given the cosmology the Fourth Gospel shared with early Gnosticism, had come down from heaven (v. 13). But it is not enough to affirm *that* Jesus is the only authentic revelation of God; *how* does this revelation take place? Jesus draws a comparison between the serpent lifted up in the desert which healed the ailments of all who gazed upon it, and the Son of Man who must be lifted up on a cross to make sense of life, both here and hereafter for all who unconditionally accept what he has told of the unseen God (vv. 14–15; cf. 1:18).

Jesus's mini-discourse (vv. 11–21) did not inform me of the *nature* of the Johannine God, but of the way *God acts*. The presence of Jesus in the human story is the result of an act of love (v. 16); God does not condemn, but saves.

It is not so much what *God* might do, but how *I* might respond to the mysterious presence of a loving God in my life. I could go on reaching into this mystery by believing in what the Johannine Jesus was telling me, or I could condemn myself to lostness by rejecting it, in favour of my long-held and well-established beliefs. I was the one responsible for my own actions, my own present and future, the rightness or wrongness of the way I responded to my world and the people and situations of that world. There was no fixed agenda, just a request to gaze upon the loving gift of God (v. 16), lifted up on a cross. Herein lay the challenge: to recognize in the cross, so horrific to some (cf. Moore 1994: 95),[2] the symbol of the Son of Man lifted up from the earth (cf. 12:32), the most exquisite way of telling me of the immensity of God's love. 'No one has greater love than this, to lay down one's life for one's friends. You are my friends if you do my commandments' (15:13–14). 'This is my commandment, that you love one another as I have loved you' (15:12; cf. 13:34–5; 15:17).

Jesus's words to Nicodemus are no longer a threat but a challenge. He might have expressed concern over my ability to understand τὰ ἐπουράνια, but he also challenged me to be responsible for the recognition of love where it can be found, and for my rejection of love made known. The Johannine Jesus concluded his words to Nicodemus (me) by further spelling out that the choice was mine: I could choose light or darkness, goodness or evil. I could walk along the established ways that led me where I wished to go (cf. 21:18), but that would leave me in darkness, afraid to come into the light of truth for fear that my sinfulness might be seen. On the other hand, I could live in the Spirit, allowing myself to seek the freedom of responding freely and responsibly to the reality of love in my life (cf. v. 8). This was the way which led into light. Whichever way I decided to go, I wrought judgement upon myself (vv. 19–21).

Are you also led astray? (John 7:47)

A new sense of freedom floods into the life of anyone naive enough to accept the authority of Jesus's words to Nicodemus. I was – and am – such a naive person, rendered naive by my belief in the ultimate significance of the God of the Bible, and the revelation of that God, which Christians believe took place in and through Jesus Christ.[3] But it is one thing to have the principles clear, and another to put them into practice. Again, I was able to identify with Nicodemus as he stated the truth but faltered when 'the institution' dared me to exercise my new-found freedom.

During the last day of the Johannine account of the celebration of Tabernacles (7:37), Temple officers (ὑπηρέται), who had been sent out by the Pharisees 'about the middle of the feast' (cf. 7:14) to arrest him (7:32), return to the leaders of 'the Jews' (cf. Moloney 1996a: 84–93). The officers have been listening and observing Jesus for several days, and are now impressed by the authority of his words (cf. v. 46). The Pharisees close ranks, accusing the officers of having been seduced by Jesus, claiming that none of the authorities (μή τις ἐκ τῶν ἀρχόντων) or the Pharisees (ἐκ τῶν Φαρισαίων) believed in him (v. 48). But Nicodemus, one of them (v. 50: εἷς ὢν ἐξ αὐτῶν), had earlier been reduced to silence (3:1–10) and in his silence promised the revelation of love and life (vv. 11–21). He speaks up and makes a lie of their claim (v. 51). Nicodemus was from among the Pharisees (3:1: ἐκ τῶν Φαρισαίων), a ruler of the Jews (3:1: ἀρχῶν τῶν Ἰουδαίων). I am aware that I have a great deal in common with him. I join him again as I look back across my own life story, recalling the times when I tried to stand for what I believed to be true. Nicodemus attempts to break ranks, and to insist that the opposition to the Jesus of the Fourth Gospel is not as unified as some might like to believe. The only people, insists Nicodemus on the basis of his own experience (cf. 3:1–21 = my experience), who understand Jesus are those who hear his word in faith and recognize his works for what they are: the action of God in his Son (Pancaro 1972: 340–61; 1975: 138–57). But abuse and the fear that he (I) might be regarded as one of the fringe dwellers of his (my) social, cultural and religious context leads to silence. Nicodemus (I) has (have) no word in response to the challenge from the approved hierarchy that has domesticated the approach to God into a system which they control (v. 52).

But there is more. As I (he) had come from the darkness into the light to approach Jesus in 3:2, I (he) now skulk (skulks) back into the darkness (cf. 3:2), probably aware that I (he) have (has) blotted my (his) copybook with the powers that be. This situation is further complicated by the fact that I (he) am (is) unable to cope with the challenge of the marginalization that the accepted culture might impose upon me (him) if I (he) were to stick to my (his) guns.[4]

Nicodemus came, bringing myrrh and aloes (John 19:39)

My journey with Nicodemus comes to an end at the tomb of Jesus (19:38–42) (cf. Moloney 1995: 25–62). Scholarly opinion ranges from a claim that Nicodemus has not progressed beyond the limited faith he displayed in 3:1–11 (e.g. Duke 1985: 110; Rensberger 1988: 40; Sylva 1988: 148–51), to a suggestion that Nicodemus's reception of the body of Jesus is a hint of the reception of the Eucharist (for example, Hemelsoet 1970: 47–65; Auwers 1990: 481–503). Neither extreme reflects my adventure with Nicodemus. There is public recognition of Jesus in the association of two previously 'hidden disciples' of Jesus (vv. 38–9: Joseph of Arimathea and Nicodemus) with the crucified Jesus.[5] They request the body of Jesus from Pilate, the authority who handed him over to 'the Jews' for execution (v. 38; cf. 19:16a), and they bury him with a massive mixture of myrrh and aloes (vv. 40–1). The quantity of fragrant oils suggests that the royal theme which was present in the account of the story from 18:1–19:37 continues (v. 39). But what of Nicodemus? Is this a sign that he has finally overcome the hesitations and the fear of 7:51? Yes, but Nicodemus still has a long way to go. It cannot be said that Nicodemus has achieved the quality of faith of earlier characters in the story: the mother of Jesus (2:5), John the Baptist (3:28–30), the Samaritan villagers (4:42), the royal official (4:50) (cf. Moloney 1993: 192–9). Nor can it be said that he matches the faith of the 'beloved disciple', who does not see Jesus in the tomb, but believes when he sees God's victory over death in the empty burial cloths (20:8). We do not know how Nicodemus might respond to the last words of the risen Jesus in the story: 'Blessed are those who have not seen, and yet believe' (20:29).[6] The 'beloved disciple' believed without seeing, and all Johannine readers are exhorted to become beloved disciples, believing without seeing (Byrne 1985: 83–97). Just as Nicodemus at the tomb of Jesus cannot come under the rubric of the 'beloved disciple', nor can I. Neither Nicodemus at the tomb in the story, nor Frank Moloney's autobiography, can lay claim to believing without seeing.

My journey with Nicodemus is open-ended. Both Nicodemus and I have come to recognize that God is made known in the loving self-gift of Jesus unto death, and thus deserves all honour and even royal respect. But that is not what the Johannine Jesus (cf. 20:29) or the Johannine author (cf. 20:30–1) demands of the readers of this story.[7] Nicodemus and I have come a long way, but more adventures lie ahead of us. The challenge to live in the Spirit (cf. 3:8), to recognize the revelation of God in loving self-gift (3:13–17), and to walk in the way of that same self-gift (3:19–21; 13:15, 34–5, 15:12, 17; 17:21–6) is still with me, in an Australian culture and society where Christian faith and practice are becoming either increasingly irrelevant (except for State occasions and national disasters), or the hope of those who think that some golden era of the past will return. My own Catholic tradition is attempting the restoration of my idealized 1950s and 1960s. Its public face and the magisterial pronouncements lack compassion, and indeed reflect the 'austere ideas' that influenced Stephen Moore. But they say very little to me, and jar when read in conjunction with Mark 10:42–5:

> You know that those who are supposed to rule over the Gentiles lord it over them, and their great men exercise authority over them. But it shall not be so among you; but whoever would be great among you must be your servant, and whoever would be first among you must be slave of all. For the Son of Man also came not to be served but to serve, and to give his life as a ransom for many.

Along with Nicodemus, I cannot go back. Often I am plagued by the issues raised by an autobiographical reading of John 7:51–2. I remain a Catholic priest, a public figure in the most politically powerful representative of Christian history, society and culture, not *because* of my involvement in biblical studies, but, quite often, *despite it*. At this moment, hopefully only beginning the latter half of my autobiography, I recognize Jesus at the tomb and wonder where my adventure with Nicodemus will lead me. But in the difficulties of this postmodern moment, which may obviously intensify, I journey on, attempting to cross the bridge constructed by the Johannine Jesus's final words: 'Blessed are those who have not seen, yet believe' (20:29). In this I am armed with a prayer which comes from another Gospel tradition: 'I believe, help my unbelief' (Mark 9:24).

Conclusion

I have mixed feelings about this exercise. I can appreciate the concerns of Janice Capel Anderson and Jeffrey Staley, who edited the *Semeia* volume on autobiographical criticism: 'We, the editors, have often found ourselves seeking to protect those very authors from themselves, asking them whether they were sure they wanted to divulge the kinds of personal information found in their essays. We were worried that perhaps they had made themselves too open, too vulnerable' (Anderson and Staley 1995: 12). My main concern about 'vulnerability', however, is not for my 'Catholic career'. I am rather more concerned that the establishment of autobiographical criticism might lead to a critical interaction between scholars that does not attack *what they said*, on the basis of certain scholarly (?) criteria, but *who they are*, on the basis of who-knows-what criteria (e.g. Moore 1995: 30–1).

Another concern starts from the undeniable truth that an autobiographical approach to the biblical text lays bare the fact that all interpretation in some way inscribes the interpreter. I have no problem with that, and Rudolf Bultmann said it quite powerfully, in his own way, forty years ago (Bultmann 1984: 145–53 [original 1957]). Indeed, this was the point of my review of Moore's *Poststructuralism and the New Testament* (1994) which set me out on this adventure. I am happy that Stephen Moore uses his autobiography to interpret the Pauline cross, but I am puzzled by his rejection of reader-response approaches to the Gospels because 'the more unity and coherence the interpreter is able to ascribe to the text, the more re-assuring will be the self-reflection he or she receives back from it' (Moore 1994: 78–9). It appears to me that both Stephen Moore and Alan Culpepper (1983) are doing the same thing: inscribing something of themselves in the texts that they are interpreting.

Autobiographical criticism lays claim to 'point the way toward a more rigorously self-reflective and contextualized biblical criticism' (Anderson and Staley 1995: 16). But are we not all aware of the strengths and weaknesses of our various interpretative traditions? As biblical scholars are generally by nature reflective people, we all have an idea where we are coming from and where we are heading (cf. John 3:8!) in biblical scholarship. I fully respect the rights of agnostic biblical scholars to interpret the biblical text, although I still wonder why they bother. I ask that they respect the rights of the believing biblical scholars to inscribe their stories in interpretations. It is easy to understand why we bother.

Is it necessary to develop more and more 'methodologies' to make this fact more and more obvious? I have my doubts, however much I have enjoyed the exercise of sharing my journey with Nicodemus with you, my reader. One of my doctoral students read an early draft of this essay and responded:

> The experience of reading such a personal encounter with the text, presented not as a personal meditation but a scholarly critique, is disconcerting. There seems to be a clash of genres which leaves the reader dissatisfied. On the one hand there is the profound privilege of sharing another human being's faith journey. This is at the one time humbling, inspiring and a challenge to reflect on one's own journey. On the other hand there is a hesitancy to apply critical analytic skills to such self-disclosure, while being conscious that this is being presented as scholarly discourse. What is the reader to do? How can the biblical scholar read such autobiographical criticism with the distance needed for a scholarly perspective? The nature of this type of writing invites the reader into the text. It calls for involvement as the reader recognizes the reality or at least the possibility of his/her own story. Autobiography invites empathy and evokes human emotions. Does this help the study of and interpretation of the text, or can it, however subtly manipulate the reader and destroy a healthy objectivity?[8]

She has put her finger on an important issue when she writes of the 'clash of genres', which runs the danger of alienating or at best confusing a reader. What is under scrutiny in autobiographical criticism: a text or the critic's life-experience? Does a reader of this essay respond to the interpretation of John 3, 7 and 19 which results from the insertion of my own journey into the interpretative experience, or to my journey, so symptomatic of many who were theologically trained in the Catholic tradition in the years during and just after Vatican II? I share her refusal to accept that there is no such thing as 'objectivity', however mixed up it might be with my own agenda and my own autobiography.

There must be a multiplicity of possible readings of the biblical text and a multiplicity of interpretations which result from such readings. But there should always be a place for the traditional attempts to produce scholarly work which does its best to do the impossible: create a horizon between the

worlds behind the text, in the text, and in front of the text in an interpretation which respects all three, as well as telling something of the story –
however well hidden – of the interpreter. It is important for Jews and
Christians that there be Jewish and Christian communities where both the
text of the Bible and interpretations of the Bible are treasured. For the
Jewish and the Christian traditions, the Bible is one of the ways God is
made known. Thus the birth, life-story and death of each one of us are more
than autobiography. For me, there is a world beyond the world of 'my story'
which impinges upon the reading process. It does not, however, validate
past decisions (despite Moore 1995: 131). 'Ever anew it will make clear who
we are and who God is, and the exegete will have to express this in an ever
new conceptuality' (Bultmann 1984: 152).

Notes

1 See especially *The Postmodern Bible*. Although most informative, it is a discour-
aging and depressing book. See Moloney 1996b: 98–101.
2 It is only fair to point out that the autobiographical moment shared by Stephen
Moore on this page prefaces his reflections on the Pauline, and not the
Johannine, understanding of the cross (Moore 1994: 95–112).
3 I am aware that sophisticated postmodern biblical criticism tends to ridicule
such naivity. The Johannine view, which I am accepting as having sufficient
authority to question everything that I stood for in the late 1960s, may only be
the result of the speculations of a late first century pseudo-Gnostic Christian
which cry out to be deconstructed. My adherence to a faith tradition and my
belonging to a faith community are the reasons for my naivity. On this see Fish
1980: 303–21. See also my Conclusion to this essay.
4 I am deliberately placing my experience in the main text and the *possibility* of
Nicodemus's sharing that experience in parentheses because I do not know of
Nicodemus's inner response to the rebuff which he receives in v. 51. Nothing is
said in the Johannine text, but I do know my experience. What *might* have
been the case for a figure in the text *is* the case in my autobiography. Does this
make it a valid reading of the text? I have sincere doubts that it does, or even if
it is relevant to ask the question. See my Conclusion.
5 They possibly represent what Brown has called 'crypto-Christians' (cf. Brown
1979: 71–3). This identification resonates with my autobiographical reading of
7:51–2.
6 Unlike most narrative critics, I maintain that John 21 was added to an already
self-contained narrative which ended at 20:31 (cf. Moloney 1998).
7 Particularly helpful in this respect is Bassler 1989: 635–46. She argues that
Nicodemus is neither 'in' nor 'out' by the time the reader comes to the end of
the story. He is a *tertium quid* whose ambiguity is never resolved. For a
summary of scholarly discussion of the role of Nicodemus, see Sylva 1988:
150–1, nn. 7 and 12.
8 I am grateful to Mary Coloe for this response, which she entitled 'Reflections
from a Bewildered Bystander'. Dr Mark Brett and Nerina Zanardo also enriched
this paper with their careful critical reading of earlier drafts. I remain very
grateful to them both.

References

Anderson, J. Capel and Staley, J. L. (1995) 'Taking It Personally: Introduction', in J. Capel Anderson and J. L. Staley (eds) *Taking It Personally: Autobiographical Biblical Criticism*, Semeia 72, Atlanta, GA: Scholars, 7–18.

Auwers, J.-M. (1990) 'Le Nuit de Nicodème (Jean 3:2; 19:39) ou l'ombre du langage', *RB* 97: 481–503.

Bassler, J. M. (1989) 'Mixed Signals: Nicodemus in the Fourth Gospel', *JBL* 108: 635–46.

Brown, R. E. (1979) *The Community of the Beloved Disciple. The Lives, Loves, and Hates of an Individual Church in New Testament Times*, London: Geoffrey Chapman.

Bultmann, R. (1984) 'Is Exegesis Without Presuppositions Possible?', in S. M. Ogden (ed.) *New Testament Mythology and Other Basic Writings*, Philadelphia, PA: Fortress, 145–53. The original German appeared in 1957 (*Theologische Zeitschrift* 13: 409–17).

Byrne, B. J. (1985) 'The Faith of the Beloved Disciple and the Community in John 20', *JSNT* 23: 83–97.

—— (1996) *Romans*, Sacra Pagina Series, 6, Collegeville, MN: The Liturgical.

Culpepper, R. A. (1983) *The Anatomy of the Fourth Gospel. A Study in Literary Design*, Faith and Facet Series, Philadelphia, PA: Fortress.

Duke, P. D. (1985) *Irony in the Fourth Gospel*, Atlanta, GA: John Knox.

Fish, S. (1980) *Is There a Text in This Class? The Authority of Interpretive Communities*, Cambridge, MA.: Harvard University Press.

Hemelsoet, B. (1970) 'L'ensevelissement selon Jean', in *Studies in John: Presented to Professor J. N. Sevenster on the Occasion of His Seventieth Birthday*, NovTSup, 24, Leiden: Brill, 47–65.

Moloney, F. J. (1978) *The Johannine Son of Man*, Rome: LAS (2nd edn).

—— (1993) *Belief in the Word. Reading John 1–4*, Minneapolis, MN: Fortress.

—— (1994) Review of Moore, *Poststructuralism and the New Testament*, *Pacifica* 7: 360–2.

—— (1995) 'The Johannine Passion and the Christian Community', *Salesianum* 57: 25–61.

—— (1996a) *Signs and Shadows. Reading John 5–12*, Minneapolis, MN: Fortress.

—— (1996b) Review of *The Postmodern Bible*, *Pacifica* 9: 98–101.

—— (1997) *A Body Broken for a Broken People. Eucharist in the New Testament*, Peabody: Hendrickson (rev. edn).

—— (1998) *John*, Sacra Pagina Series, 4; Collegeville, MN: The Liturgical.

—— (forthcoming) *Glory not Dishonor. Reading John 13–20 (21)*, Minneapolis, MN: Fortress.

Moore, S. D. (1994) *Poststructuralism and the New Testament. Derrida and Foucault at the Cross*, Minneapolis, MN: Fortress.

—— (1995) 'True Confessions and Weird Obsessions: Autobiographical Interventions in Literary and Biblical Studies', in Anderson and Staley (eds) *Taking It Personally*, 30–1.

Obermann, A. (1996) *Die christologische Erfüllung der Schrift im Johannesevangelium. Eine Untersuchung zur johanneischen Hermeneutik anhand der Schriftzitate*, WUNT, 2. Reihe, 83; Tübingen: J. C. B. Mohr (Paul Siebeck).

Pancaro, S. (1972) 'The Metamorphosis of a Legal Principle in the Fourth Gospel: A Closer Look at 7:51', *Bib* 53: 340–61.

—— (1975) *The Law in the Fourth Gospel: The Torah and the Gospel. Moses and Jesus, Judaism and Christianity According to John,* NovTSup, 42; Leiden: Brill.

Rensberger, D. (1988) *Johannine Faith and Liberating Community*, Philadelphia, PA: Westminster.

Staley J. L. (1995) *Reading with a Passion. Rhetoric, Autobiography and the American West in the Gospel of John,* New York: Continuum.

Sylva, D. D. (1988) 'Nicodemus and His Spices', *NTS* 34: 148–51.

The Bible and Culture Collective (1995) *The Postmodern Bible*, New Haven and London: Yale University Press.

8

BORDER CROSSING AND MEETING JESUS AT THE WELL

An autobiographical re-reading of the Samaritan woman's story in John 4:1–44

Ingrid Rosa Kitzberger

Standing again at the well
listening to voices
whispering murmuring crying
my heart bleeding
waters welling up
from inside and outside
communication beyond words

'What do you want?' he asked me with a look of his eyes and uneasy gestures of his hands. The unspoken question flowed out from his brain and his heart and filled the air around us, infected me, poisoned me, and my joy. He did not understand a word of what I had tried to communicate in written words before my arrival and in spoken words when encountering him face to face, sitting together. I have journeyed a long way to come here, crossing the border.

'Why don't you look for a nunnery?'; the guestmaster tried to direct my desires away from this place and towards an imaginary other where I, so he thought, might fit in better. Women are not meant to live in monasteries. Border crossing is not meant to happen.

Leaving the guestmaster behind in his office, I have come back to the well in the 'fountain house',[1] in the silence of the cloister, listening to the voices of the water and the voices of my heart on this cold day in February 1996, at noon. Snow and ice have enfolded the landscape outside, yet here the waters are flowing as ever, living waters in a constant process of giving and receiving, an endless flow of life, telling its story of almost 800 years, a glimpse into eternity from my small world of only some 40 years. Whispering voices of fathers and brothers. Their story has met with mine, but they do not

111

know yet. Listening to the voice of my heart I know: Borders are meant to be crossed because life is right, always.[2]

~ ~ ~

It was a hot day when I arrived the first time, around noon on 29 July 1995, with my luggage. I was tired from my journey and thirsty, physically and spiritually. I had come here after crossing the Hungarian–Austrian border and after a stop in Vienna, on my way from Budapest to my home-town Linz in Upper Austria, on the river Danube. I was back in the country of my mother and my father, who gave me my life and my brothers, their sons.

There was a great flood the year I was born; 1954 was a memorable year indeed. 'I came with the great flood,' I used to say sometimes, when I was still living there and had not yet crossed the border. 'The stork fished me out of the water,' I joked. Water of life, after all? It was not the stork, of course; that would have been much easier, for both my mother and me. We struggled for 40 hours for birth, for separation, until the morning of 17 November that memorable year. But it remained a life-long birthing process, completed on 16 December 1989.

She enjoyed her journey into 'Herland'. I had found the German transla-tion of the novel by Charlotte Perkins Gilman in the little bookshop near the cancer clinic in Bavaria where she was staying. 'In *that* land I would like to live,' she said when I asked her later how she liked the book. And for a moment there was a spark of light in her eyes that looked into the future to come. Death came before she could finish reading. So, after all, my mother did remain in this utopian land, which – for 2000 years – has been inhabited only by women, who live together in harmony, justice, equality, and in love for their children.

~ ~ ~

Coming home where home had not been but now was. Strange remembrance and recognition, soul-knowledge, deep, deep as the well, reaching into the eternal past. A warm welcome by the Father who is not my father. 'Abbot' they call him, though he is not yet fifty. Before I came to be, he was. 'Brother' I call him. He led me to the well, on that summer day when it was hot and I was tired and thirsty. He led me to the waters of the whispering voices and into the cool silence embraced by the old stones, echoing. Nourishing, nurturing presence of the remembered unknown. And somebody who talked with me, sharing life, giving and receiving. Living waters, both material and spiritual. No cistern water in the Cistercian monastery.

~ ~ ~

What do you want? –
I want to stay
not only for the rest of the day
Come and see
that is the key –

Although named like Mozart (his middle name) he is not an Austrian. A border crosser he is, the Dutch. But he is the monk and I am the woman, a native who does not belong.

~ ~ ~

'You are a monk at heart,' he said to me, smiling. 'How do you know?' I stammered unbelievingly, while eating the cake and drinking the chocolate the 'motherly monk' had given to me, the stranger, whom they nevertheless made feel belong in this remote place in the Irish countryside. From the 'field of the lilies' to the mountains of Knockmealdon I had to journey, and there I was, sitting at the kitchen table in the monastery, in the evening of a hot summer's day in August 1996. I had not asked, 'Give me a drink', but there he was, the 'motherly monk', with his vessels and jars. He knew I was thirsty and he knew no one had given me anything to eat. 'How do you know?' I asked the other monk who had come after him. 'I can read your heart,' he answered and disappeared, leaving me behind with my heart burning, like fire.

'What do you want?' said the one who came after the other one, 'Do you want some salad?' 'No, thank you,' I responded to the guestmaster whose name is like the good future, 'I am happy.' 'Anything else?' he tried to increase my happiness. 'Come' he had said when I had phoned him from Dublin, where somebody whom I just happened to meet during the International Meeting of the Society of Biblical Literature had given me the address. No further questions, just the invitation, 'Come.' And the 'motherly monk' had stayed up late and was waiting for me, the stranger, outside the monastery to give me one of the warmest welcomes I have ever experienced.

Motherly fathers and brothers; they are the monks and I am the woman, but who cares? Crossing borders and boundaries does happen. And God looked at the man and the woman, created in his/her image and likeness, and s/he smiled, because it was very good.

~ ~ ~

Standing again at the well, in August 1995, a few days after my first visit. The waters were still flowing, as always, but with a different voice now that life had stopped. Standing there again, trembling and crying, waters running down from my eyes, living water deploring the waters of death. And my body bleeding, since the message hit me.[3] The hemorrhaging woman at the well. And no garment to touch. Alone I stood. Blood and water flowing

113

out from deep inside. My heart was pierced and my body wounded, yet I was still alive. And the crucified, agonizing around the corner, did not hear my silent cry, 'He cannot be dead, can he?' 'I am thirsty,' I heard a dying voice. 'Give me a drink.' And the silence of the cloister echoed our pain.

Turning round and looking up I saw them, Jesus sitting at the well – I knew it was him – and a woman standing at the well, like me down here, her left hand protecting her heart, and the water jar in her right. The sun was shining through the stained-glass window, bright colours radiating life. 'I know where your wound is,' Jesus communicated to the woman, with a gesture of his right hand, invisibly touching her heart, body and soul.

He was not my husband, and I never lived with him, yet he was close to me and rich was the harvest of our friendship, sowed and tended for 23 years. He cannot be dead, can he?

And I stayed in the monastery for two days, and when the two days were over I left that place and passed through Upper Austria. After crossing three borders I finally came to the tomb. It was getting dark, and the heavens had joined me crying, merging my tears into the rain. I called out his name, but the stone did not move and the tomb did not open. He was Richard, not Lazarus. Alone I stood. Nobody was there to console me on behalf of my friend. And no angels, no Jesus asking me, 'Why are you crying?'

They had laid him into this tomb on 29 July 1995, when I was standing at the well and enjoying the living waters. Not yet knowing about the waters of death, I was wondering about my encounter with Mary Magdalene, so much present in that monastery. Before I came, I had no idea that she would be there, just waiting for me, so it seemed, waiting for me, the biblical scholar engaged in research on her. 'Synchronicity,' a voice murmured, recalling my Jungian past;[4] 'God's providence,' another voice – or was it the same? – whispered into my ears. Standing at the well on 29 July 1995 and wondering about Mary Magdalene and me, I did not yet know that he was dead, drowned in the waters of a foreign country on 22 July 1995, Saint Mary Magdalene's day. On his way home he had to cross borders but, flying above them, they did not affect him any longer. Borders are meant to be crossed, and he had a life-long desire for that.

~ ~ ~

Standing again at the well. Time has passed since 29 July 1995, an autumn, a winter and a spring. It is summer again, July 1996. Time heals wounds, mother used to say. Maybe so, but it *does* take time. It is a hot day, the waters are gushing up from the well and my heart is playing with them like a child, jumping from basin to basin. And the dead are alive.

'Give me a drink,' I hear a voice, demanding. I envision a German tourist[5] standing in front of me. 'Give me a drink,' he says, just like that, without any greeting, and no 'please'. 'Who does he think he is?' I think to myself, 'How can a German man ask a drink from me, an Austrian woman, just like that? After all, I'm on my home ground and he is the stranger, the border crosser. Doesn't he know that?'

It is the land of my mothers and fathers. We Austrians are a mixed race indeed, as heirs and heiresses to the monarchy[6] when the current borders did not exist, and Hungary and Austria belonged together, and the Bavarian duchess Elisabeth became the Austrian empress by marrying Franz Joseph (100 years before I was born, in 1854). 'Tu, felix Austria, nube.' My elder brother married a Bavarian woman,[7] too, in 1979. They have lived in Bavaria ever since and have two sons, my German-Austrian nephews. I also moved to Germany, in 1981, when I became engaged to the university and started my academic career in Freiburg, near the French and Swiss borders. I was homesick for almost two years, and the pain is still there, as a constant reminder of my roots that are becoming more important the older I grow and the longer I have lived in exile. 'Back to my roots,' but where my roots are, home is not, no longer, not really and not completely. I have crossed the border many times since my emigration, going back and forth between Germany and Austria, going 'home' each way. Going home and not home at the same time. Living in two worlds, belonging to both and to neither. I did not really choose to leave my home-country, it rather happened as a consequence of following my vocation as a biblical scholar. After all, a prophetess has no honour in her own country. Over the years, I have re-created my world and re-visioned my identity, transforming it into an identity of mixture and otherness.[8] And the more often I cross the borders, the more my new identity takes shape, as a unique mode of being in this world, where I as 'the other' come into my own. I am the woman-monk and the Austrian-German, and I embrace[9] both worlds and dance between them.[10] I am a border woman.[11]

Since moving to the north of Germany, I have lived in the city of Münster, which comes from the Latin *monasterium*, meaning monastery. Moving there in 1989 was no easy decision; the place had no meaning for me and nothing was in the name. Yet looking back, I know I had to go there. And I met the people I was meant to meet, encountering also the men who did not become my husbands. It was meant to happen, the Austrian woman meeting the German men and enjoying the drink we offered each other, though it was not meant to last for eternity.

One day
the hour will come
when I will worship
the well-spring of love
neither here nor there
in body and soul
and the sower and reaper

will rejoice together
eternally

~ ~ ~

'What do you want?' they wondered. 'How can a girl study theology? She cannot become a priest, can she?' 'She will not get a proper job and will have no money,' my teacher tried to influence my mother, 'No girl in this school has ever had such a crazy idea.' My mother and my father did not understand either, yet they accepted my wish and supported my decision.

One day I knew what I wanted. I was about 17 and I listened to my inner voice, not caring about the voices of others. In the autumn of 1973 I moved to the 'mountain of the nuns', the Benedictine nunnery high above the city of Salzburg, famous because of the nun who became a mother when she joined the Trapp family. Part of the film was cast in the nunnery, and American tourists envied me because I was allowed to walk around inside this place, while they were shut out from paradise. When I was still a child and often stayed with my great-aunt, my mother's aunt and her mother's sister, I was especially fond of a book I had found there about the Trapp family. At that time I had no idea whatsoever that I would ever live in that nunnery where the love-story started; and when I moved there I had forgotten about it. (I also had no idea that I would ever make my way to a Trappist monastery in the Irish countryside later on.) Every day, on my way from the nunnery to the theological faculty, I went through Saint Peter's churchyard, which was the shortest way and very convenient for a person in a hurry. And each time I wondered about the man and his seven wives when I passed by their graves with the wrought-iron crosses, all identical, just like the names on them.

~ ~ ~

'What do you want?' Sitting in a classroom with my fellow students, future priests and some of them monks, I am listening to a professor's voice, male and celibate. As so often, I am the only woman also in this class, a course on homiletics, the art of preaching.

'What do you want?' my colleagues signal to me, 'You will never ever have a chance to preach, you are a woman.' I gave a wedding sermon though, in class, in front of the celibate men staring at me.

But they were wrong, in the end, those voices. My hour did come, years later, when I preached in Saint Peter's in Salzburg, the church of the Benedictine monastery at the foot of the 'mountain of the monks'. (Appropriately enough my sermon was, by coincidence, on Saint Peter's attempted walk on the water.) And a few years later still I even preached by the Sea of Galilee, at Tabgha, with Magdala to my left and Capernaum to my right, and a gentle breeze from the waters strengthening my back. Upright I stood and nobody asked me, 'What do you want?'

We had come from Jerusalem to Galilee – we did not go through Samaria – seventeen women and two men, my master and me with our disciples, students of theology, now all of them teachers themselves.

~ ~ ~

I left the nunnery after my first year; I just did not fit in, not even in the guesthouse, and descended from the 'mountain of the nuns', transfigured. In my last year at the university I returned to the mountain, but this time to the 'mountain of the monks' (yet I did not live with monks).

During those years, framed by my mountain experiences, I fell passionately in love with the Scriptures and became a New Testament scholar. There was a professor of New Testament who talked with me from the beginning and never asked me, 'What do you want?' He is named like Mozart (his first name). Sitting together (opposite Mozart's birthplace on the other side of the square, and with a well in between), we were often engaged in theological dialogue and shared the personal challenge of the Scriptures in seminars with fellow students, men and women. Listening to my voice he encouraged and empowered me to trust myself. And so I did, even when I left this place, which had become a kind of home to me, and crossed the border to Germany.

~ ~ ~

Sitting at the window and looking out at the well in the garden, we were speaking with each other. I had returned to the Trappist monastery in County Waterford, at the foot of the Knockmealdon mountains, on my way home after touring County Kerry. One of the motherly fathers, the one who can read my heart, was listening to my voice and my experiences; how we went out to Skellig Michael on a stormy and rainy day, after all boat trips had been cancelled already. Waves that seemed as high as mountains were hitting hard and tossing our little boat about, a tiny nutshell in the ocean. I was with a group of German youngsters and their leader, eleven Germans and one Austrian, in an Irish boat. The captain was struggling with the waves, and so were we, the twelve. 'Does he not realize that we are perishing?' my inner voice silently cried, while I was trying hard not to fall overboard when the waves came in repeatedly. Then all of a sudden there was the smiling face of the heart-reading monk in the mountain-waves and I felt safe, in God's hands, and Richard was close, being rocked gently into death, like a baby rocked into sleep by his mother; it was no longer frightening. That day the waters of death turned into waters of life again, after all, in spite of everything.

~ ~ ~

Standing at the well we looked at each other. There was deep knowledge in his eyes as he looked right down into my soul. He was leaning against the

117

wall of the well, shaky. It had taken us all this Sunday morning to get him ready for this impossible outing. Steadily declining, he had been unable to move out of the confines of the house for weeks. But this morning we felt we had to take him out, one more time. I had journeyed a long way from Germany, crossing the borders, first to Austria and then to Switzerland, to come to this little village near the border where he was. It was a sudden decision and involved a hasty departure, for I was feeling the pressure of time. Standing at the well, the wheelchair and the illness were forgotten for a few minutes, for a moment filled with the intensity of life bursting through the clouds of death, just like the sun that came out the moment she took the picture of the two of us. Standing at the well we felt the farewell.

We had known each other for eternity. It was another Sunday morning when we first met, back in August 1973, in London. I had just finished school and was working as an au-pair girl with an English family in Westminster, near Victoria Station. After that summer I was to start my studies of theology at the university of Salzburg. He was an accomplished New Testament scholar who had just come from the annual meeting of the Studiorum Novi Testamenti Societas in Durham. But I did not yet know all of this when we met. We both had enrolled for an excursion that day, and there we were at the Austrian Centre in Hammersmith, London. (To this day, I do not know how a Swiss professor could ever end up in an Austrian Centre for young girls.) Before the outing, we were all celebrating Holy Mass early on this Sunday morning, and for the first – and last – time in my life I was invited by the priest to take the cup and give the drink to everybody. 'The blood of Christ,' I said, and gave the cup to Eugen. But I did not yet know who he was.

His niece was fond of taking pictures of him; 'my favourite photo model,' she would say. And when we came to the well she suggested taking pictures there, of him and me. A last encounter of two people who were meant to meet.

Two weeks later he died, near the well, on the other side of the lake, and only ten minutes' drive away from Richard's tomb in Vaduz, capital of Liechtenstein, just across the border. The icon of John the Evangelist accompanied Eugen on his last journey, until the very end. I had found it in a little icon shop on the hill of Buda, near the convention centre of the Society of Biblical Literature International Meeting in Budapest, in July 1995. From there, the icon had journeyed with me to the well at the Cistercian monastery, the 'lilies of the field', and on to Richard's tomb and back to Münster, from where I had sent it to my friend in Lucerne – John the Evangelist for Eugen the Johannine scholar. The cycle of a life-story was closing in this autumn, when the leaves turned into bright colours, radiating life, like when the sun shines through the stained-glass window at the well. John was present when, in the early hours of the morning of 7 October 1996, Eugen returned to the Father from whence he had come, and John did not try to hold him back when his hour had come. Both knew that life is a journey, always, not a final resting place.

~ ~ ~

Standing at the well they looked at each other. There was deep knowledge in his eyes, as he looked right down into her soul, knowledge deep, deep as the well that reconnected them with days of long ago, when Jacob, their ancestor, had come by, digging. Though they had never met before, there was strange recognition and remembrance from the moment they saw each other, unexpectedly. They had known each other for eternity, yet did not know how this could be.

It was about noon when they first met, on that memorable day, when it was hot and both were tired and thirsty.

She had come to the well from the nearby city of Sychar, as every day, to draw water, for herself and the man she lived with. He, however, had travelled a long way, crossing the border, on his journey from Jerusalem back home to Galilee.

He had stayed behind at the well when his fellow travellers decided to go to town and get something to eat. Why he did not go with them, he did not really know. But there was this strange inner voice telling him to stay, though, in fact, it did not make any sense. After all, he had no vessel to draw water with.

Approaching the well she saw somebody sitting there, unexpectedly. She had not supposed anybody would be there, not at this time of the day. Usually, she would come here in the morning, together with the other women. However, that very day she came alone, at noon, when the heat was worst. She was not sure why she did it, she just followed that strange inner voice, not listening to the voices of those who told her what she was doing was stupid.

'What do you want?' she heard voices from the distance, and was startled, all too suddenly awakened from a dream. Never before had she had such an encounter, transforming her in seconds of eternity. Her whole life-story was recognized and listened to by a wounded heart like hers. Later on, when trying to recall how it all started, she only remembered there was some casual talk about water to start with. The poor man was so thirsty and had no vessel. But then, in no time, they were speaking about theological issues. Eternal life, he mentioned. Worship on the Garizim or in Jerusalem, she put into the debate. Never before had anybody taken her interest in theological issues seriously. After all, she was a woman. But this strange man, this traveller, gave her the feeling of coming home into her very own. 'You are a theologian,' he said and smiled at her. None of her men, neither her husbands nor the man she lived with now, had ever recognized and appreciated her in such a way. Somebody listened to her and empowered her to speak with her own voice. Within seconds of eternity her life-story was changed, eternally.

'What do you want?' she heard the group of men and a few women saying, more to each other, avoiding her look, but she knew they meant her. And all of a sudden she was pushed back into the reality she knew. A woman is not meant to talk with a man in public, alone, and even less a Samaritan with a Jew. Though she soon had realized that this man was a Jew she did not care about it, nor did he. They knew the borders and boundaries between them, but they were no longer separating them. Somehow they felt that the hour had come to cross them, for the time being at least.

~ ~ ~

'Goodness me,' she exclaimed, 'what have they done to my story?' She found herself both nodding and shaking her head when reading John 4.

A long time had passed since that memorable day, and she had returned to the well, one more time. Standing again at the well it was like going back to her own roots and the place of her empowerment, where the journey into her true identity had started. Meanwhile, she had become a missionary, not only to her own townspeople but to all Samaritans, and border crossing had become her vocation. 'What do you want?' These words were still echoing in her heart, but with a different voice from when she had heard them the first time, long ago. When confronted with the group she later learned to identify as the disciples of this man and when confronted with their non-understanding mistrust, she suddenly knew what she wanted, and she followed her inner voice. Immediately, she left her water jar behind at the well and returned to the city and told her townspeople what had happened to her. After that day nothing was as it was before, not for any of them. They all came to believe in this man as the long-awaited Messiah. And looking back later she knew that all this was due to her encounter with Jesus at the well, on that memorable day, when she did what they thought was stupid. 'Life is a mystery,' she thought to herself, 'the unfolding of what is meant to be.' [12]

'But he had to go through Samaria,' she read again, returning to the beginning of the story. For sure, he could have chosen another route, thereby avoiding Samaria. However, it was meant to happen that he, the Jewish man, and she, the Samaritan woman, met that day, around noon, and at this well in the remote desert. It was then, facing the mountain, that Jesus had this border crossing vision. 'Neither here nor there,' he said, and looked into the future to come, overcoming the borders and boundaries that had separated their peoples for too long. 'Now the hour has come,' he added convincingly. And later that same day they experienced a glimpse of that future. Jesus and his disciples stayed for two days, changing their travelling plans, but when the two days were over they continued their journey home to Galilee, transformed like the Samaritans. It was the beginning of a long friendship.

'I was not that stupid,' she exclaimed in protest, 'and I never asked Jesus that question in the first place.' 'How could they do that to my story?!' she added in bewilderment. 'And he never told me to go and call my husband,' she thought to herself, because there was nobody there to listen to her. 'And I never ever said, "He told me everything I have ever done."' She could partly understand why her conversation with Jesus was rendered so inaccurate, after all they were alone then and hesitant to talk about that intimate encounter later on when they were asked. However, she was unable to understand how her own words could be so distorted. She never made that moral judgement against herself, nor did anybody else. Her life was what it was, a story of love and pain. And of a new beginning when old patterns were outgrown and old structures collapsed into a future world to come.

'But yes,' she nodded, 'I really said "our father Jacob and his sons" and "our fathers".' 'Honestly, I was not aware of what I was saying,' she continued her musings. Since then she had thought a lot about her mother and her foremothers, and their stories that had bound them together, eternally.[13] 'What about your mother?' one day another woman asked her when she was, once again, speaking of fathers. And long-forgotten memories came back to her, painfully liberating. That encounter and question changed her life again, re-connecting her with her female roots and the womb she had come from. Coming home where home had not been but now was. No longer a motherless child. Nourishing, nurturing presence of the remembered unknown.

~ ~ ~

Standing at the well they felt the farewell, when the voices came closer. They never had a chance, after that, to be alone together. And they never saw each other again after his departure. Later she learned that his journey had finally led him to the cross on Golgotha. '"I am thirsty," he said, when dying on the cross, and he mentioned your name, with a whispering voice,' the woman added, when she told her, many years later. 'I felt the farewell,' she responded, 'and the death to come.' 'There was this strange look in his eyes when he was speaking about the living waters gushing up into eternal life, from deep inside.' 'Blood and water gushed up from his side when the soldier opened it with his spear,' the other woman continued, passing on what others had told her, for she was no longer present then. When she saw him again in the nearby garden, he was standing in front of her, yet she did not recognize him. Only when he called her name, her eyes were opened. 'Goodness me, Jesus,' she exclaimed in joy and bewilderment, 'I did not know it was you!'

Meanwhile, the two women had become close friends, sharing their encounters with Jesus and the vocation he had kindled in them. And often they shared their experiences of their missionary journeys, their ups and downs in a world where men did not always believe their words because they were a woman's words. 'It is no longer because of what you said that we believe, for we have heard for ourselves, and we know that this is truly the saviour of the world,' she remembered that strange remark made even on that first day when the future had only just begun. Though she knew that those who went out to Jesus at the well came to believe because of her word, while those who stayed in town came to believe when they heard Jesus himself, she did not mind so much these words of some men. After all, they came to believe, that was what counted. But sometimes she still felt the hurt of that remark which hit her in the midst of her joy and enthusiasm. It was a bit like that remark heard earlier the same day, 'What do you want?' Words are powerful, for good and for bad.

~ ~ ~

'Now Jesus did many other signs in the presence of his disciples, which are not written in this book. But these are written so that you may come to believe that Jesus is the Messiah, the Son of God, and that through believing you may have life in his name.'

After reading these words she put down the book on the wall of the well, and her thoughts started wandering again. 'Yes,' she agreed, 'many other signs, but certainly, one sign he did not do in the presence of his disciples.' And that, for her, was the greatest of them all. 'But maybe,' she wondered, 'maybe one or the other reader of this book will think of Jesus's encounter with me when reading these words.' And she closed the book and said farewell to the well and returned to the nearby city where she had left her fellow travellers behind. 'Life is a journey, always, not a final resting place,' she said to them, and off they went.

~ ~ ~

This is the Austrian woman from the well who is testifying to these things and has written them. And it is true, there are many meaning dimensions[14] in the Samaritan woman's story. If they were all explored, I suppose that the world itself could not contain the books that would be written.

For 2000 years women and men have been either nodding or shaking their heads when reading John 4. Reading and re-reading the story over the years, I have found myself both nodding and shaking my head. Reading with the grain and reading against the grain is called for, as I have come to realize.[15]

'Goodness me,' I have often thought, both when reading John 4 and when reading or hearing readings – ordinary and scholarly readings – of John 4. The truth is, there is no 'true' reading, but the truth is always personal.

Entering into John's story-world over and over again, I have met Jesus and the woman at the well, and I have journeyed[16] on with Jesus from the well at Sychar to the tomb at Bethany, and then to the cross at Golgotha and finally to the tomb in the nearby garden. Thus, I have got involved in the christological internet of women in John[17] in general and of that between the Samaritan woman and Mary Magdalene in particular. Entering John's story-world from my own story-world and entering my own story-world from John's story-world, both have been informed and transformed intertextually. In this process a new story has emerged which is no longer one or the other, but both, a story of mixture and otherness.

One day, standing again at the well, I encountered the Samaritan woman and sided with her.[18] That was the beginning of a friendship, in struggle and solidarity, in which two border women[19] have crossed the borders and boundaries, coming home into their very own, no longer strangers, re-visioning themselves in each other's image.[20] And often, since that first encounter at the well in the 'field of the lilies', they have shared their life-stories, as women in a male world and as 'the other', always.

But sometimes it happens that they, unexpectedly, meet a border man,[21] an 'other' man. Then there is deep recognition and knowledge in their eyes when they look at each other and deep down into the wells of their stories. Sharing and speaking with[22] each other, old patterns become outgrown and old structures collapse into a future world to come. Then, sometimes, they are granted a glimpse into that future, like the sun shining through the clouds of death, radiating life, and painfully liberating. But smiling at each other they know: Borders are meant to be crossed, because life is right, always.

~ ~ ~

Notes

1 'Fountain house' is my translation of the German word 'Brunnenhaus'. According-ing to information from Prof. James Hogg the English word would be 'lavabo', but there is no true adequate translation because English monasteries do not have these fountain houses which are typical of Cistercian architecture.

2 See Rilke (1996: 69) who, in a letter dated 4 November 1904 to Franz Xaver Kappus, wrote: 'Und im übrigen lassen Sie sich das Leben geschehen. Glauben Sie mir: das Leben hat recht, auf alle Fälle.'

3 At the same time, just across the Austrian–Czech border, I was elected a member of the Studiorum Novi Testamenti Societas at the Prague jubilee meeting. Therefore, both events are forever linked in my memory.

4 Synchronicity is an acausal connecting principle, a meaningful coincidence in time, see Jung (1981, 1990). During the academic year 1986/87 I studied at the C. G. Jung Institute for Analytical Psychology in Küsnacht, near Zürich, Switzerland.

5 German tourists are a special species invading Austria, especially during the summer and winter season. The 'Piefkes' are a sub-species and the term refers to a certain type of German (tourist) from the northern parts of Germany. They

speak with a (for Austrian ears) very harsh and loud voice and act in a dominating and demanding manner. 'Give me!' 'Bring me!' they would say, for example, to a waitress in a restaurant, as opposed to an Austrian who would say (even in his/her own country), 'Could you please give me', or, 'Would you please be so kind as to bring me'. And greeting, even strangers, is a common practice amongst Austrians (different, again, from the 'Piefkes'). For the ambivalent relation between Austrians and Germans, see also James (1994: 6, 9). 'Piefke', according to James, 'implies the humourless arrogance of the militaristic Prussian' (9).

6 According to James (1994: 12), 'Collective analysis is not easily applied to the Austrians with their mixed Swabian, Bavarian and Slav provenance.' However, there are a few more, for example, Hungarian and Italian. Austrian identity is, therefore, by its very nature a mixed identity (cf. James 1994: 5).

7 Coincidentally, her name is the same as the one Elisabeth had chosen as a pseudonym, see Hamann (1995: 387).

8 I owe both the image and the inspiration to think anew about my own identity to Fernando F. Segovia, since the SNTS meeting in Madrid in 1991. See Segovia (1992, 1995).

9 See Segovia (1992, 1995).

10 Reading Gustafson (1997) on my flight to San Francisco for the AAR/SBL Annual Meeting on 17 November 1997, I was fascinated with the image and inspired to re-imagine my mixed identity in a dynamic way. The 'dancing' refers in actual reality to my commuting between Germany and Austria (including the Cistercian monastery) on the one hand, and my journeys to the Trappist monastery in Ireland on the other hand.

11 Encountering Anzaldua (1987) in the autumn of 1996, I found the appropriate designation for myself.

12 See Jung (1981, 1990) and Cousineau (1997).

13 See Virginia Woolf's insight that we women think back through our mothers (1945, 1928: 76, 96). My own thinking back through my mother and re-claiming our history was engendered by Amy-Jill Levine's critical comment on the inconsequence of my social location as presented in my lecture at Vanderbilt University (Nashville, TN) on 14 November 1996 entitled 'Reading and Re-reading the Samaritan Woman's Story. Characterization and Social Location'. Claiming the 'our' of John 4:12, 20 for my social location was and is in fact not possible because it implies, in terms of the story, a thinking back through our fathers only.

14 On 'meaning-producing dimensions' and the multidimensionality of biblical texts, see Patte (1995, 1996).

15 I first developed a feminist-theological hermeneutics of 'reading with the grain' and 'reading against the grain' in the paper presented at the AAR/SBL Annual Meeting in New Orleans on 23 November 1996, see Kitzberger (1998).

16 The motif of the journey is essential for the plot of John's story. See Segovia (1991).

17 On the 'christological internet of women in John', see Kitzberger (1998).

18 Siding with the woman who is 'the other' within the patriarchal narrative framework implies a subversion of this narrative and claiming a voice for her. See Exum (1993: 9–10). Cf. also Bach (1993: 69) and Rashkow (1993: 109). Since my en-visioning Jesus as a German tourist I have become conscious also of the colonialistic bias of the story about the Samaritan woman, who is viewed as 'the other' and the inferior both in terms of gender and ethnicity.

Generally, Germans also consider the Austrians as inferior. Besides actual behaviour, there are numerous German jokes about the Austrians, characterizing them as stupid and behind the times.

19 Like me, the Samaritan woman was a border woman by birth. She belonged to a mixed race, half-Jewish, half-pagan, due to the changing political situation after the fall of the northern kingdom to the Assyrians in 722/721 BCE.

20 On characterization as reader's construction, see Rashkow (1993) and Kitzberger (1995).

21 Jesus was a border man too. He crossed borders not only in terms of geography, but also in terms of gender, ethnicity, and class. Besides that, according to John's Gospel he lived in the borderlands, that is, in the earthly and heavenly realms simultaneously. But while walking on earth, he did not belong there.

22 I owe both the term 'speaking with' and the experience in concrete reality to Daniel Patte. See Patte (1995: 23–5; 1996: 389–96). It 'happens when one simultaneously recognizes the otherness of the other and affirms it by recognizing, thanks to it, one's own otherness, i.e. one's own different identity' (Patte 1995: 33, n.21). As different from 'speaking to', 'speaking about', and 'speaking for' somebody, 'speaking with' implies equality, justice, and respect; thus it is liberating and empowering.

References

Anzaldua, G. (1987) *Borderland/La Frontera. The New Mestiza*, San Francisco, CA: Aunt Lute.

Bach, A. (1993) 'Signs of the Flesh: Observations on Characterization in the Bible', in E. Struthers Malbon and A. Berlin (eds) *Characterization in Biblical Literature*, Semeia 63, Atlanta, GA: Scholars, 61–79.

Cousineau, P. (1997) *Soul Moments. Marvelous Stories of Synchronicity – Meaningful Coincidences from a Seemingly Random World,* Berkeley, CA: Conari.

Exum, J. Ch. (1993) *Fragmented Women. Feminist (Sub)versions of Biblical Narratives,* JSOT Supplement Series, 163, Sheffield: JSOT.

Gustafson, F. R. (1997) *Dancing Between Two Worlds. Jung and the Native American Soul*, New York and Mahwah, NJ: Paulist.

Hamann, B. (1995) *Elisabeth. Kaiserin wider Willen,* München and Zürich: Piper (7th edn).

James, L. (1994) *Xenophobe's Guide to the Austrians*, London: Ravette Books.

Jung, C. G. (1981) *Synchronicity. An Acausal Connecting Principle*, trans. R. F. C. Hull, London: Routledge & Kegan Paul (repr. 1977, first publ. 1955).

—— (1990), 'Über Synchronizität', in C. G. Jung, *Archetyp und Unbewußtes*, Grundwerk Bd. 2, Olten: Walter (4th edn), 279–90.

Kitzberger, I. R. (1995) 'Mary of Bethany and Mary of Magdala – Two Female Characters in the Johannine Passion Narrative. A Feminist, Narrative-Critical Reader Response', *NTS* 41: 564–86.

—— (1998 forthcoming) '"How Can This Be?" A Feminist-Theological Re-reading of the Gospel of John', in F. F. Segovia (ed.) *Reading John. More Interpretations than the World Could Hold*, SBL Symposium Series, 4, Atlanta, GA: Scholars.

Patte, D. (1995) *Ethics of Biblical Interpretation: A Reevaluation*, Louisville, KY: Westminster John Knox.

—— (1996) *Discipleship According to the Sermon on the Mount. Four Legitimate Readings, Four Plausible Views of Discipleship, and Their Relative Values*, Valley Forge, PA: Trinity International.

Perkins Gilman, Ch. (1992) *Herland and Selected Stories by Charlotte Perkins Gilman*, ed. and with an Introduction by B. H. Solomon, Harmondsworth: Signet Classic.

—— (1988) *Herland*, trans. S. Wilhelm, neue frau, Reinbeck b. Hamburg: Rowohlt (am. orig. ed. New York: Pantheon Books, 1915).

Rashkow, I. N. (1993) 'In Our Image We Create Him, Male and Female We Create Them: The E/Affect of Biblical Characterization', in E. Struthers Malbon and A. Berlin (eds) *Characterization in Biblical Literature*, Semeia 63, Atlanta, GA: Scholars, 105–13.

Rilke, R. M. (1996) *Briefe an einen jungen Dichter*, hrsg. und mit einer Einleitung versehen von F. X. Kappus, Frankfurt a. M.: Suhrkamp (3rd edn; orig. publ. 1929).

Segovia, F. F. (1991) 'Journey(s) of the Word: A Reading of the Plot of the Fourth Gospel', in R. A. Culpepper and F. F. Segovia (eds) *The Fourth Gospel from a Literary Perspective*, Semeia 53, Atlanta, GA: Scholars, 23–54.

—— (1992) 'Two Places and No Place on Which to Stand: Mixture and Otherness in Hispanic-American Theology', *Listening: Journal of Religion and Culture* 27: 26–40.

—— (1995) 'Toward a Hermeneutics of the Diaspora: A Hermeneutics of Otherness and Engagement', in F. F. Segovia and M. A. Tolbert (eds) *Reading from This Place. Volume 1: Social Location and Biblical Interpretation in the United States*, Minneapolis, MN: Fortress, 57–73.

Woolf, V. (1945) *A Room of One's Own*, Harmondsworth: Penguin Books (first publ. 1928).

9

READING THE LETTER TO THE GALATIANS FROM AN *APARTHEID* AND A POST-*APARTHEID* PERSPECTIVE

Bernard C. Lategan

My resistance to an autobiographical reading is due, I suppose, to a number of influences that shaped my development as an aspiring interpreter of biblical texts. The most important – which I share with many of my guild – is the conscious separation of the personal from the critical in performing what is supposed to be the professional task of interpretation. The Reformed tradition in which I grew up reinforced this reserved attitude. Displaying emotion in religious and public life was subtly discouraged. Perhaps that was also why autobiographical readings at first struck me as exhibitionistic, some even as narcissistic. Anderson and Staley describe the dilemma and dangers of autobiographical criticism very succinctly (1995: 12–15; cf. also Rohrbaugh 1995: 256–7).

To overcome my resistance I had to find reasons (or a least a plausible excuse) for attempting such a reading. The first was supplied by Rohrbaugh's very perceptive criticism of this approach. He warns that social locations must be understood for what they are, namely *heuristic* constructs, and that they should not be expected to function as explanatory ones (1995: 255). For him, autobiographical readings tell us more about the reader and his or her appropriation of the text than of the text itself and its (original) setting. Given the importance of this distinction, the interesting question to explore is how this appropriation takes place. In my case, I have been reading the text of Galatians on and off for more than two decades. In the course of time, there has been a clear shift in my understanding of the letter. Initially, these readings were very much from an *apartheid* perspective, that is, from the ideology of racial segregation and from a socio-political system that applied this ideology to all aspects of public and private life.

This has changed to a post-*apartheid* reading, that is, a reading from the perspective of a fully democratized society, based on a constitution with an entrenched bill of human rights and a constitutional court to enforce this. What caused this change? The changed political situation? A shift in my personal convictions? The persuasive power of the text? In terms of Rohrbaugh's distinction, what follows will be an attempt to use auto-biographical criticism as a heuristic device to explore these questions.

The second reason was suggested by the theory of reader-response criticism. One of its strong claims is that the receiver and the context of the receiver play an important role in what is eventually understood as the meaning of the text. The rise of contextual theologies seems to support this claim. But how does the process actually work? How much or how little of the self is involved? Is the text still a *Gegenüber* or an 'other' that can change the course of things? These are very similar questions to those prompted by the first reason.

As soon as the self comes into play in such a self-conscious manner, the warning given by Moore (1995: 26) becomes important. He reminds us that an autobiographical reading can only work if enough of the self is disclosed to make that specific reading understandable and convincing. This will be a further challenge for the reading that follows. At the same time, it must be constantly borne in mind that what we call the 'self' is in itself a construct – perhaps even more so than in the case of 'outside' history. The idea that we know ourselves better than anybody else and are therefore the best source for the 'self' obscures the arbitrary nature of our reconstructions of the self – and of how selective our memory of ourselves can be (cf. Pippin 1995: 163; Rohrbaugh 1995: 243, 255). We may have privileged information about ourselves, but this does not guarantee that we will produce a more truthful picture of the self.

With all these qualifications and caveats in mind, let us turn to the text of Galatians itself.

How can Galatians possibly be read from an *apartheid* perspective? One of the main themes of the letter is the unity of the believing community. Paul makes an emotional plea to his readers to accept believers from a gentile background as full members of the church and as rightful heirs to the promises of God. His argument reaches a climax in the programmatic statement of 3:28:

> There is neither Jew nor Greek, there is neither slave nor free,
> there is neither male nor female; for you are all one in Christ.

This surely defies any attempt to justify racial separation and a comprehensive system of legalized discrimination. To understand how an *apartheid* reading of this passage and of the letter as a whole can indeed develop, a longer run-up is needed.

If there is 'no theory that is not a fragment, carefully preserved, of some autobiography' (Moore 1995: 20, quoting Valéry), the impact of personal experience in my own case is evident on two levels. The first level relates to the transition from a society based on racial discrimination to a democratic state, embracing the values of equality, freedom, participation and the respect for human rights. The second relates to changes in personal attitudes and convictions within the context of this socio-political transition. My reading of the letter to the Galatians was affected by experiences on both these levels.

To start with the first level, my training in Classical Greek and in linguistics in the early 1960s introduced me to the system and structure of language. This soon lead to the discovery of hermeneutics as a philosophical and theological discipline and brought the wider issues of understanding and the conditions for understanding into focus. Via Bultmann, Fuchs, Ebeling, Jüngel and the 'new hermeneutic', the issue became much more than just the technical aspects of syntax and semantics. The philosophical stream flowed via Betti, Heidegger, Gadamer and especially Ricœur. The third influence was quite naturally literary theory. I became aware of reception theory in its Continental version and reader-response criticism in its North-American version almost at the end of its bloom, just before deconstruction and postmodernism became the vogue. At the same time, the work of Ricœur became increasingly important for my own thinking. His interpretation theory, his exploration of narrative and time and his insights into the transformative potential of texts, provided a framework to integrate philosophical, literary and theological perspectives. These insights were also of direct relevance for the problems of social change facing South Africa in the 1980s. My own thinking was constantly stimulated and shaped by the continuing interaction with two most valued circles of colleagues and friends – the work group on contextual hermeneutics that met regularly in Stellenbosch, and the seminar group on 'The Role of the Reader' as part of the annual meetings of the international Studiorum Novi Testamenti Societas (SNTS).

The focus on reception theory and the role of the reader coincided with the rise of the liberation movement in South Africa. This movement gathered momentum in the course of the 1980s as the repressive political system increased in severity. The strategy adopted by its exponents was very similar to that of reception theory, although it is doubtful whether any formal link ever existed. Both take as their point of departure the receiver of the message. This approach provided the tool with which exponents like Mosala (1989) and Boesak (1984) could challenge the dominant theological discourse in terms of its own premisses. Once the constitutive contribution of the receiver or audience and its role in co-determining the meaning of the biblical message are accepted, the rise of various forms of contextual theology becomes understandable and even predictable. Liberation theology, black theology, feminist theology, theology of the poor and other marginalized groups (cf. the latest study of Germond and De Gruchy 1997), are all variations of the same hermeneutical model. New reading strategies developed – 'reading against the grain', looking for the sub-text, reading from the perspective of the powerless, of women, of the marginalized. Texts read and re-read for generations in a certain way suddenly revealed dimensions that nobody noticed before. The strength of this strategy was its recognition of the *interactive* nature of understanding. A powerful critique of the dominant discourse developed (cf. West 1996). It was possible to expose the contingent nature of this discourse and how it was shaped by its own historical context. It became possible to unmask the role of power in biblical interpretation. Theologically speaking, it meant the recognition of the outsider, of the newcomer to the tradition and the important contribution he or she has to make to continue the tradition and to keep it vibrant and alive.

But this history of liberation from political and other forms of oppression is not *my* history. What I shared via my interest in hermeneutics with the liberation movement on this point was an intellectual interest, not an existential one. My own social location constituted a clear boundary (cf. Pippin 1995: 165). I was *not* part of the struggle for liberation in any physical sense. I shared the commitment to democracy, but I had no experience of what it meant to be on the receiving end of the *apartheid* system. I was part of the protected and privileged white minority, not only by historical accident, but by conviction. I was a founder member of the *Ruiterwag*. This was a secret youth organization that served as the recruiting arm of the much more influential *Broederbond* (Band of Brothers), of which I became a member in due course. The *Broederbond* was originally formed in the 1920s to protect the interests of Afrikaners, who were then a marginalized group, excluded from any real power in government, the public service, and the world of industry and finance. After the victory of the National Party in the general election of 1948, the role of the *Broederbond* changed. The Afrikaner was now in political control and the *Broederbond* became a powerful instrument to consolidate this position. It functioned as a think-tank for government policy and played a decisive role in the formulation and implementation of *apartheid* on all levels of South African society.

My membership of the *Ruiterwag* and later the *Broederbond* was only a part of the much wider social context in which I grew up. My father was deeply committed to Afrikaner nationalism and to Afrikaans as the language of this nationalism. 1938 was the year of the centenary celebrations of the Great Trek, the historic migration of Afrikaners northwards in the middle of the nineteenth century to escape from British rule in the Cape Colony. The year marked a strong upsurge in nationalist fervour. The symbolic re-enactment of the Great Trek ended just outside Pretoria, where the foundations of the

Voortrekker Monument were laid in December 1938. I was baptized at this occasion in the 'tent of assembly' – a direct allusion to the Great Trek of Israel out of Egypt to the Promised Land. This parallel between the Afrikaner people and the history of Israel in the Old Testament is just one indication of an almost total identification of the Afrikaner people with the people of Israel – not uncommon in many forms of nationalism, but very powerful in this case. (Paul's claim in Phil. 3:5 – 'circumcised on the eighth day, of the people of Israel, of the tribe of Benjamin, a Hebrew of Hebrews . . .' – always had a familiar ring to it.) The power lay in the mix of elements in this nationalism. Anti-colonialism, freedom, independence, commitment to democracy, self-reliance and a large dose of idealism combined to form a heady mix that inspired Afrikaners in their rise to political and economic power.

At the same time, this nationalism (like all nationalisms?) was fatally flawed. It was based on a narrow and deep-seated racial prejudice. Its benefits were intended for some, not all. All its idealistic attributes could neither conceal nor control its essential racist nature and the untold misery that followed in its wake. Ironically, it is exactly the ideals of freedom and recognition which it shares with the black liberation movements of the twentieth century that made it possible for Afrikaners to understand and fear the rise of black power.

From my earliest childhood, I was socialized in this paradigm. My first loyalty was to the Afrikaner people. The church, in this case the Dutch Reformed Church, supported these nationalist ideals and supplied the moral and theological justification for the policy of *apartheid* as it unfolded from 1948 and as it was implemented in increasingly severe form. The Dutch Reformed Church's theological justification for *apartheid* is well documented and cannot be discussed here in any detail (cf. Kinghorn 1986; De Gruchy 1979). It certainly influenced my reading of Galatians at critical points. To understand why this happened and why Paul's struggle to come to terms with his own past in this letter was of such significance to me, it is necessary to highlight some aspects of *apartheid* thinking and theology.

The link between Afrikaner history and the Old Testament did not only extend to the parallel with Israel as the chosen people of God and their history of liberation. It was of a much more fundamental nature, in which Gen. 11 (the story of national and linguistic diversity) and the creation stories themselves played a critical role. *Apartheid* theology is 'archaeological' in orientation – that is, its principle of explanation is via the *origin* of things (cf. Kinghorn 1986: 125–8, 139–40). If you understand the beginning of things, you understand their essential nature. It was therefore critical to establish pluriformity as a principle of creation. The exegesis of Gen. 11 is crucial in this respect. By using a form of 'reverse reading', apartheid exegetes interpret the story of Babel as God's rightful punishment of the resistance to the principle of the pluriformity of creation and of the sinful attempt to establish a unitary dispensation. The problem is that the creation story itself is much more naturally understood as the story of the unity of all humankind descending from the same original pair. The solution was to take the diversity of the *physical* world in the creation story as the point of departure and to argue that what happened in Gen. 11 was only the natural unfolding of a diversity that was already present in embryo at creation.

We will not follow the convoluted logic of this exegesis here. The important point for the reading of Galatians and for my own socialization is that cultural and ethic diversity was accorded *ontological* status. These were constituent factors determining your own existence and beyond the possibility of change. They could only be resisted, not changed – and resistance would amount to sin and rebellion against the will of God.

Apartheid ethics was at the same time an ethic of granting unto others what you claimed for yourself. That was the principle that soothed many a conscience, but was rarely put into actual practice (cf. Jas 2:15–16). *Apartheid* exegesis thus became an exegesis of *principles*. The unity in Christ, which according to Gal. 3:28 overrides differences in culture, ethnicity, social class and gender, is accepted in principle. But this is an *invisible* unity. In terms of the 'laws of creation' and the structure of existence in *this* dispensation (archaeological thinking), unity can only be anticipated in this dispensation. It can be fully realized only when this (sinful) world is replaced by the perfect world at the parousia. The new creation in Christ in fact does not cancel existing reality.

These perspectives are important when trying to understand how Galatians is read from an *apartheid* perspective and how my own reading, despite qualms about its correctness, continued in this vein. The radical impact of the programmatic statement in Gal. 3:28 (the consequences of which apparently were not fully understood and certainly not fully implemented by Paul himself) was therefore cushioned in my own mind. It was possible to bracket this statement in view of other statements emphasizing diversity and in view of my own (rather desperate) insistence on the *invisible* unity of all believers in Christ.

What triggered the shift from an *apartheid* to a post-*apartheid* reading of Galatians in my own case? In trying to reconstruct the process, two factors stand out.

The first was the exposure to students and colleagues of the Dutch Reformed Mission Church. This was one of the four churches in the family of the DR Church in South Africa – a family organized by the white 'mother' church along racial and cultural lines in accordance with *apartheid* principles – one for whites, one for blacks, one for Indians and one for 'coloureds'. The Mission Church was established to serve the needs of the latter, the 'coloureds'.

When I started teaching at the University of the Western Cape in 1969, the reception by students and colleagues of the Mission Church challenged and soon fundamentally changed all my preconceived ideas about how to deal with racial diversity in South Africa. They did not act according to the stereotypes that had been ingrained in me. They had every reason to keep a critical distance from this young lecturer from the 'mother church', but they received and accepted me as a brother in faith and in practice. In a time of the first violent protests against *apartheid*, the student uprising at UWC in 1973 and the Soweto riots of 1976, this was *not* the natural thing to do. Racial tensions were running high in an atmosphere of deep suspicion on campus. These students and colleagues demonstrated to me in practice what was just theory in my own tradition – that the unity in Christ goes before all other loyalties, that it is not merely an ideal, but something that has to be realized in practice.

The unexpected behaviour towards me was the first important factor. The second was the rediscovery of the text of Galatians itself. The change of context and the new experiences in this context changed the way in which I read the text and made me see things I never noticed before. I had a small glimpse of what women readers experience when they read 'against the grain', when they see different things because of different experiences. For me, that was convincing proof that the receivers of the message indeed have a co-constitutive role in determining the meaning of the text.

To explain in more detail how a post-*apartheid* reading of Galatians took shape, a little more needs to be said about the argumentative situation of the letter as theological text. It is generally accepted that Galatians is an argumentative text. Central to its interpretation is the issue and the audience to be persuaded – not as historical personae, but as 'the ensemble of those whom the speaker wishes to influence by his argumentation' (Perelman and Olbrechts-Tyteca 1969: 30). At least three categories of readers are addressed: gentile believers who have not adopted a Jewish lifestyle (5:2, 3:14), believers who are Jewish by birth (2:15), and what can be called a 'universal audience' (2:17–20, where Paul writes in a generic or 'timeless' way; for more detail, cf. Lategan 1992).

The complexity of the audience is an indication of the complexity of the argument. Paul has to negotiate between two modes of existence (one of slavery under the law and one of freedom in Christ) and deal with two categories of readers (Jews belonging to his own tradition with all the privileges belonging to descendants of Abraham, and gentile believers who have never been part of this tradition). Compared to Jewish believers, converts from the gentiles found themselves at a distinct disadvantage.

Are they to be accepted as 'full members'? Do Jewish believers have a privileged position? The principle of chronological priority was very powerful in Jewish thinking. The position of the firstborn and the concept of the first fruits of the harvest emphasize the importance of this principle. Something parallel to the 'archaeological' tendency of the *apartheid* philosophy seems to be working here, placing Jewish believers in an almost unassailable position. How is it possible for gentiles to become descendants of Abraham?

To find an answer to this problem, Paul adopts a very significant strategy. Instead of ignoring this claim of history, he radicalizes it by going back even further in the history of Israel. The real significance of Abraham is not to be found in circumcision or the Law – those true hallmarks of the Jewish way of life that are so closely associated with the descendants of Abraham. When Abraham received the blessing of God, it was on the basis of his *faith* alone; neither circumcision nor the Law was in operation at that time – these appeared on the scene much later. By going further back in history, Paul is able to effectively disarm the arguments of the Jewish traditionalists, without denying the validity of their claim as descendants of Abraham. In a similar manner, the challenge for *apartheid* apologists is to retrace their steps and go further back in their own history – before 1948 and before the distortion caused by nationalism – to re-discover the initial commitment to the ideals of democracy, equality and freedom.

Paul therefore found *faith* and only faith to be the bonding factor between God and believers and between believers themselves. It is faith that stamps believers as descendants of Abraham and as legitimate heirs of the promises of God.

The discovery that faith and not tradition is the deciding factor, opens the possibility to break through the seemingly unalterable structures of history and re-think the family of God. In fact, it exposes any 'history' for what it really is, namely a *construct* – a selection of certain events taken from a much larger reservoir and structured in such a way that it makes sense and reveals lines and patterns. Changing the dominant view of history therefore depends on finding *other* traces in this history – clues to alternative ways of how it can be re-constructed. The discovery of an Abraham without circumcision and without the Law was such a clue. It suddenly highlighted the fact that *faith* was the defining factor in Abraham's righteousness (3:6). But that in its turn presented the possibility of redefining the concept 'sons of Abraham'. The link is neither tradition nor physical descent, but the bond of faith. 'Therefore know that only those who are of faith are sons of Abraham' (3:7).

This way of re-structuring history to include those who came onto the scene later and to recognize their status as heirs who have an equal claim to the blessing given to Abraham (4:7), has far-reaching consequences for the way in which *apartheid* deals with history and reality. For many who were socialized in a different context, these insights might seem self-evident. In my case, it provided two important rhetorical strategies to move beyond the constraints of my own tradition.

First, it made it possible to break the tyranny of history and the power of archaeological thinking. These two can be combined (as in my own tradition) to form a formidable combination. This happens when history is understood as providing the script for how the future should unfold. How things were at the beginning thus attains normative status. I was therefore fascinated by the way in which Paul did not turn from his tradition but faced it, subjected it to critical scrutiny, discovered hitherto unnoticed or suppressed traces that offered clues to an alternative understanding of this history. He then articulated this understanding in a way in which the unthinkable became possible. Instead of being marginalized outsiders, believers from the gentiles were in fact on an equal footing with their fellow Jewish believers – sons of Abraham through faith, children of God and full heirs of the promises of God.

The second strategy was related to how the concept of an 'alternative world' can be used as a shifting mechanism in a time of social transformation. One of the important insights that emerged from the debate about paradigms is that one uncertainty and one alternative possibility is not enough to cause a paradigm switch. Not only do the internal contradictions have to reach a certain level, but there must also be an alternative way of making sense of the available facts. This is precisely what happens when Paul develops the concept of the 'family of God' in Galatians as an 'anti-structure'. 'Anti-structure' is a term used by Petersen (1985) to refer to alternative patterns of social relations and social behaviour. The functioning of any society depends on such a system of hierarchical relations and clearly understood roles that can be played by members of that society. At the same time, anti-structures develop that are often the inversion of these prescribed roles. These anti-structures mediate between existing fixed structures and emerging new relations (Petersen 1985: 152).

In the New Testament, one of the most prominent 'anti-structures' used to demarcate and characterize the emerging community of faith is the concept of the 'family of God'. This is the case in the Gospels (cf. Dormeyer 1987), but also in Galatians. Here the starting point is different, but Paul explores the same anti-structure (descendants of Abraham, children of God) in his quest to include the gentiles on an equal basis in the new community of faith.

A deeper understanding of the mediating function of these anti-structures was the direct result of the interaction with colleagues in the SNTS seminar on 'The Role of the Reader' and of discussions in the Stellenbosch group on contextual hermeneutics. This was enhanced by important insights of Paul Ricœur. His explanation of how texts offer 'proposed worlds' as alternative ways to self-understanding and making sense of the world, and his views on the role of imagination in this process, marked turning points in my own development. But perhaps the most influential was the work of Eberhard Jüngel and especially an often neglected essay that first appeared in *Evangelische Theologie* (1969). In this study he argues for the priority of the possible in relation to what is real. This consolidated in my own mind the switch from archaeological thinking, focused on origins, to eschatological thinking. The latter entails not only thinking about the present from the perspective of the end (or the future). It also means that reality (past and present) does not ultimately determine the shape of the future. Priority in this case must be accorded to what is possible. That meant not only liberation from the stranglehold of the past, but a setting free of creative, innovative and imaginative forces for thinking the unthinkable and shaping a future along lines that were never regarded as possible. The programmatic statement in Gal. 3:28 sums up the essence of Paul's experience in these matters and gives a glimpse of just what this alternative world might look like. It represented a fundamental shift that changed the nature of the believing community forever. The differences between the situation Paul had to deal with and modern transitions to democracy are so fundamental that it rules out any comparison. But there is one similarity. The peaceful transition to a democratic dispensation in South Africa – against all odds – seems to be a change of the same nature. It happened in a way that nobody really thought would be possible.

For me, the text of Galatians then became alive with possibilities and with strategies that could be used for persuasion and change. But seeing possibilities is still not implementation. An alternative reality only emerges when we act in terms of the new possibilities presenting themselves. The *social consequences* of this new understanding have still to be realized.

Gal. 3:28 therefore became a challenge for implementation. Paul is clearly dealing primarily with relations within the community of believers, and although that remains an important area in the present South African context, the transition to democracy required a much wider application. This raises the question whether relations in the believing community could be used as a model for society as a whole. In this respect, David Tracy's distinction between three publics for theology (the university, the community of faith, and the public arena) proved to be very helpful. The challenge was not only to develop an alternative understanding of the church, but also to find effective ways to reshape civil society. It is a formidable task, fraught with difficulties, but that is exactly the purpose of initiatives like the Reconstruction and Development Programme, the Truth and Reconciliation Committee, and a whole series of new laws to formalize the transition.

The overriding thrust of Gal. 3:28 is the unity of all believers in Christ, which relativizes the differences of race, culture, class or gender. The challenge was to go beyond the acknowledgement of this unity in *principle*, the talk about the *'invisible* unity' of the believing community. My students and colleagues in the DR Mission Church made it possible for me to cross this threshold and to act in terms of this new 'semantic universe'. But that did not mean that cultural diversity came to an end. The three examples Paul uses in 3:28 presupposes the continuing existence of culture, class and gender. The real challenge was to find a way in which diversity was no longer used to divide and destroy, but in which its creative and constructive potential is released. As far as the first of these examples are concerned, that of cultural or ethnic diversity, the issue became concrete in an unexpected way. An opportunity presented itself in the 'third public' in the form of a request to develop common values in a large South African gold mine, where the extremes of cultural diversity threatened the continuing operation of the mine. This is a story in itself, but a process was developed to deal constructively with cultural and other forms of diversity. The key was the discovery – through representative participation of employees - that despite fundamental differences, they do share a set of basic values. On this basis, it became possible to use diversity as a resource and to change its role from being a liability to become an asset. The work subsequently spread to other companies and organizations. A concept that was originally developed for the 'second public' became functional in the context of the 'third public'.

The second example in Gal. 3:28 ('neither slave nor free') refers to differences of class and social status. The history of slavery and the attitude of the church to this institution certainly does not make good reading. Right up to the nineteenth century, formal slavery persisted in many so-called Christian countries. Ironically enough, in the New Testament the social consequences of the new relationship in which believers found themselves were already spelt out in concrete terms. In the letter to Philemon the faith of the recipient is put to the test. His slave, Onesimus, ran away from his master. Apparently, his travels brought him into contact with Paul. Under the apostle's influence, Onesimus became a believer, but he did not dare return to his former master for fear of what might happen to him. The purpose of the letter to Philemon is *inter alia* to prepare Philemon for this return. If the re-interpretation of the 'family of God' means anything, then the status of Onesimus has changed. He is no longer a slave, but a brother. The critical test at his return will not be his attitude, but that of Philemon. Paul challenges him to accept Onesimus for what he now has become – a member of the family. On trial is not the faith of Onesimus, but that of Philemon; or rather, the challenge is whether Philemon will act in terms of the new reality constituted by faith. His acceptance or rejection of Philemon becomes the acid test of his own faith. This was the same challenge posed to me by my newly discovered family in the DR Mission Church.

The third of the contrasts in Gal. 3:28 that faith is supposed to overcome is that of gender. In many ways, this presents the ultimate challenge of the new paradigm of faith. Paul himself certainly did not fully realize the consequences of his own statement. For many, the apostle remains the notorious upholder of male chauvinist ideas. There is little doubt that the main thrust of his statements about women is in line with the ethic of his time and reflects the inferior social position of women. The revolutionary impact of Gal. 3:28 was slow in coming. At the same time, cracks do appear in his own reasoning about the matter. In 1 Cor. 11, he starts out by confirming the dominant position of men and tries to prove that with reference to the fact that Adam was created first. But as his argument develops, the logic becomes confused. Man was created before woman, yes, but then . . . no man came into being without a woman. . . . His argument trails off and he reverts back to the basic unity in God: 'In any case, all come from God!' Without claiming to understand the position of women or to be able to read from their perspective, a post-*apartheid* reading of Galatians changed my whole thinking about their position.

Trying to reflect on one's own reading and to trace the shifts that occurred in this process is indeed a complex and perhaps an impossible task. The re-construction of the act of reading requires at the same time a re-construction of the self. The question remains: What was the dominant influence in the process, the experience of a new situation that contradicted my preconceived ideas, or the alternatives that I discovered in the text? My own under-standing is that the latter was triggered by the former. At the same time, without the discovery of the alternatives in the text, it would probably not have been possible to make the shift in a context where the text still exercises persuasive power. In my experience, the text *does* function as a *Gegenüber*, as a foil, but does so only when confronted with 'real' questions. As Ernst Fuchs once said, to know what a cat is, you must put a mouse in front of the cat. It is through the dialectic tension that exists between text and experience that new understanding emerges. But let the reader decide, who most probably will read my reading differently . . .

References

Anderson, J. Capel and Staley, J. L. (1995): 'Taking It Personally: Introduction', in J. Capel Anderson and J. L. Staley (eds) *Taking It Personally: Autobiographical Biblical Criticism, Semeia* 72 Atlanta, GA: Scholars, 7–26.

Betti, E. (1972) *Die Hermeneutik als allgemeine Methodik der Geistenwissenschaften,* Tübingen: Mohr.

Boesak, A. A. (1984) *Black and Reformed. Apartheid, Liberation and the Calvinist Tradition,* Johannesburg: Skotaville.

Bultmann, R. (1965) *Glauben und Verstehen* III, Tübingen: Mohr.

De Gruchy, J. W. (1979) *The Church Struggle in South Africa,* Cape Town: David Phillip.

Dormeyer, D. (1987) 'Die Kompositionsmetapher "Evangelium Jesu Christi, des Sohnes Gottes" Mk. 1.1', *NTS* 33: 452–68.

Ebeling, G. (1959) 'Hermeneutik' in *Religion in Geschichte und Gengenwart III,* 242–62. Tübingen: Mohr.

Fuchs, E. (1958) *Hermeneutik,* Bad Cannstatt: Muellerschoen.

—— (1965) *Glauben und Erfahrung,* Tübingen: Mohr.

Gadamer, H.-G. (1975) *Wahrheit und Methode,* Tübingen: Mohr.

Germond, P. and De Gruchy, S. (1997) *Aliens in the Household of God,* Cape Town: David Phillip.

Heidegger, M. (1976) *Sein und Zeit,* Tübingen: Niemeyer.

—— (1959) *Unterwegs zur Sprache,* Pfullingen: Günther Nestle.

Jüngel, E. (1969) 'Die Welt als Möglichkeit und Wirklichkeit. Zum ontologischen Ansatz der Rechtfertigungslehre', *EvTh* 29: 417–42.

Kinghorn, J. (ed.) (1986) *Die NG Kerk en Apartheid,* Johannesburg: Macmillan.

Lategan, B. C. (1984) 'Current Issues in the Hermeneutical Debate', *Neotestamentica* 18: 1–17.

—— (1992) 'The Argumentative Situation of Galatians', *Neotestamentica* 26: 257–77.

—— (1994) 'Aspects of a contextual hermeneutics for South Africa', in J. Mouton and B. C. Lategan (eds) *The Relevance of Theology for the 1990s,* Pretoria: HRSC, 17–30.

—— (1996) 'Styles of theological discourse', *Scriptura* 57: 139–48.

Moore, S. D. (1995) 'True Confessions and Weird Obsessions: Autobiographical Interventions in Literary and Biblical Studies', in J. Capel Anderson and J. L. Staley (eds) *Taking It Personally: Autobiographical Biblical Criticism, Semeia* 72, Atlanta, GA: Scholars 19–50.

Mosala, I. J. (1989) *Biblical Hermeneutics and Black Theology in South Africa,* Grand Rapids, MI: Eerdmans.

Perelman, C. and Olbrechts-Tyteca, L. (1969) *The New Rhetoric. A Treatise on Argumentation,* Notre Dame, IN: University of Notre Dame Press.

Petersen, N. R. (1985) *Rediscovering Paul. Philemon and the Sociology of Paul's Narrative World,* Philadelphia, PA: Fortress.

Pippin, T. (1995) 'A Good Apocalypse is Hard to Find: Crossing the Apocalyptic Borders of Mark 13', in J. Capel Anderson and J. L. Staley (eds) *Taking It Personally: Autobiographical Biblical Criticism, Semeia* 72, Atlanta, GA: Scholars, 153–71.

Ricœur, P. (1976) *Interpretation Theory*, Fort Worth, TX: Texas Christian University Press.

—— (1981) *Hermeneutics and the Social Sciences*, Cambridge: Cambridge University Press.

Rohrbaugh, R. (1995) 'A Social Scientific Response', in J. Capel Anderson and J. L. Staley (eds) *Taking It Personally: Autobiographical Biblical Criticism*, Semeia 72, Atlanta, GA: Scholars, 247–58.

Villa-Vicencio, C. (1988) *Trapped in Apartheid*, Maryknoll, NY: Orbis Books.

West, G. (1991) *Biblical Hermeneutics of Liberation. Modes of Reading the Bible in the South African Context*, Pietermaritzburg: Cluster Publications.

—— (1996) 'Reading the Bible differently: Giving shape to the discourse of the dominated', in G. West and M. W. Dube, (eds) *'Reading With': An Exploration of the Interface Between Critical and Ordinary Readings of the Bible. African Overtures*, Semeia 73, Atlanta, GA: Scholars, 21–42.

West, G. and Dube, M. W. (1996) 'An introduction: How we have come to "read with"', in G. West and M. W. Dube, (eds) *'Reading With': An Exploration of the Interface Between Critical and Ordinary Readings of the Bible. African Overtures*, Semeia 73, Atlanta, GA: Scholars, 7–17.

10

MY READING OF
1 JOHN IN AFRICA

Jan Gabriel van der Watt

Introduction

My reading of 1 John in Africa started nearly two decades ago when I was Head of the Departments of New Testament and Practical Theology at the University of Fort Hare, the oldest and probably the best known predominantly black university in Southern Africa. I am a white scholar, who was, at that stage, basically trained in Western theology. When I started lecturing on the historical–critical method, dropping names like Bultmann or Jeremias, or emphasizing the importance of the synoptic problem, I realized – mainly because of the response of the students – that I was barking up the wrong tree. Together with my colleague, Rev. Solomon Sibanyoni, a black scholar, we started a programme to develop a New Testament syllabus which our students from Africa could relate to. We as lecturers took the lead, but with the cooperation of our students.

Our Department of New Testament began an intensive research programme to determine the nature of religious thinking among the African people. Since Fort Hare is situated in a predominantly black rural area, the students, who were as excited as we were, went to old people and gathered information that was transmitted orally in those African traditional communities. They then prepared assignments on different religious topics which were discussed in class.[1] The results were systematized and gave us very good insight into the African traditional way of thinking. (Some of these remarks will be indicated by means of italics in this article.)

With these results in mind we (the students and lecturers alike) read the New Testament afresh. Suddenly much of what we read sounded similar to what the students actually reported. The worlds of the New Testament and traditional Africa merged as if they belonged together. Notions such as the 'strong group awareness' and a 'weak sense of individuality', concepts of time, the intense awareness of the spiritual world, etc., seemed to be very close to one another. But there were also differences. Could one relate the role of Jesus to that of the ancestors? And what about notions such as 'salvation' and 'sin'?

This research project sensitized me by making me aware of the role of culture in transmitting a religious message, of the different faces of Christianity and how arrogant any form of Christianity is when superiority is claimed on the basis of a particular culture, as was often seen in certain missionary efforts in the past. It also made me aware of the unique position of Christianity among the other religions. What follows is a personal reading of 1 John in the light of the realities of the African traditional religion (ATR) with which Christianity was confronted in Africa in previous centuries. Both religions will be treated as systemic realities and will be compared as such.

Symbolic narratives

African traditional religion (ATR) is a coherent system of ideas in which 'cultural elements' and religious ideas are intimately related. The same applies to the Christianity brought to Africa by the missionaries. In the process of the assimilation of European religious culture by African religious culture, interesting phenomena resulted, ranging from a total rejection of Christianity by Africans in an attempt to turn back to their 'roots', to different degrees of acceptance and integration of certain aspects of Christianity into the African religious ethos,[2] through to a total acceptance of the Western form of Christianity. It is important to understand the structural dynamics of these religions if one wants to understand the effects of the process of interaction.[3]

In an attempt to formulate the essence of each respective religion, I opted for a symbolic-narrative approach. 'Symbolic' implies that the different objects (characters, cultural objects, etc.) are seen as 'symbols' that refer to particular qualitative contents. 'Narrative', again, implies that these objects or symbols relate and interact in a dynamic fashion with one another. Although the narrative is ever-developing, it is determined by dominant rules (tradition), which implies that meaningful events from the past are 're-played' in this ongoing narrative, and this gives the process the status of a meta-narrative that is acted out within the lives of believers. In an endeavour to find an acceptable way to compare ATR and Christianity by using 1 John as an example, I first describe the symbolic narratives of both these religious traditions and then compare them critically.

Before proceeding any further, I should point out that these symbolic narratives function on a high level of abstraction. Different tribes and groups in Africa have different viewpoints and practices of their beliefs. The same applies to Christianity. By working on a high level of abstraction, certain central elements can be identified and used effectively in a comparison.[4]

A brief survey of certain elements of the symbolic narrative of ATR

Members of ATR coexist in a spirit of *collective solidarity* and *interdependence*. Individual members are determined by their group (Crafford 1996: 11) and can 'only be a person through others' (Mbigi 1997: 31). The ATR believers' world is that of *ubuntu*, or belonging. In other words: 'I am because we are.'[5] Cosmologically, the reality may be divided into two spheres: the spiritual (unseen) and the physical (seen), which are closely related. The dominant spiritual world directly influences and determines the physical world of the believer. Believers are constantly exposed to a world full of spirits and powers (symbols) stronger than themselves.

Death does not imply the end of life, but the transition into a new mode of life (Mulemfo 1995: 51–2). When people die, they become ancestors ('living-dead'), meaning that they are still alive, but in a spiritual way (Mulago 1969: 137–58). Ancestors are regarded as part of the family (the 'living-living') and are still intimately involved in the lives of their children, both in matters of joy and sorrow, health or disease, prosperity or adversity. The family still has to care for, and appease, their ancestors by keeping them happy. If an ancestor becomes unhappy, (s)he can punish the family (through sickness, bad crops, and so on). That is why ancestor veneration is central within ATR (Crafford 1996: 14–16). It is not a matter of 'worship', but of venerating an important person. As one would show a father or a king respect, one would keep on showing one's 'living-dead' father respect, and that is not worship in the Christian sense (Fasholé-Luke 1974: 209–21). Ancestors are a central symbol in ATR narrative, playing a central role in the everyday life of the family.

Concreteness is a key concept in ATR. The activity of the spiritual world (including ancestors) can be perceived in concrete events; for instance, negatively in the failure of crops, in sickness or death, or positively in good crops or health, and so on.[6] This implies that these activities of the spirits should be regulated in a concrete way. For this, the system of *'diviners'* (*iSangoma*) *inter alia* exist (Ezeanya 1969: 30–46; Crafford 1996: 16–17). One basic function of diviners is to regulate the interrelation between the spiritual and physical dimensions of reality (Mulemfo 1995: 51–67; Crafford 1996: 5–6; Mugambi 1989: 57). This is done in different ways, for instance by the casting of bones, and by inducing spiritual experiences such as going into trances, as well as certain cultic and ritual actions. But there is also a negative group of diviners (Crafford 1996: 16–17), who manipulate negative powers in order to harm people.[7] Diviners are important symbols in ATR narrative.

As was already mentioned, the family in traditional Africa is *group orientated*; it functions through a network of mutual interdependence between an individual and his or her community (Maimela 1985: 66).

The father or king 'rules' the family, which is structured hierarchically. *The most important practice is to observe, with respect, the hierarchy in society. At the acme of this hierarchy is God, followed by ancestors, traditional healers, kings and chiefs, adults, the last category being the children.* Tradition (transmitted orally) represents the nature, values and norms of the family.

'Africa has an optimistic view of humanity' (Crafford 1996: 11). People are not born with sin, but as valuable members of a community who have to live their lives in a world of conflicting powers. *Among Africans you are born sinless and have to live in harmony with the ancestors, complying with their needs.* Members have to act in such a way that their actions will result in positive effects for the community. Individuals find themselves within a network of dynamic forces and powers, both positive and negative (Mugambi 1989: 64–6), which have the potential of influencing and affecting them. Members' responses within the dynamic process of living within this network lead to 'sin' or exoneration (see Maimela 1985: 67).

'Sin' (as an important symbol) is to be understood as trespassing against the group (tradition), and thus harming the group by affecting the relations within the group negatively.[8] Failure to do what is required will release evil forces, which in turn will result in misfortune for the group as a whole (Maimela 1985: 67). As long as this distorted relationship exists the person is guilty and something should be done to correct the wrong, since the whole group suffers from this wrong.

'Salvation' takes place when the wrong is corrected and anxiety is relieved. Diviners play an important role in pointing out the wrong and suggesting a 'cure'. There are also specific procedures by means of which the 'sinner' may confess and be accepted back into the family. *Since any anti-social act is sin in ATR, salvation can be procured by satisfying social needs and demands. To be saved, is to be accepted by society.* This is, of course, the decision of the head of the family, in consultation with his advisors. The 'sinner' has to convince the family of his or her undivided loyalty, which exclude similar negative actions in future.

'God' can also be seen as a symbol, *inter alia* as creator (Idowu 1969: 17–29; Crafford 1996: 8). In ATR, the ancestors are regarded as mediators and God does not play such a direct role in the ordinary lives of the group. *Africans are aware of the existence of God, however vague this idea is. There is no direct contact between God and the living humans. They do not think of him as engaging himself in daily life* (Mugambi 1989: 59–63; Crafford 1996: 13–14).

In summary, the symbolic narrative is gradually unfolding. Persons are born into a community and their lives are determined by that community. Their world is full of spirits (including ancestors) and powers that constantly have to be satisfied and even manipulated. Certain cultic actions, like sacrifices, as well as the presence of diviners, ensure that relations stay sound. Therefore, the game of life demands that one stays within the limits of one's group and if, by chance, one trespasses, the wrong must be dealt with so that the group is not harmed. After death a person simply lives on as ancestor and is still involved in the well-being of the group.

A brief outline of the symbolic narrative of 1 John

Only a very brief outline of the most important symbols and their relations in 1 John will now be given. 1 John was chosen by chance as my main field of interest lies in Johannine studies and my students also had a strong affinity with John and his writings. It seemed the ideal choice. However, it could just as well have been a Pauline letter, but if a Pauline letter had been chosen, the emphasis in the co-reading process would have fallen on different aspects, according to the restrictions of that particular text. The procedure of the reading process, as it is suggested later on, would nevertheless have been the same.

God as creator is the source of truth, love and life. Humanity is by nature sinful and needs salvation. By believing in Jesus one becomes a child of God and obtains eternal life (4:14; 5:11–13). The believer is received into the family of God.[9] This is a patriarchal family and is strongly group orientated. God, the Father, is the head. His will should be done, and all members are bound to one another by means of loyalty and responsibility as the expression of love (3:16; 3:23–4). Through the power of the Spirit of God, members of the family are guided in truth. Within this family the members also have confidence to communicate with God. Their eschatological future lies in their eternal relation with God, which is the result of eternal life.

Life within this 'spiritual' family of God coincides with life in the physical realm, but the values and norms of the communal life (*koinonia*) of the 'spiritual' family take precedence over that of the physical realm. Obviously, a Christian can sin, but sin is dealt with by means of confession (1:8–10), which implies the restoration of relations and the confirmation of the sinner's loyalty to the family. Through the atonement work of Jesus, as well as through his mediation, the believer is forgiven and can live as a child of God in restored relations (2:1–2).

My reading of 1 John in Africa in the light of the symbolic narratives of 1 John and ATR

A comparison between the symbolic narratives of 1 John and ATR points to interesting similarities, but also to crucial differences. My reading strategy entails starting with the similarities to establish common ground, and then moving to a gradual understanding of the differences. This is achieved by keeping the organic structure of both narratives in mind, and by indicating how a new structure might arise that can still be regarded as biblical.[10] This procedure will be carried out in a dialectical manner which implies that the text should be 'entered' through concepts that are common to both symbolic narratives. Thereby, the platform for further dialectical discussion is provided. It is a matter of 'reading with' and not 'reading for' (Mugambi 1989: 8–9). 'Reading with' people of ATR becomes an adventure, because this dialectical discussion in the end involves the readers in an existential way. Questions about the road ahead challenge beliefs and traditions, which is formative as far as the faith systems of the participants are concerned. It is not only an intellectual procedure, but is emotive too. This I have often seen and experienced among my students.

One possible misunderstanding should be avoided. Because of about 350 years of contact between Western Christianity and ATR in South Africa, the religious scene is quite varied, ranging from 'pure Western Christianity' to 'pure ATR'. Portraying the entire picture is complicated. The best way of doing this, I believe, is to describe the two focal points, which are the symbolic narratives of ATR and 1 John respectively, and then to endeavour to understand and describe what happens with the movement between these two focal points. Schematically this may be illustrated as follows in figure 10.1:

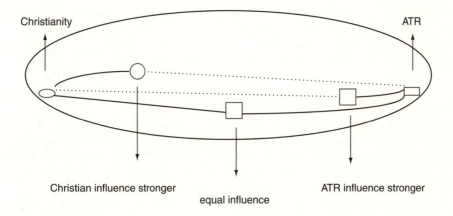

Figure 10.1

This schema shows that a person can find him- or herself anywhere within this ellipse. [11] Such a position is not to be determined on a straight line, but in an elliptical sphere. In this way the reality can be illustrated that several different Christian movements might move closer to the Christian focal point, but that these movements' way of absorbing the Christian symbolic narrative might differ from other movements who have moved equally close to the focal point (Mugambi 1989: 52–3; Mosala 1983: 23).

I will now offer a brief description of how I read the text dialectically. Only a few examples are offered, and the various issues will of course not be discussed in depth. This description should illustrate my reading strategy, as a white Christian academic, together with that of my fellow African Christians who might find themselves somewhere else in the ellipse in Figure 10.1.

1   In both symbolic narratives *group orientation* (*ubuntu* or *koinonia*) forms the socio-structural core. The pattern of the patriarchal family, with obedient members, whose existence is totally determined by their group adherence, exists in both. Members of both groups should be loyal to their respective group, and if they harm their own group or group relations in any way, the harm should be remedied. Both symbolic narratives depend strongly on this social norm, in other words, if group adherence and its corollaries are negated, the respective narrative structures will collapse. Therefore, I regard group adherence as the ideal 'entrance into the texts' of the respective symbolic narratives, which provides a basis for a dialectical discussion.

'Entering' into 1 John in this way sensitizes one to sections like the following: In 1 John 3:11–18 a treacherous brother's (Cain's) *anti-group behaviour* is explained and denounced. This behaviour shows that he does not really belong to the family, since family members will have regard for one another (3:16–17) and will definitely not harm one another. Family cohesiveness and corresponding loyalty will manifest itself through positive behaviour towards one another (3:9–10). No member of a group can or may have a pattern of behaviour that will reflect anti-group behaviour. (See also texts like 5:1–2.) Obviously, this is also the social world familiar to ATR.

But there are even more far-reaching correspondences. In 1 John 1:6–2:2 the problem of *violating the conventions of the group* (sin) receives attention. If such a wrongdoer still claims to be a member of that particular group, confession is required (1:9), so that the relations within the family may be restored.[12] However, the Father deals with this matter in conjunction with the παράκλητος, who acts on behalf of the group, as 2:1–2 indicates. Although variations might occur among different groups, this basic pattern is also common in ATR (Mulemfo 1995).[13]

2   In dialectical interaction, members adhering to both symbolic narratives will recognize the correspondences that can form a basis for further discussion. It will, however, become clear that there are also dissimilarities between these two families. This is crucial, since it is at the point of dissimilarity that people are confronted with new realities that will require them to switch or adapt their symbolic universes. 1 John 1:3–4 deals with this 'switch'. According to my reading of 1 John 1:3–4, the reader is invited into κοινωνία (fellowship) along with the group of the writer (μεθ᾽ ἡμῶν) and the Father and his Son (μετὰ

τοῦ πατρὸς/υἱοῦ – these are familial terms). An invitation is extended to enter into *fellowship with God's family*. This is a spiritual family, which coexists, but supercedes existentially and ethically the physical family to which a person belongs. Thus, Christianity has a structure where physical and spiritual life are *parallel* to one another, as opposed to ATR's *linear* structure of physical life now and spiritual life only after death. The fact that, according to 1 John, a person lives spiritually while he or she is still on earth, is crucial, because it implies that a person has a different mode of being on earth – he or she already has eternal life. This implies membership of another, spiritual, family but also of an ordinary earthly family. That reminds one of the words of Jesus: 'My mother and brothers and sisters are those who believe in me' (Matt. 12:50). Highest loyalty is therefore owed to the spiritual family. By accepting this demand, a new tradition, new rules, and new values relativize previous traditions, rules and values. This is what conversion is all about. To live according to a family, a particular person must accept that he or she forms part of this new family and *vice versa*.[14] Within the parameters of the dialectical interaction, members of the ATR should accept this datum. There should be the realization that there is another, yet more important, spiritual reality of which one should become part.

3   The idea of having eternal life already on earth (*realized eschatology*), the idea of simply remaining in the spiritual family after death (cf. *eternal life*) corresponds with ATR's idea of becoming an ancestor. In the latter, the deceased family member lives on, as is the case with the member of the family of God who has *eternal* life. This must, therefore, be readily accepted in a dialectical interaction between ATR and 1 John.[15] However, care must be taken to point out that life after death is not identical in these two instances.[16] A Christian does not return to remain involved in the earthly family after death, as is the case with ancestors in ATR.

4   A crucial question, of course, is how one becomes part of the family of God. This involves another notion that could easily be understood by ATR. To belong to a group/family, you have to be part of that group/ family. To become part of a family, you need to be *born into that family*. In this respect one may note the extensive use of γεννᾶν in 1 John (2:29; 3:9; 4:7; 5:1, 4, 18). New birth into a new spiritual family re-orientates one's loyalties and way of thinking. Different rituals (not necessarily those we read of in the Bible, but which have the same meaning) mark this event of transition from ATR into African Christianity. From the perspective of ATR, the necessity for another birth might be questioned. No change in nature or being is required to become an ancestor, only a change in the mode of existence. The

concept of 'becoming part of a different family' (of God), however, requires being born again.

5   This brings us to 1 John's treatment of the *Spirit*. How can the new existence be experienced in a concrete way? God now stays with, and in, the believer by means of the Spirit (3:24). The Spirit becomes the guiding influence in the lives of believers (2:20–7; 5:7), influencing their concrete behaviour. This concept fits well into the frame of reference of ATR. In ATR, people's lives are dominated by the presence of spirits and powers, which cause people to live in anxiety. If members of ATR had the mighty Spirit of God *in* their lives (not just close to them), they would not have to fear any longer. They would have God's power at their disposal in a concrete way. The Spirit influences and leads a person to act correctly. He frees a person from fear and endows a person with boldness. In my reading of 1 John with members of the ATR, I emphasized the power of the Holy Spirit, as well as the way in which the Spirit works. (The description of the role of the *Paraclete* in John 14–16 is also relevant here, and is indeed helpful in discussing contact with the spiritual world.) In Africa, I would, therefore, accentuate the references to the Spirit within the context of a world dominated by spirits. In ATR a person is totally exposed and even helpless, if he or she is without some kind of protection; in ATR this protection is generally provided by the help of the diviner by means of his or her medicine. However, for the Christian, the Spirit of truth represents the truth, and together with Jesus (5:18) the Spirit protects the believer against evil. This datum should thus have appeal, especially to a member of ATR. A father has to care for his family; God, as Father, does exactly that through his Spirit.

Caution should, however, be taken not to confuse all spiritual experiences as coming from God's Spirit (4:1–2). The Spirit will guide the believer according to the content of the Gospel of Jesus. Correspondence between the two symbolic narratives is found in the *spiritual involvement* in the lives of people, while dissonance resides in the difference in nature of the 'Spirit' and 'spirits'.

6   The fact that the Spirit is *in* a person, will most probably create tension with the *role of the diviners* within the symbolic narrative of ATR. The diviners are responsible for contact with the spirits and with the ancestors. Therefore, the question arises whether diviners should be retained at all within the Christian narrative. This is a sensitive point in the co-reading process, since the abstract presence of the 'Spirit in you' functions in the place of a concrete presence of the diviner. Most often, the concrete presence of the diviner is preferred, because of the concreteness with which African people approach the world around them. However, in other instances, their liturgy is developed in such a way that the manifestation of the Spirit

can be experienced concretely in some way or another. Concrete ways of protecting the believer against evil spirits are also common (like holy water, badges that have been blessed, and so on). Since ancestor veneration is not seen as worship,[17] it is often linked to Orthodox and Roman Catholic practices of the communion with saints (Fasholé-Luke 1974: 209–21).

7   What would the *role of Christ* be in ATR? According to 1 John, Jesus is the revealer and bringer of the realities of God into this world (1:1–4), *inter alia* of salvation (1:7; 2:1–2; 3:16; 4:10). ATR emphasizes the role of tradition. You are what you are born to be and what your ancestors made you, according to the tradition of your family. A similar idea is found in 1 John. When you are born into the family of God, you should not only be what you are born to be, but you should *also live* according to the tradition of that new family. ATR and 1 John correspond in this regard. But where do we learn about 'tradition' in Christianity? Tradition is to be found in Jesus, 1 John emphasizes the role of tradition in 1:1–4 (cf. also 5:20; 2:24). One should follow this 'Jesus tradition' in one's behaviour and actions. Jesus's behaviour and actions came directly from God, who is described as love (4:16). This is why a member of the family of God should also love (4:7–8). Therefore, once it can be accepted that *rebirth* is necessary, and that this results in belonging to a *new family*, it becomes clear how one should live in that new family, namely according to the traditions of that family. This could be well understood by a person who knows how an African traditional family lives. The complicating factor, however, is that these requirements of the spiritual family might be in conflict with that of the earthly family. Obviously, the spiritual family should take preference.

8   According to 1 John, children may *freely approach their Father* in the new family, which is not always allowed in African traditional families. This approach involves the issue of prayer (5:14–15). Prayer, as Western Christians understand and know it, is not so common in African traditional situations.[18] It usually takes place only at crucial points in history, and then the father or another important represen-tative of the family will mediate. It appears that contact is made instead with the spiritual world through dancing or dreams. This way of establishing contact could possibly serve as a parallel to prayer, which implies that dancing might serve as an important substitute for prayer in the African practice of Christianity.

To sum up: the idea of a strong *group orientated family* forms the basis of both symbolic narratives, and it determines the basic organization and interrelatedness of symbols. Because of this, common ground for dialectical interaction exists. The notion that one belongs to a family, that the family expects loyalty which implies obedience, that wrongs committed against the family should be corrected, and that one lives forever in a family, and so on, are all corresponding elements. However, because two essentially *different families* are under discussion, there are crucial differences. The notions of Father, tradition, expectations of the family, relation to the spiritual world, and so on, of 1 John differ from that of ATR.

The critical question is how both the correspondences and the differences between the two narratives could be internalized by, for instance, a co-reader from ATR? The acceptance of the *necessity for transition* from one symbolic narrative to the other constitutes the bridge. Once members of ATR accept that they have to be part of a *new family* who will demand new loyalties and obedience (exactly as was the case in the old family) then the transition begins. '*New birth*' is the concept that indicates this transition. The moment a person sees him- or herself as a member of a new spiritual family, he or she is on familiar ground again (a group orientated family), although different rules and values (of the new family) are now valid. Jesus and the Spirit become the functionaries and mediators between God and his people, thereby taking over the functions of the ancestors or diviners. That is why new life is required of the believer. From this point onwards, the gradual introduction into the finer details of 1 John's symbolic narrative can take place. By now not only a new identity and a new life have been embraced, but also a new symbolic narrative, which needs to shape the person's entire life.

In practice, however, it is not so easy for a person to change his or her symbolic narrative. There are numerous practical problems. For instance, loyalties of the physical family and the spiritual family might be conflicting, and it might be difficult to exchange symbols such as the ancestors with Jesus or the Spirit when functions overlap. The reading process is therefore a gradual process. Initially it involves introducing the text (*via* familiar elements) to the person who is interested in reading with you. When interest is incited, it becomes a process of 'reading along with'. At first in the reading process a member of the family (i.e. Christian family) is reading to a member of another family (i.e. a member of ATR). Patience should be exercised in this process, since it may happen that one 'family' does not accept 'the other family'. When new birth or conversion takes place in a person, this person becomes a co-reader, since he or she now is a member of the new family.

'Reading together' or 'reading with' is to embark on an adventure, since it implies the creation of a new symbolic narrative for the co-reader. Different readers, however, have different problems in this reading process, as was illustrated earlier with the figure of the ellipse. The adventure is to move away from the familiar to the new, in such a way that it makes sense to the co-reader. This will result in a definite, and not just a cosmetic, change of symbols.

Conclusion

Due to the limitations of this article, the above is only a brief illustration of my reading of 1 John in Africa. The same approach is followed with other New Testament books. The elements that are similar to both symbolic narratives are used as common ground for starting the dialectical process. The differences, however, require a value judgement and, accordingly, a decision. For a Christian the symbolic narrative of 1 John should take precedence. However, it is important that the structural function of a particular element in the symbolic narrative be replaced in such a way that it makes sense. This transformation of symbols should lead to the acceptance of the symbolic universe of Christianity. For example, Christ and the Spirit can replace certain functions of the ancestors. The ancestors can be *re-defined* within the structure of the Christian narrative. This does not mean that John's symbolic narrative can simply be transferred *in toto* and without problems on to the new co-reader, but that a 'new symbolic narrative' will result in which, for instance, 'prayer' might be expressed in dancing, or ancestors may be seen as saints. The basic requirement is, however, that the key symbols like God, Jesus, Spirit, salvation (eternal life), and so on, are not devalued to the extent that they become meaningless. These *'pillars of the Christian symbolic narrative'* should still constitute the core of narrative.

This is probably what Crafford (1996: 18–24) has in mind when he points out that African ideas still play an important role in Christian communities in South Africa. This is not necessarily a negative state of affairs at all, since indigenous African Christianity contains many positive elements, but there are still elements that need to be transformed if a sound synchronization with the biblical symbolic narratives is the aim. It must constantly be borne in mind that certain Christian elements cannot be changed or ignored without changing the essential nature of the Gospel. 'The solution lies in a vital African Christianity which so reconciles the two worlds that Christianity is no longer alien to Africa and Africa is no longer alien to Christianity' (Crafford 1996: 24).

For me personally this reading process meant that the New Testament, as ancient document, should no longer just be read within the restraints of Western theology or interests. New questions are put to the text that result in fresh answers. I am even convinced that a discussion with ATR helped me to understand the text of 1 John better. I had to ask what the role of the New Testament in Africa and its religious experience should be. I have realized what the communicative potential of the New Testament really is, especially in cross-cultural situations. Dogmatic and cultural presuppositions should not be allowed to determine this reading process. By accepting the 'guidance' of the New Testament text in the co-reading process, but also allowing an openness for ideas foreign to my own frame of reference, a very enriching and challenging reading experience resulted for me. This indeed makes the reading of the New Testament a new, exciting and lively procedure.

Notes

1 No questionnaires were used. It soon became clear that if you ask a traditional person to fill in a questionnaire, you get the answer that person thinks you want; not what he or she really thinks. We therefore worked on a basis of consensus among the students. Figures of authority, like the lecturers, were withdrawn from the discussion in class, for the same reason. In a traditional society the figure of authority is usually correct and should not be challenged. A report returned by the group of black students was then computerized and systematized.

2 For example: Initiation into Christian faith is by the sacrament of baptism. According to ATR, however, a beast is slaughtered and ancestors are notified of the new arrival. This is called 'imbeleko'.

3 Setiloane (1975: 34) points out that the basic norms of the African world view did not disappear with the acceptance of Christianity, but that traditional insights and values are perpetuated in everyday lives.

4 There will be exceptions and differences when one moves to a detailed discussion (Mosala 1983: 24). I am, however, convinced that the Weberian approach is valid in dealing with this kind of material. See Mugambi (1989: 56) and Crafford (1996: 8–9).

5 Setiloane (1975: 31) quotes Mbiti by saying, 'I am because I belong and because I belong I am'.

6 These (negative) things do not happen because the ancestors act in a capricious fashion. They take place because ancestors take the interests of the family seriously.

7 Kibongi (1969: 48–9) mentions six causes of evil that indicate the differentiation which traditional Africans identify regarding the realities which confront them.

8 'To traditional Africans . . . sin is the destruction of the stability of the community . . .' (Maimela 1985: 70–1).

9 The family metaphor in John is described by, for instance, Rusam (1993) and van der Watt (1991; 1992).

10 As a Christian my assumption is that the Gospel of Jesus takes precedence over ATR.

11 Crafford (1996: 8–9) underlines the diversity.

12 Masiala (1986: 129) sees this as a typical African way of dealing with conflict.

13 Initially, it will also not be experienced as a problem that God is called the Father in 1 John, since ATR sees God as part of their group hierarchy.

14 In an individualized Westernized (European or North American) situation, these strong communal ideas are difficult to concretize.

15 Mbiti (1969: 166–9) sees futuristic eschatology as a problem, but does not give due attention to the realized eschatology of 1 John.

16 The cosmology of ATR is 'mono-sectional' (Mugambi 1989: 51). The person dies and then returns to the family. 1 John differs on this point of returning. The Spirit of God (God himself) will look after the family, because it is God's family. The Father of the family should do that.

17 There are Christian groups among Africans who maintain that it is 'worship' in the proper sense of the word.

18 That anyone can pray by himself or herself to God is not generally accepted.

References

Crafford, D. (1996) 'African traditional religions', in P. Meiring (ed.) *A World of Religions. A South African Perspective*, Pretoria: Kasigo, 1–26.

Ezeanya, S.N. (1969) 'God, Spirits and the spirit world', in K. Dickson and P. Ellingworth (eds) *Biblical Revelation and African Beliefs*, London: Lutterworth, 30–46.

Fasholé-Luke, E. W. (1974) 'Ancestor veneration and the communion of saints', in M. E. Glasswell and E. W. Fasholé-Luke (eds) *New Testament Christianity for Africa and the World. Essays in Honour of H. Sawyer*, London: SPCK, 209–21.

Idowu, E. B. (1969) 'God', in K. Dickson and P. Ellingworth (eds) *Biblical Revelation and African Beliefs*, London: Lutterworth, 17–29.

Kibongi, R. B. (1969) 'Priesthood', in K. Dickson and P. Ellingworth (eds) *Biblical Revelation and African Beliefs*, London: Lutterworth, 47–56.

Kriel, A. (1996) *Eenders dink, eenders doen?* Kaapstad: Lux Verbi.

Maimela, S. S. (1985) 'Salvation in African traditional religions', *Missionalia* 13: 63–77.

Masiala, M. S. (1986) 'La confession, un processus psychothérapeutique individuel and communautaire', *Revue Zaïroise de Théologie Protestante* 1: 117–42.

Mbigi, L. (1997) 'Images of Ubuntu in global competitiveness', *Flying Springbok* April 1997: 31–5.

Mbiti, J. S. (1969) 'Eschatology', in K. Dickson and P. Ellingworth (eds) *Biblical Revelation and African Beliefs*, London: Lutterworth, 159–84.

Mosala, J. (1983) 'African traditional beliefs and Christianity', *Journal of Theology for Southern Africa* 43: 15–24.

Mugambi, J. N. K. (1989) *African Heritage and Contemporary Christianity*, Kenia: Longman.

Mulago, V. (1969) 'Vital participation', in K. Dickson and P. Ellingworth (eds) *Biblical Revelation and African Beliefs*, London: Lutterworth, 137–58.

Mulemfo, M. M. (1995) 'Palaver as a dimension of communal solidarity in Zaïre', unpublished PhD thesis, University of Pretoria.

Rusam, D. (1993) *Die Gemeinschaft der Kinder Gottes*, Stuttgart: Kohlhammer.

Setiloane, G. (1975) 'Confessing Christ today. From one African perspective: Man and community', *Journal of Theology for Southern Africa* 12: 29–38.

Van der Watt, J. G. (1991) 'Die Woord het mens geword: 'n Strukturele uiteensetting van die teologie van die Johannesevangelie', in J. H. Roberts, W. S. Vorster, J. N. Vorster and J. G. van der Watt (eds) *Teologie in Konteks*, Midrand: Orion, 93–130.

Van der Watt, J. G. (1992) '"Julle moet mekaar liefhê": Etiek in die Johannesevangelie', *Scriptura* S9a: 74–96.

11

A SELF-CONSCIOUS READER-RESPONSE INTERPRETATION OF ROMANS 13:1–7

James W. Voelz

Part I: Introduction

Preliminary thoughts

In this essay I will attempt a self-reflective reading/interpretation of Romans 13:1–7. I will seek to do so from my own personal and social location. I am a 52-year-old white male of German extraction who was raised in a traditional home and educated according to the traditional German 'gymnasium' model. I am a clergyman of the Lutheran Church – Missouri Synod, a conservative confessional Lutheran denomination in the USA. I have taught at the seminary level for well over twenty years, have served as a parish pastor for 4 years, and participate regularly and extensively in meetings of scholarly societies on the local, national, and international levels. I am a Christian and a Lutheran by both birth and conviction. I have chosen this text because it has been a *sedes doctrinae* for a so-called Christian view of the state, for all Christians in general and for Lutherans in particular, and, as such, it has been something of a problem, especially for us Lutherans since the time of the Third Reich, given that quietism *vis-à-vis* Nazi atrocities can be attributed to a standard interpretation of it.

Theologically, I believe the book of Romans to be the inspired Word of God, written by an apostle of my Lord, Jesus Christ, a book that may be set within a matrix comprising other words of God, which may be used to interpret it. As a Lutheran Christian, I am also aware that I stand in a tradition of positive assessment of the State as such (cf. Luther), which inclines me from the start to give a congenial, not resistant, reading of the text. Furthermore, I have been trained in the humanities and classics, which gives me a positive view of ancient texts, inherently receptive, generally not suspicious, with little readiness to see contradictions in every verse.

Fundamental presuppositions

To a great extent the interpretation of any text is 'predetermined' by the reader's/interpreter's fundamental presuppositions, not only about reality in general, but also and especially about the nature of language, the nature and function of texts, and the process of reading and interpretation. I will, therefore, attempt to detail in this section my own fundamental presuppositions concerning these issues, which will function explicitly in the actual interpretation of Rom. 13:1–7.

1. Language

Texts comprise, principally, language. What is language like? In my view it is a systemic construct of human beings and serves to reflect reality as they perceive it to impinge upon them. It is to be understood synchronically not diachronically, so that etymological study, while having, perhaps, some mnemonic value, is not to be looked at as a source for the meaning of words in given contexts. Language comprises a system of signifiers that are designed to evoke conceptual signifieds in the minds of receptors. Such signifiers, embraced by a given community and learned by its members at various stages in life, are called forth as people attempt to express conceptual signifieds, which themselves arise in their minds, as they interact with their environment.

2. Texts

THE NATURE OF TEXTS

General characteristics I see texts, essentially, as a means of communication. Through them authors communicate with readers. Texts, in my view, are not essentially (though they may be in some part) catalysts for the development of meaning by receptors, much as a piece of so-called modern art produced by throwing paint upon a canvas may be conceived of as a catalyst to stimulate the thoughts and feelings of its viewers. Rather, they attempt to convey thoughts and stimulate reactions within receptors with a greater or lesser degree of intentionality. For this reason, I conceive of the 'processing' of texts essentially as *interpretation* not (simply) as 'reading' – as an attempt to convey what an author wishes to communicate, not as an attempt to stimulate personal reaction to signifiers perceived.

Specific characteristics: Levels of signifiers and interpretation I strongly believe that texts exist and should be interpreted on several levels. This is because they comprise several levels or orders of signifiers. The marks on the page that constitute words, including their forms and arrangement, provide the most *basic level* or order of signifiers, and give a text its *'sense'*. The thoughts or ideas that are evoked in the mind of the interpreter as the words are processed provide the *second level*/order of signifiers; these, too, may be read and interpreted, even as words are read, and give the *'significance'* of the text.[1] A *third level*/order of signifiers may also be read and interpreted, namely, the fact that an author has produced what has been produced. The very existence of such signifiers and conceptual signifieds tells interpreters about the author and the circumstances surrounding the writing's production, giving the *'implications'* of a text.[2] It is by reading on this third level that one 'determines' the so-called 'implied author' and 'implied' readers of a work (cf. Fowler 1991: 31–6).

A text must be read on all three levels for full interpretation.

Specific characteristics: Shorthand On all of its levels texts are also, it seems to me, communications in shorthand. An author does not say everything that could have been said, so signifiers on level 3 are not as complete as they might have been. Furthermore, not every idea that could have been expressed within a presentation is actually expressed, so thoughts and ideas on level 2 must be filled in to complete the total argument. Further still, a text is incomplete on level 1 as well. Sentences may contain blanks that remain largely undetected. (For example, Paul says in 1 Cor. 11:6 concerning a woman: κατακαλυπτέσθω; but, *by what means* should she be covered?). Or, more important, nouns and adjectives based upon verbal roots may conceal, as *external entailments*, entire sentences within their fold. (For example, Paul describes himself as ἀπόστολος in Rom. 1:1; but *who* sent him, *to whom* was he sent, *for what* was he sent?, and so on – these are external entailments of the word.)[3]

Much of interpretation involves filling out the shorthand (cf. Iser), and that on every level of the text.

THE FUNCTION OF TEXTS

Texts function to inform. But, in accord with Speech–Art theory, I believe that the information they provide (locutionary force) has a further function, for example, to rebuke to warn, to command, and so on. (illocutionary force). Such rebuking, warning, and commanding itself has a further function, which is to urge the interpreter to action (perlocutionary force). Thus, the meaning or semantics of a given text will naturally issue in a function or pragmatics of that text.

3. *The process of interpretation*

As should be clear from what has been said so far, in my view an interpreter on any text is hardly passive as the interpretation of that text takes place.

Such a reader activates the signifiers detected in a text, matrixing them and their meanings with other signifiers and their meanings and filling in the blanks – and all this on every level of the text. The interpreter is, therefore, in a very real sense, constructing (and not only re-constructing) the text which is being read.

But there is even more. Receptors themselves are complexes of beliefs, knowledge, attitudes, experiences, and so on. When readers interpret, these factors are brought into connection with a text, as interpretation itself proceeds; they become part of the very matrix for textual interpretation. In other words, a reader is, as it were, a 'text' him- or herself, and the interpretation of any given text thus involves two texts, namely, the 'target' text (e.g., Rom. 13:1–7), and, as part of the matrix for its interpretation, the interpreter as 'second text'. And it is 'against' the features of this 'second text' that the features of the 'target text' are, in face, understood (Voelz 1997: 208–11).

The application of a text is a move in the opposite direction. To apply a given text is to read the interpreter's 'second', personal text as target text against the features and meaning of the original target text.[4] This application move applies to both the semantic and pragmatic dimensions of the text alike.

My personal second text has already been described in my preliminary thoughts (p. 156).

Part II: Issues and assumptions relating to Romans 13:1–7

The reading and interpretation of a given text must be done against a certain historical background (= context) and within a certain literary matrix. Therefore, in order to interpret Rom. 13:1–7, certain decisions must be made concerning issues that are not related to the meaning of the words as signifiers (level 1). Included in the context will be a (re-)construction of the historical situation and a (re-)construction of the implied readers and impled author; and literary considerations will include decisions on matters pertaining to genre, co-text, and pragmatics. It is to these that we now turn.

Issues

1. Contextual

HISTORICAL SETTING

In what context was the book of Romans written historically? Is the apostle Paul the author? Is he the author of all of it? If he is the author, when and where was it composed?

IMPLIED READERS/IMPLIED AUTHOR

Who are the implied readers of the text? First of all, who are the implied readers in terms of *referent*? That is to say, are the people for whom these verses were written the total membership of the congregation at Rome? Or, are they a certain segment of that congregation? Or, are they even Roman governmental authorities? One may also ask: Are there primary and secondary implied readers? That is to say, is the author intending these words to be read or heard primarily by the members of the Roman congregation but secondarily by Roman authorities (who might chance to see and read this missive)? Or, perhaps, are these words addressed primarily to one segment of the congregation, with others (secondarily) 'listening in'? Indeed, if one is thinking of implied readers and not actual readers, a party who one thinks will overhear a communication may be conceived of as the primary audience, though the addressees may be the congregation as a whole.[5]

Second, what is the nature of the implied readers in terms of *character*? That is to say, what is the modality of the implied readers, their attitudes, beliefs, and so on? Whether all of the congregation, part of the congregation, or the civil authorities are implied, are these readers or hearers receptive to a message of one like Paul? Or, are they suspicious of what he (as they conceive of him, i.e., as implied author) might say? Or, are they non-receptive to his address to them?

Who is the implied author of the text? The decisions made on questions relating to the implied readers of our text have ramifications for our conception of the implied author of its words. We may note how interconnected these issues are. Are Paul's implied readers receptive? Then, perhaps, he – really, the implied author – is instructive. Are Paul's implied readers suspicious? Then, perhaps, he is self-conscious or somewhat afraid, fearful and 'walking on eggshells'. Are his implied readers non-receptive? Then he may be stern, admonishing those who are not prepared to listen to his words. What he has in mind (which we construct) determines, as it were, the state of his mind (which we also (re-)construct) and, therefore, the implied author of our text.

2. Literary

One's views of the historical situation and the readers and author implied in the text will help to determine certain literary features of the text.

First, there is the question of the *genre* of the text. Is this a set of *Haustafeln* (cf. Eph. 6;1ff., 1 Pet. 2:13ff.)? Is it an original composition by St Paul? The answer to this question may affect our interpretation, especially in the matter of the level 3 'implications' of the text.

Second is the matter of the *co-text* of the text at hand. With what other signifiers are these signifiers to be interpreted? How wide-ranging is the co-text seen to be? Does is include the verses of chap. 12? The verses of chap. 14? Even the entire book?[6] Indeed, the question of canon becomes crucial here, for the question of co-text is essentially the question of intertextuality, and the question of canon is nothing other than the same question in larger scope.

Third, the matter of the *rhetorical function* of the text must be examined. If the Epistle to the Romans was written at a relatively peaceful time, it is not likely to function as a rebuke, with the implied readers being thought of as involved in rebellion against the state. If the implied readers are seen as receptive to the letter's address, the letter may well be informative in function. If the implied readers are seen as suspicious, it may well be explanatory, especially as it is designed to tell the implied readers about the nature of the author (whom/which they are to imply).[7] If the implied readers are seen as non-receptive, it may be an admonition (virtually a rebuke), to correct or to forestall their false understandings. This is, in standard Speech–Act terms, not an issue of meaning but of illocutionary force, and it is critical to our understanding of the text.

Assumptions

I will proceed to interpret the text at issue with the following assumptions regarding (re-)constructed context and literary factors. It must be said, however, that it becomes readily apparent, upon rigorous self-reflection, that the basis for the decisions in each case involves interrelationships and crossings between categories, so that questions cannot be distinguished neatly and conveniently in virtually any case.

1. Contextual

HISTORICAL SETTING

I follow the historical reconstruction of Bo Reicke,[8] which takes seriously and in a straight-forward manner the evidence of the epistle and of the book of Acts. It understands Romans as written by the apostle Paul from the city of Corinth during his third missionary journey, in 58 CE.

IMPLIED READERS/IMPLIED AUTHOR

Given the argumentation of the author only several chapters later (15:22), and given the fact that he tackles sensitive issues, especially the problem of Jewish–Greek relationships in chap. 14 (and that in a full and thorough way), it seems reasonable to conclude that the implied readers of the text of

Rom. 13:1–7 are receptive readers or hearers, who will receive the words of instruction given. It is, therefore, likely, in view of his treatment of the themes in chap. 14 and throughout the book, that the entire assembly is in view as the implied readers in referential terms. This leads us to an implied author who is confident in himself, self-asssured (not defensive), who is prepared to instruct his implied readers as he sees them ready to receive his words.

2. Literary factors

GENRE

The verses under discussion seem to exhibit a form similar to that of the *Haustafeln* in general, which may indicate that they are an adaptation of previously existing material. This may not be critical to an understanding of these verses' content, but if this analysis is correct, it would show Paul to be positive toward traditions (cf. 1 Cor. 15:3) and an integrated member of the Christian community at large (level 3 'implication').

CO-TEXT

The meanings of the signifiers of our text must be understood against the background of which other signifiers and their meanings? Narrowly focused, it would seem that the narrow co-text comprises the chapters following chap. 9–11 (specifically 12; 13:8ff., and chap. 14), given the 'structure' of the book. I take the book as a unity (the placement of the last verses of chap. 16 is not relevant for this discussion), which makes the whole book of Romans the intermediate co-text. Wider co-text comprises, first, the epistles of Paul,[9] then the books of the NT,[10] and finally the entire Bible, to make one total, canonical whole. This intertextual perspective is critical to the interpretive task, for the limits of one's literary co-text are a major factor in the shape of one's interpretive result. Note that this inevitably raises the question of the Spirit and inspiration, which factors are critical to any cross-book, cross-author, and cross-testament literary analysis – a question related to one's experiential 'second text'!

PRAGMATICS

The function of the text may well be dependent upon my own reading of the text. That is to say, the actual impact which it has upon me – does it, in fact, inform, rebuke, defend, and so on? – will be a major factor in my understanding of its intended impact upon the implied readers that the author conceives. Here again the issue of the implied readers presses to the fore. Given the implied readers detailed above, it is likely that the intended function of the text was to be informatory (a confident statement of fact), rather than an admonition or a fearful self-defence.[11]

Part III: The interpretation

In what follows, first I will analyse the meaning of Rom. 13:1–7 according to the various aspects of meaning that I have delineated. I will try to record my experience of the interpretive process, as far as that is possible, and I will try to keep separate the various aspects of meaning, but, as will become readily apparent, the actual process of interpretation involves moving between aspects continuously, and, almost, unwillingly. Second, I will discuss the pragmatics of the text. Finally, I will discuss briefly the application of the text to myself.

Meaning (semantics)

1. Level 1/sense

BASIC EXEGETICAL CONSIDERATIONS

Verse 1. As I begin consideration of the pericope, the problem of the external entailment (see specific characteristics: shorthand, page 158) of ἐξουσίαι, i.e., who does 'ἐξουσιάζω-ing', is immediately apparent. The previous context, especially 12:3ff., seems to suggest that the 'ἐξουσιάζω-doers' may be in the church, and certainly neither the remainder of v. 1, nor v. 2 militates against this thought. V. 3, with its talk of φόβος, however, seems to limit 'ἐξουσιάζω-ers' to secular powers, a reading 'confirmed' by the middle of v. 4 (cf. μάχαιραν) and vv. 6 and 7 (φόρους τελεῖτε and τῷ τὸ τέλος). The middle and end of v. 1 seems to say that all powers/ authorities are God-ordained, as does the beginning of v. 4 (θεοῦ διάκο-νος). Quick mental jumps to the aspect of level of significance (level 2) and to application raise questions about this understanding, however. Is every action of all governments to be seen as divine activity? Does God work equally in the secular sphere as he does in the church? Is Paul saying that to resist the government in Rome in any way is to resist God? What does this mean for me? What about the Third Reich or Kampuchea? But the words 'seem clear' on the level of sense.

Verse 2: The interpretation of v. 1 seems to be confirmed by v. 2, for it is stated that to resist the authority is to resist the command of God, which earns judgement.

Verse 3: seems to explain (γάρ) in part the beginning of v. 1 (why one is to be subject) and v.2b (why those who resist will get judgement for themselves). For me, this 'clear sense' of the verse re-inforces the positive view of government in vv. 1–2. At this point, however, it is impossible to prevent several 'second text' caveats from creeping in. First, is Paul really talking about government here, with the assertion that government always dispenses proper judgement? Perhaps seeing the external entailment of ἐξουσίαι as involving church officials is right after all! But, no, my experience in the church is not totally positive either, so this will have to wait for further consideration. Second, one begins to wonder about application once again. These two caveats lead to a consideration of the possibility that the external entailment of ἐξουσίαι and ἄρχοντες is narrower than I had thought previously. Perhaps only those authorities that act in the way delineated in v. 3 are really ἐξουσίαι ὑπὸ θεοῦ τεταγμέναι (v. 1). But, trying to be somewhat 'objective' (sic!), that does not seem to be what the sense of these verses is. This type of double-think often occurs in passages such as this.

Verse 4: continues the pattern of positive statements begun in vv. 1–3. But a problem of referent now arises. To what does εἰς τὸ ἀγαθόν refer? Is Paul's reference here simply meting out justice positively and negatively? Or, do these words refer to something broader for Paul's readers, for example, to positive social engineering, so that the state should be involved in such activities for the welfare of its citizens? Or, is the referent broader still, encompassing spiritual as well as physical dimensions? The latter part of v. 4 (ἔκδικοας εἰς ὀργήν) seems to indicate a narrow interpretation of referent, relating to the administration of justice, not to a welfare state.

Verse 5: The interpretation of v. 4 is 'confirmed' by the beginning of v. 5, which continues the theme of practical obedience begun in v. 4. The end of v. 5 (διὰ τὴν συνείδησιν) seems to pick up the theme of v. 1 again and may well be designed as a 'corrective' to the *Tendenz* of the last several verses, which have given practical reasons for obedience, picking up, as it does, the basic truth that actions *vis-à-vis* the government are actions *vis-à-vis* God himself.

Verse 6: begins with a clause that includes a γάρ, but it is not immediately apparent to me how this γάρ functions, or, more precisely, how the (meaning of the) words of this clause can relate causally to the (meaning of the) words of the main clause. Is Paul saying that his readers do pay taxes because they have fear and are conscience-bound? If so, why do the first five verses contain imperatives and/or expressions of compulsion (cf. ἀνάγκη, v. 5)? This raises a question that was not raised in v. 1 of the 'blank' in the text (cf. Issues – Literary, pages 160–1) at ὑποτασσέσθω. is the 'dative of means' by which one obeys not so wide as to include taxes? Does it include only obedience to laws of personal conduct, movement, and so on, and not include taxes? This, in turn, raises the question of the interpretation of the signifier τελεῖτε. Is it really indicative, as all translations understand it? Within the context of the meaning of the whole, perhaps it should be understood as an imperative ('Pay!'). It seems to me, though, that the inclusion of γάρ in the clause militates against such an understanding. I will, therefore, conclude –

allowing concerns of level 3/'implication' to intrude – that the people were, in fact, paying their taxes quite gladly, probably seeing its overall benefit to them. But could they do this for conscience's sake and not be obedient in other areas (cf. vv. 1–5)? The judgement of my 'second text' is that they could not. And such an interpretation provides an 'anchor', as it were, for the understanding of our text as a whole in other areas (cf. Voelz 1997: 136–8), as far as both its 'implications' and its pragmatics are concerned.

Verse 7: seems to provide an adequate summary of the previous six verses, with the only question being the referent of πᾶσιν: is it still governmental authorities, or, does it now encompass all authorities? Considering the nouns that follow (φόρον, τέλος, φόβον and τιμήν), it seems 'logical' to limit πᾶσιν to governmental authorities.

THEOLOGICAL CONSIDERATIONS

It is apparent to me at this point that, unlike narrative or story, the theology of this type of text is, basically, expressed on level 1 by the words as signifiers.[12] What is that theology? Proceeding with the assumption that they are consistent both internally and with their co-text, these verses seem to say to the addressees that governmental authorities are in league with God, not with the forces of evil, and so must always be obeyed. (On the basis of the sense detailed above, it does not seem that the theology of these verses is that God is at work only in those governments that act as his διάκονοι, i.e., which are truly a terror to evil and a boon to good.) Applications immediately intrude at this point for me, not so much as a middle-class citizen of the United States with either little or no experience of government oppression, but as one who has an historical consciousness, and it strikes me that a reader/hearer within a different governmental context would find applications intruding with a very great force, indeed. Nevertheless, the 'theology' does not seem opaque at all. A key question, however, is the relationship between this text and other canonical texts dealing with governments and/or other activities of God (the issue of larger co-text/intertextuality). The negative view of the Apocalypse comes to mind, but so does the positive view in the Gospel of Matthew (22:17ff.). My own 'second text' causes me to consider Acts 5:29 (πειθαρχεῖν δεῖ θεῷ μᾶλλον ἢ ἀνθρώποις), as well. A matrix of these verses gives the following to me: In Rom. 13:1–7 the addressees are told that government is of God and is his 'arm' in the world. However, Paul would say that, in the total context of things, there are other higher actions or powers of God (1 Cor. 2:6; cf. Acts 5:39), or, possibly, that an authority may become corrupted (1 Cor. 2:8; 2 Tim. 4:18; cf. Apocalypse). Thus, the fact that governmental authority is a διάκονος of God in this text, does not mean that its powers are conceived of as unlimited, for other authoritative expressions of God's will can and may take precedence in other contexts. But, am I drawing this conclusion to avoid 'harmonizing' this text's message with the terrible capitulation of so many Lutheran pastors to the authorities of the Third Reich only 60 years ago? This text is much more awkward than we Lutherans ever care to think!

2. Level 2/significance

If I consider the theological significance of the thoughts and ideas expressed by the words as signifiers, several provocative significances arise for me from this text. For example, the fact that, for Paul, it is true that governmental authorities are an 'arm' of God itself means/signifies that this age has not been abandoned by God but is still under his control. This, in turn, means/signifies that the judgement of standard Jewish apocalyptic is incorrect, namely, that this age is an evil age which must simply be destroyed. It means/signifies that the view of the profligates in several of Paul's congregations (cf. Phil. 3:2; 1 Cor. 5:8) is incorrect, for order in this world is not an expression of godlessness but an expression of godliness and is to be affirmed. Here too, applications immediately suggest themselves to me, not the least of which is a greate optimisms about the possibilities of a quiet existence in this life than some events (for example, the slaughter in Algeria on 23 September 1997) might suggest. Most of my colleagues see the Western world as descending into chaos. Perhaps it is not so hopeless after all!

3. Level 3/implication

What do the 'sense' and 'significance' of these verses say about the state of the implied readers and the implied author of this text? From what I have said, especially with regard to the sense of v. 6, I 'read' the situation of the readers and the author, which I detect as a settled one, with a positive relationship to the state. V. 6 strongly suggests that taxes are being paid, also for conscience's sake, which, in turn, has importance for the pragmatics of this text.

Pragmatics

How does the text from Rom. 13 function? Is it informative, a rebuke, or apologetic? In historical terms, I conclude that Paul intended the impact of this work to be informative, not a rebuke or an apology. If this is so, it would solidify Paul's authority and convey a positive image of him to them.

Application

How I may apply this text, with its three previously delineated aspects of meaning and its pragmatics, depends in such large measure upon my personal 'second text'.

1. Semantics

Since I perceive myself to be in a situation very similar to that of the readers and the author I see implied in this text, the transfer of its meaning will be fairly direct for me. Others, especially those in much different contexts, will respond differently, I know. I can also say that the theological significances (cf. Meaning – level 2, page 166) cause me, as a Lutheran Christian, to see involvement in the governmental process not only as possible but as God-pleasing, in actual fact. This is an application which I, as an American, will certainly not resist!

My experience of reading is also semantically significant, however, and something I apply to myself (cf. Voelz 1997: 316–21). Because I am aware of the world around me, the 'moves' which I have had to make in the interpretive process, and the fact that I have had to consider serious options in that process, have exposed 'vacancies' (cf. Iser) in my 'second text', causing me to question my own theological understandings. Have my understandings simply been too comfortable, too convenient for a middle class American who is not all that badly placed in socio-economic terms? This inevitably leads me to raise questions, both about my interpretation and also about my actions in rather different, more difficult situations: is my 'congenial' reading sustainable, for example, in North Korea, Algeria, Serbia, and so on? It goes without saying that this has inevitably enlarged my 'second text'.

2. Pragmatics

In terms of application for me as the current reader, this passage is also instructive and informative. But for me as a Lutheran interpreter specifically, it functions primarily as a rebuke: as a citizen I have not acted toward governmental authorities as I ought to have and, therefore, must repent. It cannot help but so function, since, for (me as) a Lutheran, words of command function as Law, and *lex semper accusat* (the so-called 'second use of the Law'). This is a critical part of my theological and, therefore, interpretive consciousness. Pragmatically, the text does not function for me as a Lutheran primarily as a source of information (and therefore as the so-called 'third use of the Law'), because, generally, I see my problem as a Christian not as lack of proper information but as having a self-centred and resistful heart.

Notes

1 For example, the fact that it is so, as Paul asserts in Gal. 5:17, that the spirit and the flesh are at odds with one another, may itself be read to signify that in this age the ὁ μέλλων αἰών is never fully present. (I am not using 'significance' in the way that it is used by E. D. Hirsch; cf. Voelz 1997: 156).

2 So Paul's assertion in Gal. 5:17 may be read to show that he himself endured severe inner struggles after his conversion.

3 They are not part of the meaning of ἀπόστολος as such, as many interpreters suppose. For the external entailments of ἀπόστολος, see Acts 26:16–18.

4 Cf. Ricœur (1981: 178), who says that we understand ourselves 'in front of the text, in front of the world of the work'.

5 This is similar to what may happen in a marriage, namely, talking to a child 'for the benefit of' one's spouse, i.e., so that he or she will overhear.

6 This raises the question of integrity in a critical way, though integrity is, essentially, an historical question.

7 This is, again, the matter of level 3 'implication'.

8 Articulated in his *neutestamentliche Einleitung* lectures delivered in the *Winter-semester* at the University of Basel, 1982.

9 One might distinguish the deutero-Pauline epistles here; I do not.

10 One might distinguish homolegoumena from antilegomena, standard for centuries in the church.

11 There is virtually no way to gauge the perlocutionary force of the passage. It has an informatory effect upon me personally as I read.

12 Unlike narrative or story, in which the words as signifiers depict acts/events that can themselves be interpreted as signifiers (i.e., one reads the deeds depicted as [level 2] signifiers), arguments in texts such as epistles states its theology on the level of the words.

References

Fowler, R. M. (1991) *Let the Reader Understand: Reader-Response Criticism and the Gospel of Mark*, Minneapolis, MN: Fortress.

Iser, W. (1974) *The Implied Reader: Patterns of Communication in Prose Fiction from Bunyan to Beckett*, Baltimore, MD: Johns Hopkins University.

Ricœur, P. (1981) 'Metaphor and the Central Problem of Hermeneutics,' in J. B. Thompson (ed. and trans.) *Paul Ricœur: Hermeneutics and the Human Sciences: Essays on Language, Action and Interpretation*, Cambridge: Cambridge University Press, 165–81.

Saussure, F. de. (1969) *Cours de Linguistique Générale*, Paris: Payot.

Voelz, J. W. (1997) *What Does This Mean?: Principles of Biblical Interpretation in the Post-Modern World*, St. Louis: Concordia (2nd edn).

12

A RE-EVALUATION OF HOSEA 1–2: PHILOLOGY INFORMED BY LIFE EXPERIENCE

Mayer I. Gruber

My romance with the book of Hosea began when I was 15 years old, a member of the confirmation class at the Tree of Life Temple, a Reform synagogue in Columbia, South Carolina, where my father, may his memory be for a blessing,[1] was the rabbi. Among the duties that my father particularly loved was teaching the confirmation class. That particular year, the academic year 1959–60, my father chose the history of the Jewish religion as his theme for the class. It was a triumphalist version of Judaism's history, beginning with the patriarchs (who even dreamt of foremothers in those politically incorrect times?) and culminating with Reform Judaism as practised at the Tree of Life. I especially remember my father explaining to us how Hosea, the Prophet of Love, learned from his own personal tragedy how to empathize with God's heart-break. My father pointed out that it might seem as if it was Hosea's dialogue with God – who was distraught that His wife, as it were, the nation of Israel, had been unfaithful to God, her beneficent husband – that made Hosea understand why he could not simply put his faithless wife Gomer out of his head and out of his life and move on. As a rationalist Reform rabbi my father could not possibly imagine that it was something that God told Hosea that might change Hosea's thinking about Gomer. On the contrary, my father explained, it was Hosea's personal experience with a faithless wife, for whom his love was unconditional, that made the prophet understand how it is that God never gives up on his spouse, the nation of Israel, even when that spouse's flirtation with other deities may be compared, metaphorically, to a wife who engages in promiscuous sex with a series of lovers.

What I did not know then was that my father's interpretation of the Israelite prophet as a kind of philosopher, who learned about life and about God and the universe through contemplation, derived from the quasi-canonical David Qimhi (1160–1235 CE), a medieval Jewish commentator

170

on the Early (Joshua, Judges, Samuel, Kings) and Later (Isaiah, Jeremiah, Ezekiel and the Twelve [Minor]) Prophets; that Qimhi's view of prophecy as a form of philosophy derived from Moses Maimonides (1135–1204 CE) *Guide to the Perplexed* Book II, Chapters 36–8; and that Qimhi's conviction that Hosea came to empathize with God's obsession with Israel because of his own obsession with Gomer derived from the Babylonian Talmud, Tractate Pesahim 87b.

Koheleth (the book of Ecclesiastes) says, 'There is nothing new under the sun' (Eccl. 1:9). It should not be altogether surprising, therefore, that in the Jewish exegetical tradition the eternal message of the prophet Hosea derives not only from the prophet's dialogue with God but also from the prophet's own personal voice criticism. In the context of Hos. 1–3 that personal voice criticism means a view of social and cosmic reality informed by the prophet's own life experience.

After the confirmation class in 1959–60, my next serious encounter with the book of Hosea came about as a result of my going to study for the rabbinate at the Jewish Theological Seminary of America (hereinafter JTS), sometimes called the fountainhead of the Conservative movement in Judaism. There I came under the spell of Professor Harold Louis Ginsberg, of blessed memory, who – following Y. Kaufmann (Kaufmann 1964: vol. 6–7, 93–107) and H. Graetz (Graetz 1891: 240, 251) – argued convincingly that the issue of choosing between God (Yahweh) and Baal (Hadad) was tied up with Jezebel's patronage of the prophets of Baal during the reign of her husband King Ahab of Israel (869–50 BCE), and that this issue is absent from Hos. 4–14 and from other collections of the speeches of the eighth century BCE prophets, who are concerned not with apostasy but with social injustice.

Yehezkel Kaufmann divided the book of Hosea into the work of two distinct Israelite prophets – one speaks in Hos. 1–3 and the other in Hos. 4–14. According to the theory espoused and elaborated by Ginsberg (1972: 1010–24), the so-called First Hosea (of Hos. 1–3) belongs to the middle of the ninth century BCE while the so-called Second Hosea (of Hos. 4–14) belongs to the middle of the eighth century BCE. According to the theory, the so-called First Hosea shared with his contemporary Elijah the passionately-held belief that worship of God (who is called by the proper name Yahweh in the Elijah narratives of 1–2 Kings as in the book of Hosea) along with devotion to the Canaanite storm god Baal (actually an epithet meaning both 'lord' and 'husband' applied to the Canaanite deity whose proper name is Hadad) is intolerable.

Early in the course of my studies at the JTS, I decided to become a Jewish confessional biblical scholar. The professors and administrators of the JTS from Chancellor Louis Finkelstein, of blessed memory, downwards went out of their way to encourage me in this endeavour. These professors all agreed that the proper training for such a worthy profession was to study all of the dead languages of the ancient Near East – Akkadian, Aramaic, Hebrew, Moabite, Ugaritic – in order that I might establish the precise meaning in context of the many homonyms and obscure *hapax legomena* in Hebrew Scripture, and thus establish once and for all exactly what it was that Moses, the prophets, the sages and psalmists said. From the Bible faculty at JTS and from my PhD sponsor at Columbia University, Professor Moshe Held, of blessed memory, I learned all kinds of fascinating tidbits. Among these tidbits that stick in my memory I learned that Ugaritic proves that the Hebrew word *yāpûah* in Ps. 27 and elsewhere means 'witness' rather than 'such as breathe out' (King James Version). Another important tidbit was that, contrary to the Septuagint, *salmāwet* in Ps. 23 does not mean 'shadow of death' but simply 'darkness', as does the etymological equivalent in Akkadian, *salmūtu*. Another very important tidbit, about which my late and revered teacher Moshe Held used to shout with the passion of an Old Testament prophet, was that Isa. 3:17 does not say, 'Yahweh will uncover their pubic triangles'. Held would painstakingly show us that read in the light of Jer. 48:45 and Num. 24:17, Isa. 3:17 can be shown to refer only to removing the women's hats in public, not, God forbid, their skirts or panties! It was only in the summer of 1997 that I learned from spending some quality time with my son David, now the Orthodox rabbi of Wellington, New Zealand, and his wife Liat that in some cultural contexts such as that of Jewish Modern Orthodoxy in the late twentieth century CE, removing a woman's hat in public has connotations not far removed from the uncovering of breasts and genitals referred to in Hos. 2:5. Hence, it may turn out that Held's philological analysis of Isa. 3:17 contributes very little to understanding the verse in its cultural context.

However, I remember that back when my son David was not yet a toddler I had taken time out from conjugating Akkadian verbs, and I saw the star of the film *Deep Throat* interviewed on television, explaining that she had given up believing in God because the Bible in Isa. 3:17 portrays God as a voyeur. I was not even 30 years old at the time, and, therefore, I knew everything. What I knew most of all was that by spreading the Gospel of Held and Ginsberg and clearing the God of the Old Testament of the false charge of voyeurism I could bring back many from atheism to faith and thus do what Levi did according to Mal. 2:6, ' . . . and he did turn many away from iniquity'.

Fortunately, however, in the course of my studies at the JTS my classmate Byron L. Sherwin, now Vice-President for Academic Affairs of Chicago's Spertus Institute of Judaica, arranged for me to prepare a study guide for Abraham J. Heschel's *The Prophets* (Heschel 1962) for the Women's Division of the American Jewish Congress. As Sherwin, following JTS's then party-line concerning what makes one a proper biblical scholar, explained to Professor Heschel, of blessed memory, 'Mayer is especially qualified to do this work because he is studying Akkadian and Ugaritic!'

Heschel said in his last television interview, aired shortly after his untimely death in December 1972, that writing the English version of his book *The Prophets* had changed his life. The prophets' passion for justice had forced him to leave his study and get involved in the issues of the day – the fight against racism in Selma, Alabama, and later the struggle to put an end to the Vietnam War. *Mutatis mutandis*, writing the study-guide entitled *What is Prophecy?* (Gruber 1970) changed my life because I came to recall what I had written to Harvard University Professor John Strugnell, with whom I had studied Aramaic during my final undergraduate year at Duke University, in order to explain to him why I wanted to undertake the study of dead languages at Columbia University in the City of New York. I explained to Strugnell that I saw the study of dead languages as the primary means of acquiring the credentials necessary to find employment as a Jewish confessional biblical scholar. I explained that I fully understood that the real work of a biblical scholar is to help the divine message contained in Scripture to speak intelligibly to modern audiences who thirst for that message.

I read and re-read Heschel's *The Prophets*, first in preparing *What is Prophecy?*, and later in teaching a course entitled 'The Prophetic Experience' at the Spertus College of Judaica in Chicago (1972–80), and still later in teaching prophetic texts including Hosea at Ben-Gurion University. I came to understand, and succeeded in conveying to others, the conviction that prophetic books seen as collections of prophetic speeches[2] came into being because a prophet sincerely believed that he/she had been summoned against his/her will to be God's confidant and to express first to one or more of the peoples of the ancient Near East and ultimately to all human-kind God's passion for love and for justice. Like Heschel, I cannot prove that Hosea actually heard God. I cannot even prove that there was a Hosea, or someone else by another name, who actually lived in the ninth century BCE and composed Hos. 1–3. Nor can I prove that there was a Hosea, or someone else by another name, who actually lived in the eighth century BCE and composed Hos. 4–14. It is quite possible that archaeologists or road builders or construction workers will one day uncover an inscription or inscriptions that will tell us much about the personal life of the human author of Hos. 1–3. What I have learned, however, over the course of time, is essentially what I knew at the beginning when I asked Professor Strugnell to recom-mend me for admission to the PhD programme in Semitics at Columbia, namely, that most but not all the things we can actually prove about biblical data – the kinds of things about which Held, of blessed memory, would rant and rave – are matters of very little consequence. What does matter is the attempt of a few men and women who lived in the Middle East in the ninth, eighth, seventh, sixth and fifth centuries BCE to convey some-thing of what they heard from on high in order to make this world a better place in which to live. One of the things we learn is that some of what these prophets heard, or thought they heard, can be hazardous for men and women. One of the things that we should learn is how creating a dialogue between our personal experience, the prophetic experience and the ever-expanding discipline of biblical studies may help us see further beyond what the prophet/ess saw and thereby supply the antidote to some of the poison that those the prophet/ess may have mistaken for medicine.

Read through the eyes of Kaufmann and Ginsberg, Hos. 1 tells us that a certain prophet was summoned at the very beginning of his prophetic career to provide himself with an adulterous wife and children born of adultery to symbolize the Israelites' disloyalty to God her husband. This disloyalty is thus compared to a married woman's having extra-marital sex, which was considered 'the great sin' in the ancient Near East (see Moran 1959: 280–1). As the rather brief chapter 1 of the book of Hosea unfolds, we are told that in response to God's request to him the prophet married Gomer, daughter of Diblaim, who bore him three children. These children were each given symbolic names: Jezreel, meaning 'God will fructify'; Unloved; and Not My People.

The core of Hos. 1–3 is the long prophetic speech contained in Hos. 2, which begins and ends with words of comfort, consolation and encouragement. In this speech the children of Israel – that is the individual members of the corporate body called Israel – are identified with the three children borne by Gomer: Jezreel, Unloved and Not My People. There is a fundamental difference between Hos. 1 and Hos. 2. In Hos. 1, which serves as prologue, the three names all have negative meanings. In chapter 2, on the other hand, the three names – or rather Jezreel and the permutations of the other two names – have positive meanings. These positive meanings point to God's reconciliation with the previously unfaithful Israel, both in its corporate body and in its individual humanity, as symbolized by Jezreel, and his sister and brother. The sister and brother are re-named 'Loved' and 'My People' respectively. Jezreel, who is associated in chapter 1 with the place where a terrible atrocity was perpetrated in the name of the God of Israel, is associated in chapter 2 with its etymological meaning, 'God will fructify'.

Hos. 2 ends with God saying:

I will fructify the sky [by filling the clouds with water],
And it [the sky] will fructify the earth [by means of the rain],
And the earth will fructify grain and wine and oil,
And these will fructify Jezreel [the place-name which means literally 'God will fructify'].
I will sow her [a play on the name Jezreel] in the land as My own,
And I will take back in love Unloved
And I will say to Not My people, 'You are My People',
and he [i.e., Israel collectively and individually represented by Gomer's third child 'Not My People'] will declaim, '[You are] [3] my God'.

(Hos. 2:23–5)

Inspired by Ariella Deem (1978: 27–8), I came to understand that in each of its five occurrences in Hos. 2:23–4 the Hebrew verbal root *'ny* means 'fructify'. It is the same verbal root that is attested in Deut. 22:23–4 in the sense 'have sex with':

> In the case of a virgin who is engaged to a man – if a man comes upon her in town and lies with her, you shall take the two of them out to the gate of that town and stone them to death: the girl because she did not cry for help in the town, and the man because he had sex with [Heb. *'innāh*] another man's wife.[4]

According to Hos. 1:4, through the prophet, God promises to punish the dynasty of Jehu for the bloody deeds it perpetrated in the Valley of Jezreel. As I suggested in my unsigned entry 'Hosea' in the *Illustrated Dictionary and Concordance of the Bible* (Wigoder 1986: 457), the bloody deeds perpetrated by the dynasty of Jehu in the Valley of Jezreel may well refer to Jehu's annihilation of the survivors of Ahab's dynasty (2 Kgs 10:11) in Jezreel. Ginsberg, may his memory be for a blessing, knew that the deeds of King Jehu (842–815 BCE) in the Valley of Jezreel were treated as praiseworthy by the narrator in 2 Kgs 10:30, according to whom God spoke to Jehu in a prophetic revelation and said,

> Because you have done well to do what is just in my eyes in doing what I wanted to the dynasty of Ahab, four generations of your descendants will be enthroned upon the throne of Israel.

It should not be altogether surprising that the evaluation of King Jehu's treatment of the descendants of Ahab found in Hos. 1:14 is at variance with the one reflected in 2 Kgs 10:30. It is indeed the glory of Hebrew Scripture that it constantly records variant evaluations of the same events. For example, Gen. 11:31 asserts that it was through the initiative of his father Terah that Abram set out from his native city on his journey to the land of Canaan, while Gen. 12:1 asserts that it was Yahweh who directed Abram to leave his native land and his father's house and to set out for 'the land that I will show you'. Nevertheless, in his characteristic manner Ginsberg sought to eliminate Hosea's negative evaluation of Jehu's annihilation of the descendants of Ahab in Hos. 1:4 by emending 'the blood of Jezreel' to 'the [festival] days of the Baals' and Jehu to Israel.

Ginsberg believed that by making the Hosea of Hos. 1–3 into a single-issue prophet concerned only with apostasy, he made this prophet look more like his near contemporary Elijah. In fact, it is the unemended text that invites the comparison of Hos. 1–3, who condemns both bloodshed and apostasy, to Elijah, who condemns both the bloodshed perpetrated by Jezebel against Naboth and the apostasy she fostered.

For at least ten years, between composing the entry 'Hosea, Book of' in the *Illustrated Dictionary and Concordance* and the summer of 1995, I was fully convinced that Hos. 1–2 rightly compares Israel of the mid-ninth century BCE to a woman who has been unfaithful to her beneficent and long-suffering husband. In fact, I understood Hos. 2:16–17 in the light of Jer. 2:2. Now, in Hos. 2:16–17 we read as follows:

> Assuredly I will entice her, and I shall take her out into the wilderness, and I shall speak tenderly to her . . . There she shall call out [Hebrew verbal root *'ny* in the same sense as in Ps. 119:172][5] as in the days of her youth when she ascended from Egypt.

Jer. 2:2 reads as follows:

> I [God] give you [Israel personified as God's wife] credit for your devotion [to me] in your youth, your love [for me] as a bride, how you followed Me in the wilderness, in a land not sown.

Reading Hos. 2:16–17 in light of Jer. 2:2, I gave much credit to God as portrayed by Hosea. I saw Hos. 2:16–17 as a portrayal of God as a husband who realized that his wife had been unfaithful to him in order to bring home to him that he had taken her for granted. Realizing this, God portrayed as husband in Hos. 2:16–17, does what many a reasonable husband might do after some marital counselling, namely, take his wife away for a weekend, a kind of second honeymoon in the place where they celebrated their first honeymoon. What may have escaped Jeremiah and what certainly escaped me was the simple fact that inviting the wife to a weekend in the wilderness where there are few amenities and where she might well die of thirst can well reflect the very same abusiveness that is portrayed in Hos. 2:4–6 quoted below.

I suggested again and again to my students with abundant examples from literature on marital counselling that God as portrayed in Hos. 1–2 was being the perfect husband, repentant of his earlier neglect of his wife's need for emotional intimacy. In fact, I drew the parallel from eighth century BCE Hos. 4, in which God defends the right of women to be unfaithful to husbands who neglect them and chase after sexual playmates (Gruber 1995: 176–8). However, during all the years that I so interpreted and taught the book of Hosea, my colleague Naomi Graetz kept telling me that, despite my perception of the book of Hosea as medicine for marital instability, it contains poison. She referred me again and again to Hos. 2:4–6, in which the prophet, speaking in the name of God, says the following:

> Rebuke your mother, rebuke her –
> For she is not my wife

And I am not her husband
She must put her fornication away from her face
And her adultery from between her breasts
Else I will strip her naked
And leave her as on the day she was born;
And I will make her like a wilderness,
Render her like a desert land,
And let her die of thirst.
I will also disown her children;
For they are children conceived through adultery.

This is hardly the prophet of love about whom my father had taught us in that confirmation class back in 1959–60. Yet, I confess, I chose to gloss over this as God's tentative, angry musings before he decided that the best solution is to pay the wife more attention and just take her away for a second honeymoon. I simply could not take seriously Naomi Graetz's contention (N. Graetz 1992, 1995) that divinely-sanctioned violence directed against women in Hebrew Scripture constitutes a divine sanction of violence by Bible-reading men against women. I believe that the main reason I could not take Naomi Graetz's frequent diatribes seriously is that during twenty-three years of marital bliss I didn't seriously associate domestic violence against women as having anything to do with the world I lived in, which consisted of happily married, Bible-reading urban professionals. Moreover, I agree now with J. Cheryl Exum (1996) that many men tend to read biblical texts that abuse women differently from women, unless they are shocked into seeing first life and later on literature from a woman's point of view.

The world I lived in changed drastically in the summer of 1993 when my beloved wife Judith died a few months after being diagnosed with pancreatic cancer. In the faith community to which I belong it is largely taken for granted that when one's spouse dies one tries to find another partner. And so it was that at first very discreetly and later less discreetly I began dating. One of the things that I found to be shared by a very high percentage of the young or middle-aged urban professional women with whom I went out – widows, women who had never been married, and divorcees – was tales of domestic violence: sexual assault of a teenager by a sister's boyfriend; child abuse; physical violence directed against the urban professional woman by her father, and so on.

Not infrequently, I would be told or perceive that women I dated would have flashbacks to scenes of sexual abuse brought on by something as simple as the colour of my hair, which reminded one woman of something she had not talked about for almost four decades. I never really believed that people like these existed among the people of the world in which I work and play. There were days and weeks when the pain I felt for some of these women was my constant obsession. In the middle of all this I was reading, in connection with a research project, two very important books that dealt with the subject of domestic violence, especially childhood sexual abuse (Bass and Davis 1990; Herman 1992). I began to understand fully that I had on several occasions been experiencing countertransference, which is commonly experienced by caring professionals who counsel victims of domestic violence.

Just at this point I attended the Society of Biblical Literature International Meeting in Budapest in July 1995, and I heard J. Cheryl Exum present her paper 'Prophetic Pornography'. She began her presentation with a hand-out. The first quotation in support of her contention that Hebrew Scripture contains pornographic material which appears to condone sexual violence against women was Isa. 3:17. Of course, I remembered Held's brilliant insight (see page 172 above). However, as I later told Professor Exum, her abundant examples made Held's insight a matter of little consequence. Having been pained so greatly by the violence perpetrated against women whom I had met and befriended, I came to see that for all the largesse of God in Hos. 4 and in Hos. 2:16–25, the moral dilemma represented by God's verbal abuse and threat of physical abuse against His wife and her children in Hos. 2:4–15 is not a figment of Naomi Graetz's imagination.

It is a matter that must be confronted seriously by all who believe, as I do, that God could not possibly condone the verbal abuse and threat of physical abuse against His wife and her children (contrast with Weems 1989: 97–8). Having realized the ubiquity of violence by men against women, especially in the home and in intimate relationships, I came to see that in being a human male I belong to the 49 per cent of humanity which has and exercises control over the other 51 per cent who are female, and I must share in the collective shame of that powerful minority. I also came to believe that insofar as Hebrew Scripture and Jewish exegetical literature and liturgy by and large picture God as father and husband and much less rarely as mother or wife (see Trible 1978; Gruber 1983; Eilberg-Schwartz 1994: 129–30), not only must the comparison of God to man take into consideration the divine phallus (Eilberg-Schwartz 1994) but must also consider the hypostatization of male violence against daughters, sisters, girlfriends, wives and unnamed women. To portray God accurately as father and husband means that God must embody all that father, husband and boyfriend all too often entail, including abuse, exploitation and degradation. I would go so far as to suggest that the socially and theologically redeeming value of prophetic pornography in Hebrew Scripture (contrast with Exum 1996: 122) is to reveal fully the shortcomings of the use of male imagery in referring to God. Just as Jews, and in some circles especially Jewish women, assemble on the new moon to help atone on God's behalf for His act of abuse directed, as it were, at the moon,[6] so must all Israel – both after the flesh and after the spirit – help the God of Hebrew Scripture both

178

to model the listening, repentant husband portrayed in Hos. 2:16–25 and to own up to the full implications – many of them not pleasant at all – of portraying God as father and husband rather than mother and wife.

Had I not learned through close encounters of the human kind of the ubiquity of domestic violence and the toll it takes, I am not certain that I would have understood what J. Cheryl Exum was talking about in Budapest. Therefore, I do believe, with perfect faith, that personal experience is no less important to the understanding of biblical texts than Palestinian archaeology, Semitic philology, and literary criticism. The cultivation of what King Solomon called 'a listening heart' (1 Kgs 3:9) in response to other people's personal voice criticism may, I hope, spare colleagues and students the need to experience for themselves abuse, which none of us would wish even upon our worst enemies.

Notes

1 Jewish scholars who endeavour to make themselves and their subjects mainstream characteristically reveal their being on the margin of what Elisabeth Schüssler Fiorenza aptly calls the white male Euro-American academy (Schüssler Fiorenza 1989: 1) when they use this formula following the name of the deceased rather than the definite article and attributive adjective 'late' preceding the name of the deceased. Similarly, when they mention in the same sentence a living and a dead scholar they will invariably set apart the name of the living scholar with the words 'may he/she be distinguished for life' lest the writer be guilty of encouraging the Angel of Death to take prematurely the living scholar along with the deceased one to the Academy on High. Interestingly, those most quintessentially mainstream white male Euro-American scholars, those of the Anglican persuasion, similarly marginalize themselves when they refer to the head of the Roman Catholic Church not as 'the pope' but as 'the bishop of Rome'. In a sense, therefore, all academic scholars of the Scriptures deliberately both marginalize themselves and mainstream themselves and their subjects. What unites us is that all of us find in Holy Scripture read objectively, scientifically, historically, and philologically divine sanction for the convictions born of very personal joys and tragedies.

2 Jewish biblical scholars of the first seven decades of the twentieth century almost took it for granted that the books of Isaiah, Jeremiah, Ezekiel and The Twelve (Minor) Prophets with the exception of the book of Jonah contain the speeches of the prophets of the mid-eighth to late sixth centuries BCE, see, for example, Haran 1963; passim in Kaufmann 1964; Gitay 1983. Mainstream Euro-American biblical scholarship of the closing years of the twentieth century CE tends to see in the prophetic books literary creations, which are the product of hundreds of years of accretions to whatever core may emanate from the speech of an Isaiah or Hosea or Jeremiah. See, for example, Sweeney 1988 and Clements 1990. I regard it as my privilege as a Jewish confessional biblical scholar to believe that the prophetic books are essentially speeches of the so-called Old Testament prophets just as I regard it as my privilege to believe that these prophets dialogued with God. I fully know that I cannot show either of these claims to be true. However, I am comforted to know that those who

engage in the newer forms of biblical criticism cannot prove that their approaches rest upon fact any more than can I with respect to mine.

3 Bracketed expression supplied with brackets from *Tanakh*, 1985; the corresponding 'thou art' appears without brackets or italics in the Revised Standard Version while the King James Version characteristically supplies 'Thou art' in italics to indicate that the Hebrew is elliptical but that English style requires making explicit what is implicit in the Hebrew.

4 This text, which speaks of a woman's culpability for consensual adultery, should put to rest the notion that the verbal root *'ny* refers to rape; contrast with Moshe Greenberg (oral communication) cited in Weinfeld 1972: 286, n. 5.

5 The verbal root *'ny* is a homonym of both the verbal root rendered 'fructify' five times in vv. 23–4 and also a homonym of the verbal root *'ny* meaning 'oppress, subjugate' attested, for example, in Gen. 15:13; 16:6, 9; Deut. 26:6; etc. The verbal root *'ny* 'to declaim, declare, sing aloud' is exemplified in Deut. 21:7; 26:5; 27:14; etc. See dictionaries and the standard critical commentaries on those verses. In the present context it probably refers to the metaphoric woman's crying out in ecstasy at the moment of orgasm both on her wedding night and during the proposed second honeymoon envisioned in Hos. 2:16–17.

6 In the Jewish tradition of biblical exegesis represented by the canonical biblical commentary of Rashi (1040–1105 CE) it is explained that the he-goat, which was to be sacrificed at the new moon according to Num. 28:15, was to enable God Himself to atone for his having abused the moon by diminishing the moon in size relative to the sun. The perception of an act of abuse on behalf of God derives from the fact that early in Gen. 1:16 God is said to have created 'the two great lights' – the sun and the moon – while later in that same verse the sun and moon are called the great light and the small light respectively. Rashi explains in his commentary on Gen. 1:16 that when the moon asked, 'How are two sovereigns going to share the same crown?', God responded by diminishing the size of the moon. In other words, like many a parent frustrated by a child's behaviour, God is said to have responded with an act of physical abuse. The traditional Jewish exegesis of Num. 28:15 indicates that abuse of those less powerful than us, which is taken for granted in so many homes and places of work, in public life and in voluntary associations of every sort, is not to be taken for granted. Its sinfulness must be acknowledged, and atonement must be made for it.

References

Bass, E. and Davis, L. (1990) *The Courage to Heal*, New York: Harper and Row.

Clements, R. E. (1990) 'The Prophet and His Editors', in *The Bible in Three Dimensions*, JSOT Supplement Series, 87, Sheffield: JSOT.

Deem, A. (1978) 'The Goddess Anath and Some Biblical Hebrew Cruces', *Journal of Semitic Studies* 23:25–30.

Eilberg-Schwartz, H. (1994) *God's Phallus*, Boston: Beacon.

Exum, J. C. (1996) 'Prophetic Pornography', in J. C. Exum, *Plotted, Shot, and Painted: Cultural Representations of Biblical Women*, JSOT Supplement Series, 215; Gender, Culture, Theory, 3, Sheffield: Sheffield Academic.

Ginsberg, H. L. (1972) 'Hosea', *Encyclopaedia Judaica* 8: 1010–24.

Gitay, Y. (1983) 'Reflections on the Study of the Prophetic Discourse, the Question of Isaiah i 2–20', *Vetus Testamentum* 33: 207–21.

Graetz, H. (1891) *History of the Jews,* vol. 1, trans. B. Löw, Philadelphia, PA: Jewish Publication Society of America.

Graetz, N. (1992) 'The Haftarah Tradition and the Metaphoric Battering of Hosea's Wife', *Conservative Judaism* 45,1: 29–42.

—— (1995) 'God is to Israel as Husband is to Wife: The Metaphoric Battering of Hosea's Wife', in A. Brenner (ed.) *A Feminist Companion to the Latter Prophets*, The Feminist Companion to the Bible, 8, Sheffield: Sheffield Academic.

Gruber, M. I. (1970) *What is Prophecy?* New York: American Jewish Congress, National Women's Division, and Commission on Jewish Affairs.

—— (1983) 'The Motherhood of God in Second Isaiah', *Revue Biblique* 90: 351–9.

—— (1995) 'Marital Fidelity and Intimacy: A View From Hosea 4', in A. Brenner (ed.), *A Feminist Companion to the Latter Prophets*, The Feminist Companion to the Bible, 8, Sheffield: Sheffield Academic.

Haran, M. (1963) 'The Literary Structure and Chronological Framework of the Prophecies in Is. XL–XLVIII', in *Congress Volume: Bonn 1962*, Vetus Testamentum Supplements, 9, Leiden: Brill.

Herman, J. (1992) *Trauma and Recovery: The Aftermath of Violence; from Domestic Abuse to Political Terror*, New York: Basic Books.

Heschel, A. J. (1962) *The Prophets,* New York: Harper & Row.

Kaufmann, Y. (1964) *History of the Israelite Religion*, 8 vols, Jerusalem: Bialik Institute (in Hebrew).

Moran, W. L. (1959) 'The Scandal of the "Great Sin" at Ugarit', *Journal of Near Eastern Studies* 18: 280–1.

Schüssler Fiorenza, E. (1989) 'Introduction', in K. Geneva Cannon and E. Schüssler Fiorenza (eds) *Interpretation for Liberation*, Semeia 47, Atlanta, GA: Scholars, 1–8.

Sweeney, M. A. (1988) *Isaiah 1-4 and the Post-Exilic Understanding of the Isaianic Tradition*, BZAW, 171, Berlin and New York: Walter de Gruyter.

Tanakh: A New Translation of the Holy Scriptures (1985), Philadelphia, PA: Jewish Publication Society.

Trible, P. (1978) *God and the Rhetoric of Sexuality*, Philadelphia, PA: Fortress.

Weems, R. J. (1989) 'Gomer: Victim of Violence or Victim of Metaphor', in

K. Geneva Cannon and E. Schüssler Fiorenza (eds) *Interpretation for Liberation*, *Semeia* 47, Atlanta, GA: Scholars, 88–104.

Weinfeld, M. (1972) *Deuteronomy and the Deuteronomic School*, Oxford: Clarendon.

Wigoder, G. (1986) *Illustrated Dictionary & Concordance of the Bible*, New York: Macmillan.

13

REVOLTING REVELATIONS[1]

Stephen D. Moore

Where I come from, the third word in the title of this collection could only be pronounced as 'vice'. But it is not the personal vice in biblical scholarship that I wish to ponder here, nor even my own personal vice (though I shall hardly be able to resist the temptation), so much as that of the only New Testament narrator to employ the personal voice throughout his narrative ('I, John . . .'). I speak, of course, of the narrator of Revelation.

In any case, there is by now relatively little of my own vices and vicissitudes left to reveal. Buried in books that, if my royalty cheques are anything to go by, are seldom exhumed and opened up, my published secrets are slowly decomposing, thin nourishment for the occasional prurient bookworm. For these secrets are a sadly unsensational lot. Still, had your own life been so desperately dreary during the past decade or so as to cause you to dig out and devour my every published word, you would have read of:

1   My roots in the soggy soil of rural Ireland. My father was a butcher; you'd be weary of hearing that. Later on he became a farmer; you might also have caught that. But you wouldn't yet know that my mother was a hairdresser; that is to be the subject of my next monograph.
2   My LSD-induced psychosis in the summer of 1974, which led, simultaneously, to
3   my conversion to Christianity, and
4   my incarceration in St Joseph's Mental Hospital, Limerick.
5   My subsequent incarceration (voluntary, this time) in Mount Melleray Cistercian Abbey, County Waterford.
6   My current agnosticism. (Or is it atheism? I'm never quite sure.)
7   My 10-year affair with another man, which began in the spring of 1972, and persisted even through my period in the monastery (we entered the novitiate together). On second thought, you wouldn't yet know about that, because I haven't written about it before. The other party has, however; see Anon., *The Boys*, unpublished manuscript concealed in the bottom drawer of the grey file cabinet in my office,

beneath my (equally unpublished) doctoral dissertation. It appears that the latter favours the missionary position (as befits a work whose main title is *Narrative Homiletics*). Last year this unlikely couple conceived and gave birth to a book, *God's Gym: Divine Male Bodies of the Bible*, which ends with a preliminary exploration of the book of Revelation.

And it is to Revelation that I wish to return here. For my essay title is not intended to be a reference to my own 'revolting' revelations, as I have already intimated, so much as those of this bizarre book – *the Book of Revelations*, as it is most commonly called, at any rate in the English-speaking world. Even among Bible-reading Christians, surprisingly few refer to the book by its actual title, 'Revelation', much preferring the plural. 'Revelations' has a titillating ring to it, I suppose, that the more theological 'Revelation' cannot match. 'Revelations' doesn't conjure up the tablets of the law so much as the law of the tabloids. And what *is* the law of the tabloids – the tabloid press, and now tabloid TV as well, epitomized by the talk show? It is simply that secrets sell. Revelations is the *grand dénouement* of the world's biggest bestseller. So whose sordid secrets is it supposed to be peddling? God's or merely John's? Let's see.

'So what is Revelation actually about?' I ask myself.
'Easy', the answer comes back. 'It's about the establishment of God's kingdom on earth.'
'God's "kingdom", eh? Not his dukedom or his fiefdom, then? And "on earth". As opposed to Mars, say, or Uranus?'
'My *what*? What on earth are you mumbling about?'
'No need for alarm. I'm merely marvelling at your propensity to shroud your theological thought in archaic political and cosmological metaphors.'
'Oh, the shroud isn't mine, I borrowed it from John.'
'You look so comfortable in it. So just how is the kingdom of God to be established on earth, according to John?'
'How are kingdoms or empires ever established?'
'Through military conquest, no doubt.'
'Well, there you have it.'
'You mean Revelation is all about war?'

'Yes, messianic war. Richard Bauckham is excellent on this. Now, if I can only find his discussion of it . . . Ah, yes, here we are:

> The prominence of Davidic messianism in Revelation can be gauged from Jesus' self-designation, 'I am the root and the descendant of David, the bright morning star' (22:16). The first of these two titles comes from Isaiah 11:10 ('the root of Jesse') and is used of the Davidic Messiah. . . . The second refers to the star of Numbers 24:17, which (in the context of 24:17–19) was commonly understood to be a symbol of the Messiah of David who would conquer the enemies of Israel. 'The root of David' is found also in Revelation 5:1, alongside another title evoking the image of the royal Messiah who will defeat the nations by military violence: 'the Lion of Judah' (cf. Gen. 49:9; 4 Ezra 12:31–2). Further allusions to the Messiah of Isaiah 11, a favourite passage for Davidic messianism, are the sword that comes from Christ's mouth (1:16; 2:12, 16; 19:21) with which he strikes down the nations (19:15; cf. Isa. 11:4; 49:2) and the statement that he judges with righteousness (19:11; cf. Isa. 11:4).'

'Stirring stuff. But does all this mayhem have a purpose – other than the establishment of 'God's kingdom', that is (a phrase which, as you know, sends a small shiver up my spine)? What if its real purpose were to engender masculinity, to make men?'

Revelation *is* a book of war, a book of warriors, but not an especially vivid one, at least to my mind. My own internal standard for an ancient war book is the *Táin Bó Cuailnge* (The Cattle Raid of Cooley), the oldest vernacular epic in Western literature, ancient Ireland's answer to the *Iliad*.[2] Between the ages of 7 and 12 (numbers to which John accords sublime significance) I had but a single teacher in the tiny school that I attended in the village of Adare in County Limerick, and he happened to be an ardent nationalist. Ancient Irish mythology took precedence over biblical mythology in my early formation as a result, even though the school was run by a religious order. The *Táin*, in particular, the centrepiece of a pre-Christian(?) cycle of heroic tales, made an overwhelming impression upon my fledgeling imagination years before I even knew that John's war book existed.

Every page of the *Táin* is a paean to war. Even its accounts of warriors mentally preparing themselves for battle are marked by an exuberance and excess that I have yet to encounter in any other ancient literature. Judge for yourself; in the following excerpt, the hero of the *Táin*, Cúchulainn, prepares to take on an entire army singlehandedly:

> The first warp-spasm seized Cúchulainn, and made him into a monstrous thing, hideous and shapeless, unheard of. His shanks and his joints, every knuckle

'Ah, so we're to obsess about de-essentialized manhood again, are we? The lament of the matchstick man. Or is it the gender construct blues? Muddy Waters had it all wrong, no doubt. Instead of bellowing "I'm a man!" he should have sobbed "I'm a subject whose gender identity is purely performative, the product of a compulsory set of rituals and conventions, which conspire to engender retroactively the illusion that my masculinity is natural and innate, merely 'expressed' by the actions, gestures and speech that in fact produce it –"'

'Sorry to interrupt your own performance, but I'd like to share the following snippet with you in exchange for the Bauckham: "[U]ntil recently, critical discussion of violence, warfare, and the sacred in the Hebrew Bible has failed to consider the constitutive role of gender categories for these texts. This, I think, is remarkable, for what could be more acutely gendered than war, an activity historically described as performed by men only, in a space containing nothing but men?" (that's Harold Washington, paraphrasing Miriam Cooke). Now, given that it's the Davidic Messiah we've been discussing, let me cut to another essay, "David the Man" by David Clines.'

'The "man" of the title is not Clines himself, then?'

*'No, or at least not entirely so. He notes: "The essential male characteristic in the David story is to be a warrior, a man of war (*מלחמה* אישׁ) or a mighty man of valour (*נבור חיל*) . . . It is essential for a man in the David story that he be strong – which means to say, capable of violence against other men and active in killing other men." Later he adds:*

Or, to take another example, from a little outside the David story itself, in 1 Sam. 4:9 the Philistines say to

and angle and organ from head to foot, shook like a tree in the flood or a reed in the stream. His body made a furious twist inside his skin, so that his feet and shins and knees switched to the rear and his heels and calves switched to the front. The balled sinews of his calves switched to the front of his shins, each big knot the size of a warrior's bunched fist. On his head the temple-sinews stretched to the nape of his neck, each mighty, immense, measureless knob as big as the head of a month-old child. His face and features became a red bowl: he sucked one eye so deep into his head that a wild crane couldn't probe it onto his cheek out of the depths of his skull; the other eye fell out along his cheek. His mouth weirdly distorted: his cheek peeled back from his jaws until the gullet appeared, his lungs and liver flapped in his mouth and throat, his lower jaw struck the upper a lion-killing blow, and fiery flakes large as a ram's fleece reached his mouth from his throat. His heart boomed loud in his breast like the baying of a watch-dog at its feed or the sound of a lion among bears. Malignant mists and spurts of fire – the torches of the Badb[3] – flickered red in the vaporous

186

one another, having learned that the ark of Yahweh has come into their camp: 'Take courage (lit. be strong), and acquit yourselves like men, O Philistines, lest you become slaves to the Hebrews as they have been to you; acquit yourselves like men and fight.' This phrase 'acquit yourselves like men', literally 'become men' (לאנשים היה, repeated as (והייתם לאנשים)), means, very simply, that to be a man is to fight. The whole ideology surrounding this utterance is a little more complex than that, no doubt; for the purpose of fighting is to resist slavery for oneself and to continue to keep others in slavery . . . But as far as the gender issue is concerned, it is simple: men fight.'

'Enough! My testosterone level is shooting off the scale. I vow never again to wear my wife's dressing gown to breakfast. But how does it all connect with the Davidic Messiah?'

'Don't pretend you don't see it. The Davidic Messiah, as the ultimate warrior, would also have been the ultimate icon of masculinity.'

'A male fantasy of phallic proportions?'

'Funny you should mention the phallus –'

'Well, I was missing it, rather. You usually insist on beating me over the head with it.'

'– because Bauckham himself makes the following point about John's preoccupation with Psalm 2. Hang on a minute . . . Yes, here it is: "One of John's key Old Testament texts, allusions to which run throughout Revelation, is Psalm 2, which depicts 'the nations' and 'the kings of the earth' conspiring to rebel against 'the LORD and his Messiah' (verses 1–2) . . . God promises to give this royal Messiah the nations for his inheritance (verse 8) and that he will violently subdue them with

clouds that rose boiling above his head, so fierce was his fury. The hair of his head twisted like the tangle of a red thornbush stuck in a gap; if a royal apple tree with all its kingly fruit were shaken above him, scarce an apple would reach the ground but each would be spiked on a bristle of his hair as it stood up on his scalp with rage. The hero-halo rose out of his brow, long and broad as a warrior's whetstone, long as a snout, and he went mad rattling his shields, urging on his charioteer and harassing the hosts. Then, tall and thick, steady and strong, high as the mast of a noble ship, rose up from the dead centre of his skull a straight spout of black blood darkly and magically smoking like the smoke from a royal hostel when a king is coming to be cared for at the close of a winter day.[4]

When that spasm had run through the high hero Cúchulainn he stepped into his sickle war-chariot that bristled with points of iron and narrow blades, with hooks and hard prongs and heroic frontal spikes, with ripping instruments and tearing nails on its shafts and straps and loops and cords. The body of the chariot was spare and slight *a rod of iron (verse 9). Allusions to this account of the Messiah's victory over the nations are found in Revelation 2:18, 26–8; 11:15, 18; 12:5, 10; 14:1; 16:14, 16; 19:15."'*

'And your own point is what, precisely?'

'Oh, come on! Rod of iron?'

'Well, you know what Freud said, "Sometimes a rod of iron is just a rod of iron."'

'Freud aside, I submit that what John is really saying is that the Messiah, when he comes, will fuck the nations into submission.'

'You have such an exquisitely delicate way of putting things. Any nation in particular, though?'

'I think we both know the answer to that: "Babylon the great, mother of whores." Which brings me back to Washington: "[I]n the ANE cultural milieu violence against a feminine object is intrinsic to masculine gender. . . ." And again: "The language of war in the Hebrew Bible and other ancient Near Eastern literatures is acutely masculinist. Warfare is emblematically male and the discourse of violence is closely imbricated with that of masculine sexuality. . . ." He goes on to quote Harry Hoffner: "The masculinity of the ancient was measured by two criteria: (1) his prowess in battle, and (2) his ability to sire children. . . . [T]hese two aspects of masculinity were frequently associated with each other. . . . [T]hose symbols which primarily referred to his military exploits often served to remind him of his sexual ability as well. . . ." Here I am reminded of an edifying scene in the movie Full Metal Jacket. *You know the one I mean? The marine recruits are required to clutch their M16s firmly in one hand and their crotches firmly in the other, all the while chanting, "This is my dick an' this is my gun, one is for fightin', the other's for fun!"'*

'You can let go of your crotch now. I wouldn't want you to injure yourself.'

and erect, fitted for the feats of a champion, with space for a lordly warrior's eight weapons, speedy as the wind or as a swallow or a deer darting over the level plain. The chariot was settled down on two fast steeds, wild and wicked, neat-headed and narrow bodied, with slender quarters and roan breast, firm in hoof and harness – a notable sight in the trim chariot-shafts. One horse was lithe and swift-leaping, high-arched and powerful, long-bodied and with great hooves. The other flowing-maned and shining, slight and slender in hoof and heel.

In that style, then, he drove out to find his enemies and did his thunder-feat and killed a hundred, then two hundred, then three hundred, then four hundred, then five hundred, where he stopped – he didn't think it too many to kill in that first attack, his first full battle with the provinces of Ireland. Then he circled the outer lines of the four great provinces of Ireland in his chariot and he attacked them in hatred. He had the chariot driven so heavily that its iron wheels sank in the earth. So deeply the chariot-wheels sank in the earth

'Washington also notes:

The male is by definition the subject
of warfare's violence and the female
its victim. For example, the language
of the siege instructions of Deut.
20.10–20 is densely supplied with
syntactical groups joining a masculine
singular verbal subject with a city as
(feminine) object of attack. . . .
Given a linguistic milieu where cities
are so often portrayed in the figure of a
woman – either mother (Isa. 66.8–
13), queen (Isa. 62.3), or virgin
daughter (Isa. 37.22), a woman
married (Isa. 62.5), widowed (Isa.
47.8, 9; 54.4; Lam. 1.1), or raped
(Jer. 6.1–8; 13.22; Isa. 47.1–4;
Nah. 3.5–6) – the concentration of
feminine forms in Deut. 20.10–20
inescapably evokes the figuration of
the city as an assaulted woman. In
issuing the command to draw near to a
city 'in order to attack it', this text
effectively enjoins the soldiers 'to
attack her' (להלחם עליה, 20.10).
The description of the submissive city
'opening' to the warrior (ופתחה לך,
20.11) evokes an image of male pen-
etration. Similarly, the law uses the
verb תפש to describe the military
seizure of a city (להלחם צלוה לתפשה,
20.19), the same term used for the
forcible seizure of a woman in sexual
assault (ותפשה ושכב עמה, 22.28).'

'And all of this is relevant to Revelation, I take it?'
'Quite possibly. Compare, for example, Tina
Pippin's reading of Babylon in Revelation as a
sexually assaulted woman. Her prooftext, as
you may recall, is Rev. 17:6, "they will make
her desolate and naked; they will devour her
flesh and burn her up with fire."'

that clods and boulders
were torn up, with rocks
and flagstones and the gravel
of the ground, in a dyke as
high as the iron wheels,
enough for a fortress-wall.
He threw up this circle of
the Badb round about the
four great provinces of
Ireland to stop them flee-
ing and scattering from
him, and corner them
where he could wreak ven-
geance for the boy-troop.[5]
He went into the middle of
them and beyond, and
mowed down great ram-
parts of his enemies'
corpses, circling completely
around the armies three
times, attacking them in
hatred. They fell sole to
sole and neck to headless
neck, so dense was that
destruction. He circled
them three times more in
the same way, and left a
bed of them six deep in a
great circuit, the soles of
three to the necks of three
in a ring around the camp.
This slaughter on the Táin
was given the name Seis-
rech Bresligi, the Sixfold
Slaughter. It is one of the
three uncountable slaugh-
ters on the Táin: Seisrech
Bresligi, Imslige Glennam-
nach – the mutual slaughter
at Glenn Domain – and the
Great Battle at Gáirech and
Irgáirech (though this time
it was horses and dogs as
well as men). Any count

189

'I also recall that the perpetrators of these dire deeds are the "ten horns", together with the beast, not Christ, your phallic warrior.'

'*Admittedly, but ultimately it's the commander-in-chief who is responsible for Babylon's rape: "For God has put it into their hearts to carry out his purpose . . . (17:17)."*' 'I'm nervous that you'll have him leaping out naked from behind the curtains next to join in, so let's move on. So far you've been talking as though John's Jesus were a one-man army –'

'*Or a one-lamb army, at least.*'

'– but he doesn't wage war alone; instead, he leads an army against the enemies of God. Here's Bauckham again:

Also derived from this militant messianism is Revelation's key concept of conquering. It is applied both to the Messiah himself (3:21; 5:5; 17:14) and to his people, who share his victory (2:7, 11, 17, 28: 3:5, 12, 21; 12:11; 15:2; 21:7). Once again we note the importance in Revelation of the Messiah's army. That the image of conquering is a militaristic one should be unmistakable, although interpreters of Revelation do not always do justice to this. It is closely connected with language of battle (11:7; 12:7–8, 17; 13:7; 16:14; 17:14; 19:11, 19), and it is notable that not only do Christ's followers defeat the beast (15:2), but also the beast defeats them (11:7; 13:7), so that this is evidently a war in which Christ's enemies have their victories, though the final victory is his. We should note also that the

or estimate of the number of the rabble who fell there is unknown, and unknowable. Only the chiefs have been counted. The following are the names of these nobles and chiefs: two called Cruaid, two named Calad, two named Cír, two named Cíar, two named Ecell, three named Crom, three named Caur, three named Combirge, four named Feochar, four named Furechar, four named Cass, four named Fota, five named Aurith, five named Cerman, five named Cobthach, six named Saxan, six named Dach, six named Dáire, seven named Rochad, seven named Ronan, seven named Rurthech, eight named Rochlad, eight named Rochtad, eight named Rinnach, eight named Coirpre, eight named Mulach, nine named Daithi, nine named Dáire, nine named Damach, ten named Fiac, ten named Fiacha, and ten named Feidlimid. In this great carnage on Murtheimne Plain Cúchulainn slew one hundred and thirty kings, as well as an uncountable horde of dogs and horses, women and boys and children and rabble of all kinds.[6] Not one man in three escaped without his thighbone or his head or his eye being smashed, or language of conquering is used of all the three stages of Christ's work: he conquered in his death and resurrection (3:21; 5:5), his followers conquer in the time before the end (12:11; 15:2), and he will conquer at the parousia (17:14). Thus it is clear that the image of the messianic war describes the whole process of the establishment of God's kingdom as Revelation depicts it –'

'Permit me to interrupt. May I hazard a précis of the plot thus far?'

'The plot? I was unaware that there was one.'

'Here goes. Revelation can plausibly be said to be about the establishment of God's kingdom on earth. How is this kingdom to be established? Through the messianic war. And what is the messianic war? An activity which, on the symbolic level, is conducted exclusively by male subjects (note the notorious 14:4), and is constitutive of the masculinity of those subjects, since it is ultimately directed against the feminine (note, again, the no less infamous 17:3–6).'

'Stunning. But there's one small matter you've overlooked. This is an army that does not kill; on the contrary, it allows itself to *be* killed.'

'How noble. Your friend Bauckham, too, makes much of the fact that – let me see, where is it? – "just as 5:5–6 depicts Jesus Christ as the Messiah who has won a victory, but has done so by sacrificial death, not by military might, so 7:4–14 depicts his followers as the people of the Messiah who share in his victory, but do so similarly, by sacrificial death rather than by military violence". Well, what else should we expect John to say? A military campaign against "the enemies of God" is

without some blemish for the rest of his life. And when the battle was over Cúchulainn was left without a scratch or a stain on himself, his charioteer or either of his horses.

I must confess to finding John's parallel account of Jesus battling the beast, 'the kings of the earth', and their armies singlehandedly (for although he commands an army, apparently he doesn't need one) a tad insipid by comparison:

> Then I saw the beast and the kings of the earth with their armies gathered to make war against the rider on the horse and against his army. And the beast was captured, and with it the false prophet who had performed in its presence the signs by which he deceived those who had received the mark of the beast and those who worshiped its image. These two were thrown alive into the lake of fire that burns with sulfur. And the rest were killed by the sword of the rider on the horse, the sword that came from his mouth; and all the birds of the air were gorged with their flesh.
> (19:19–21, NRSV; cf. 20:7–10)

Whereas the *Táin* is a garish celebration of war, Revelation is a *hardly an option for Christians at the time in which he is writing. That will have to await the Parousia, he supposes, when Christians will have Christ, as invincible Divine Warrior, present in person to lead them forth into battle. (I understand the "armies of heaven" in 19:14 to be the Christian faithful, especially in light of 17:14.) What hasn't even occurred to John, of course, is the possibility that Christians might be in a position to triumph over their enemies — not symbolically, though sacrificial martyrdom, but literally, through military might — long before the Divine Warrior returns. And if the slaughter of the "ungodly" should be permissible at the Parousia, then why not before? (Whether or not Jesus is literally whacking off heads with his sword in 19:21 is a moot point, given the frightful fate of the owners of those heads: eternal death, or worse, in the lake of fire that burns with sulphur.) The Crusades, the Inquisition, and even the Holocaust are but some of the more notable manifestations of the militarism that animates Revelation; indeed, any one of those campaigns might have claimed a warrant for their genocidal fantasies in the sinister logic of this most dangerous of biblical books.'*

'Sorry, but the title "Most Dangerous Biblical Book" has already been awarded to the Gospel according to Luke.'

'By Jane Schaberg, you mean? Well, Luke is more subtle, and to that extent more sinister, but when all is said and done he doesn't have as many notches on his gun. Even Bauckham concedes that the body count in Revelation is astronomical: "So the series of judgments affecting a quarter of the earth (6:8) and the series affecting a third of the earth (8:7–12; 9:15, 18) are not, as we might expect, followed by a series affecting half the earth. . . . But there is now to be only the final judgment, the sixth trumpet (10:7). When the content of the sixth trumpet is spelled out in detail as the seven bowls (15:1), they are total, not limited, judg-

muted celebration of war. Superimposed upon Revelation, the *Táin* colours in its blanks with lurid hues. Revelation is a war scroll, as Richard Bauckham has argued. But the *Táin* is what this war scroll would look like fully unrolled.

(Fearful of exposure, Revelation resorts to threats: 'I warn everyone who hears the words of the prophecy of this book: if anyone adds to them, God will add to that person the plagues described in this book . . .' (22:18). The *Táin*, for its part, feeling its colours bleed into Revelation, ends on an equally nervous note: 'A blessing on everyone who will memorize the *Táin* faithfully in this form, and not put any other form on it'.)

As will by now be readily apparent, perhaps, my own attitude towards violence is rather ambivalent. That might or might not be evident to you should you happen to run into me. For the most part I am what I appear to be, a generally placid, not to say passive, guy, sometimes shy, in a word, harmless. But harmlessness is merely my default mode. There is actually nothing of which the God of Revelation is guilty — torture, rape, mass murder — of which I myself would not also be capable, given certain (extreme) environmental stimuli. Which is why I fear this God as much as I do, and resist him for all I am worth. [7]

But there is another kind of resistance that I wish to bring into the discussion. On the annual school excursion from Adare to Dublin, our Ireland-for-the-Irish schoolmaster would lead us in

ments (16:2-21), accomplishing the final annihilation of the unrepentant."'

'Yes, arguably the unrepentant are to be annihilated in toto, according to John. But by whom? Not by the Lamb, apparently –'

'Or not yet, at any rate.'

'– nor by the army he commands, but by the one seated on the throne and those whom *he* commands, his heavenly host. But these spectacular military strikes cannot induce repentance in the enemy (to paraphrase Bauckham). For that an altogether different kind of army is required – one designed not to kill but to be killed, as I remarked earlier.'

What's interesting to me is the way military metaphors are withheld from the one seated on the throne and his angelic agents – their most qualified recipients – and lavished instead on the crucified one and his fellow martyrs. John presents Christ and his Christians as icons of masculinity, reserving feminine imagery for the enemy. Smells suspiciously like a smokescreen to me, suggesting – yes, I see from your supercilious smile that you've anticipated what I'm about to say – a certain anxiety on John's part regarding his own masculinity.'

'Ah, so the last book of the Bible is the result of its author's acute anxiety about the size of –'

'No, the dimensions of the Saint's sacred member is probably not the issue – I'm sure that in his own mind its measurement was a multiple of seven – but domination versus submission might well be the issue, or rather the cultural proclivity to construe the former as masculine and the latter as feminine in the ancient Mediterranean world. I mean, consider the fate that John is convinced awaits him and his fellow martyrs-in-the-making, the prospect of having to submit themselves passively to being fucked with physically, unto death if necessary . . .'

solemn procession through the cavernous interior of the General Post Office, where the Irish rebels set up their general headquarters during the armed revolt of 1916 against British colonial rule. He would deliver a hushed but heated speech by the statue of Cúchulainn enshrined in the building on 21 April 1935, to commemorate the uprising, a speech sodden with intoxicating excerpts from the proclamation of Irish independence. The act that ignited the 1916 rebellion was the public reading of this proclamation from the steps of the building. We were obliged to memorize the proclamation at school, in common with most Irish schoolchildren of that era. As though fearful that the Irish public had forgotten the symbolism of the statue, the authorities recently had it framed with a lengthy quotation from the proclamation:

We declare the right of the people of Ireland to the ownership of Ireland, and to the unfettered control of Irish destinies, to be sovereign and indefeasible. The long usurpation of that right by a foreign people and government has not extinguished the right, nor can it ever be extinguished except by the destruction of the Irish people. In every generation the Irish people have asserted their right to national freedom and sovereignty; six times during the past three hundred years

'Not a very manly way to go out, at least without a certain amount of rationalization. Actually, you find the same gendered rationalization of martyrdom in another roughly contemporary text, *4 Maccabees*. There the atrociously abused martyrs are lauded as true men in the most explicit terms – even, or especially, the female martyr, the mother of the seven brothers – and at the expense of their tormentors, especially Antiochus Epiphanes, whose own masculinity is subtly but effectively called into question.'[8]

'*You're saying that* 4 Maccabees *inhabits Revelation's textual unconscious, just as texts such as Daniel and Ezekiel inhabit its textual consciousness?*'

'So that's what I said! I wonder what I meant by it.'

'*One thing still troubles me.*'

'And what might that be?'

'*Surely you're not really persuaded by my reading of Revelation?*'

'Of course not, I'm merely patronizing you.'

'*Thank goodness, you had me worried.*'

they have asserted it in arms. Standing on that fundamental right and again asserting it in arms in the face of the world, we hereby proclaim the Irish Republic as a sovereign independent state, and we pledge our lives and the lives of our comrades-in-arms to the cause of its freedom, of its welfare, and of its exaltation among the nations.

The statue in question represents a calculated combination of vulnerability and indomitability. Too weak to stand through loss of blood, the hero has strapped himself to an upright stone, sword still gripped in his now lifeless hand, defiant to the end and beyond, even in the face of unimaginable odds.[9] Padraig Pearse, poet and pillar of the 1916 rebellion, argued that the spilling of Irish blood was at least as important to the cause of Irish freedom as the spilling of English blood:

Life springs from death; and from the graves of patriot men and women spring living nations. The Defenders of this Realm have worked well in secret and in the open. They think that they have pacified Ireland. They think that they have purchased half of us and intimidated the other half. They think that they have foreseen everything, think that they have provided against everything; but the fools, the fools, the fools! – they have left us our Fenian dead, and while Ireland holds these graves, Ireland unfree shall never be at peace.

(Pearse 1996 [1915]: 40)

The authorities proceeded to demonstate the truth of Pearse's claim by summarily executing him, together with the other captured leaders of the rebellion, thereby unwittingly creating a cadre of martyrs and transforming an unpopular and apparently unsuccessful uprising into a popular and ultimately successful one, in that it eventually led to Irish independence.

John, too, knew the importance of martyrs. Indeed, his calculation of the symbolic value of martyrdom was to prove uncannily accurate. Christian martyrdom would eventually purchase a vast empire 'for God' on earth, the Great Persecution under Diocletian ushering in Imperial Christendom under Constantine. Understandably enough, John failed to foresee Constantinian Christianity, precisely. But the motif of the millenium ('I also saw the souls of those who had been beheaded for their testimony to Jesus. . . . They came to life and reigned with Christ a thousand years', 20:4–6), which he smuggles into the climactic sequence of his eschatological scenario, neatly anticipates its advent. For the symbolic economy of martyrdom in Revelation can be reduced to a simple exchange. In order to be deemed worthy to dominate others Christ and his followers first have to show, in good Graeco-Roman fashion, that they are able to dominate themselves.[10]

And so we arrive at *4 Maccabees* which, like the *Táin*, is a paean to war, but this time to war with oneself. For *4 Maccabees* is a paean to martyrdom, understood as ultimate self-mastery. The Roman Catholic children's Bible used in Christian doctrine class in that same small school in Adare did not contain the book of Revelation, even in abridged form. But it did contain something still more disturbing, the story of the scalping, dismembering and roasting of seven brothers, watched by their mother, from 2 Maccabees 7, which is to say *4 Maccabees* in miniature.[11] And so my childhood was innocent of Revelation but haunted by the *Táin Bó Cuailnge* and the tale of the Maccabean mother and her butchered sons. But perhaps providence was merely preparing me for Revelation. For it strikes me now that what I earlier said of the *Táin* in relation to Revelation would apply *mutatis mutandis* to *4 Maccabees*: Whereas *4 Maccabees* is a garish celebration of martyrdom, Revelation is a muted celebration of martyrdom. Superimposed upon Revelation, *4 Maccabees* colours in its blanks with lurid hues . . .

Notes

1 A shorter, shyer version of this essay was presented at a colloquium at the University of Glasgow on the ethics of apocalyptic held on 4 May 1997. The proceedings of the colloquium are scheduled to be published by Trinity St Mungo Press, Glasgow. The present version has benefited from some pointed – and rather personal – criticisms that were levelled at it by Susan Graham.
2 The cattle raid of the title, which provides the pretext for all the epic's battles and single combats, is the invasion of the province of Ulster by the armies of the province of Connaught, along with their allies from the other three provinces, in pursuit of the Donn Cuailnge, a gigantic brown bull that Medb, queen of Connaught, is determined to possess to match the gigantic white bull that her husband Ailill owns.
3 One of the three goddesses of war who feature in the *Táin*.
4 Later the narrator will be at pains to stress that although hideous in combat, Cúchulainn cut a strikingly handsome figure otherwise:

> You would think he had three distinct heads of hair – brown at the base, blood-red in the middle, and a crown of golden yellow. This hair was settled strikingly into three coils on the cleft at the back of his head. Each long loose-flowing strand hung down in shining splendour over his shoulders, deep-gold and beautiful and fine as a thread of gold. A hundred neat red-gold curls shone darkly on his neck, and his head was covered with a hundred crimson threads matted with gems. He had four dimples in each cheek – yellow, green, crimson and blue – and seven bright pupils, eye-jewels, in each kingly eye. Each foot had seven toes and each hand seven fingers, the nails with the grip of a hawk's claw or a gryphon's clench.

The translation of the *Táin* used throughout is that of the poet Thomas Kinsella (see Kinsella 1969).
5 The boy-troop, together with Cúchulainn himself, still a boy of 17, were left to defend Ulster against the invaders after a curse had left all the adult men of Ulster bedridden. Now the boy-troop has been massacred and Cúchulainn has set out to avenge them.
6 Dogs and horses, women and children . . . A misogynistic gem, to be sure. For what it's worth, however, the *Táin* does accord prominent roles to certain women, such as the formidable and memorable Queen Medb, or the woman-warrior Scáthach, from whom Cúchulainn received his training in arms.
7 And yet I love Revelation for its beauty – a male sentiment, surely? Its intricate lacework of images has never failed to thrill me. Of course, my impression that Revelation is an exquisite work of language is wilful illusion on my part. The English translations in which I normally read it are cosmetic coverings concealing from view all of Revelation's bizarre grammatical blemishes. The translators take John's broken Greek and beautify it, excising all its irregularities, a nip here, a tuck there. I know enough Greek to spot John's stunning solecisms, but not quite enough to hear them. I wish I could hear John's exotic Aramaic accent, listen as he fumbles in the warm Aegean night for the correct grammatical boxes in which to lock his glittering visions, occasionally picking up the wrong one in the deep, velvety darkness.
8 When I first penned the above, suggesting that the martial imagery applied to the martyrs in Revelation was an apologia for passive resistance as a legitimate

masculine stance, and appealing to *4 Maccabees* for support, I was groping for closure and felt I was overreaching. But I have subsequently stumbled upon some parallel claims that have persuaded me of my own suggestion. First, a recent article by classicist Brent D. Shaw. Of *4 Maccabees* Shaw asserts:

> Praises of active and aggressive values entailed in manliness (ἀνδρεια) by almost all other writers in the world of [*4 Maccabees*] could easily fill books. The elevation to prominence of the passive value of merely being able to endure would have struck most persons . . . as contradictory and, indeed, rather immoral. A value like that cut right across the great divide that marked elite free-status male values and that informed everything about bodily behaviour . . .
>
> (Shaw 1996: 278–9)

Shaw finds in *4 Maccabees,* and not only in *4 Maccabees* (he also appeals extensively to Seneca, for example), 'the conscious production of a rather elaborate conception of passive resistance', or, more precisely, 'the explicit cooptation of passivity in resistance as a fully legitimized male quality – a choice that could be made by thinking, reasoning and logical men' (280).

Second, a paper by another classicist, Tessa Rajak, which I chanced to hear last week in Birmingham at the annual meeting of the *Studiorum Novi Testamenti Societas*. Independently of Shaw, Rajak notes that there is evidence that in the Graeco-Roman world 'the inflexible and obdurate mind-set of the martyr was perceived by some logical spirits as the epitome of unreason' (Rajak 1997: 13). Philo, for example, 'says that opponents might consider the Jews' readiness to die for their laws as "barbaric", while in reality it was an expression of freedom and nobility (*Leg.* 215). Later, Marcus Aurelius, in expounding the Stoic way to die, was to observe that this should be with considered judgment (λελογισμένως) and not, in the Christian manner, obstinately and showily (11.3)' (ibid.; that the observation might be a gloss does not reduce its relevance, as Rajak remarks). Concerning 'the terminology of male heroism' in *4 Maccabees*, therefore, with its evocations of warfare and athletic prowess (e.g., 17:11–17), Rajak claims: 'These images are intrinsic to martyrology, as the agents which effect the transmutation of shaming passivity into the highest of masculine virtues. What we are offered is a concentrated inversion of the competitive physical values which constructed masculinity for Graeco-Roman society, a triumphant reversal of the power-structure with the victim as the winner' (pp. 16–17). (My thanks to Professor Rajak for kindly allowing me to quote from her paper.)

9 A raven has settled on his shoulder, a signal to the armies assembled around him that it is now safe to approach him. But whence this fatal loss of blood, you may well ask, given that Cúchulainn earlier took on these armies single-handedly without incurring a single scratch? Well, it was inflicted by Cúchulainn's 'adored foster-brother' Ferdia, 'the horn-skinned warrior from Irrus Domnann', 'the burden unbearable and the rock fatal in the fray', who was shamed into challenging Cúchulainn to single combat. Ferdia lost, eventually finding himself at the wrong end of the *gae bolga*, the belly-barb, Cúchulainn's ultimate weapon, which, cast from the fork of his foot across the waters of the ford in which they were fighting, sliced through Ferdia's 'deep and sturdy apron of twice-smelted iron', and shattered in three parts the stout strong stone the size of a millstone [which he had earlier stuffed inside the apron for good measure, "for fear and dread of the *gae bolga*"], and went

coursing through the highways and byways of his body so that every single joint filled with barbs'. Thereupon Ferdia is moved to remark, 'That is enough now. I'll die of that', Cúchulainn's javelin, which he had already thrust through Ferdia's heart so that 'half its length showed out through his back', having failed to impress Ferdia sufficiently. But Ferdia got his licks in too. At the height of the contest, which raged for four days, the heroes were 'piercing and drilling each other' with their 'big burdensome stabbing-spears' (Freud would have a field-day with the *Táin*), and a bewildering assortment of other heavy weaponry. 'If even birds in flight could pass through men's bodies they could have passed through those bodies that day and brought bits of blood and meat with them out into the thickening air through the wounds and gashes,' avers the narrator. And that was only the third day; the fourth was even worse.

10 Paradoxically, however, the enemies of God in Revelation embrace a course of action that is structurally parallel to Christian martyrdom. Certain Christian martyrs refused to curse Christ even under pain of death, as we know from Pliny the Younger's famous letter to Trajan (*Letters* 10.96–7), composed around 112 CE when Pliny was governor of Bithynia. But the unrepentant in Revelation dare to curse God under pain of death (16:9, 11, 21) – even eternal death-by-torture (14:9–11) – unlike the temporary torment endured by the Christian martyrs, their gesture thereby exceeding that of the latter.

11 Assuming that *4 Maccabees* is a free expansion of *2 Maccabees* 6–7.

Works cited, or obliquely alluded to,
or otherwise presupposed

Anderson, J. Capel and Moore, S. D. (1998) 'Taking It Like a Man: Masculinity in 4 Maccabees', *JBL* 117: 249–73.

Bauckham, R. (1993a) *The Climax of Prophecy: Studies on the Book of Revelation*, Edinburgh: T. & T. Clark.

—— (1993b) *The Theology of the Book of Revelation*, Cambridge: Cambridge University Press.

Butler, J. (1990) *Gender Trouble: Feminism and the Subversion of Identity*, London and New York: Routledge.

—— (1995) 'Melancholy Gender/Refused Identification', in M. Berger, B. Wallis, and S. Watson (eds) *Constructing Masculinity*, London and New York: Routledge.

Clines, D. J. A. (1995) 'David the Man: The Construction of Masculinity in the Hebrew Bible', in D. J. A. Clines *Interested Parties: The Ideology of Writers and Readers of the Hebrew Bible*, JSOT Supplement Series, 205, Gender, Culture, Theory, 1, Sheffield: Sheffield Academic.

Cooke, M. (1993), 'Wo-man, Retelling the War Myth', in M. Cooke and A. Woollacott (eds) *Gendering War Talk*, Princeton, NJ: Princeton University Press.

Hoffner, H. A., Jr. (1966) 'Symbols for Masculinity and Femininity: Their Use in Ancient Near Eastern Sympathetic Magic Rituals', *JBL* 85: 327–32.

Kinsella, T. (ed. and trans.) (1969) *The Táin*, Mountrath, Ireland: The Dolmen.

Moore, S. D. (1996) *God's Gym: Divine Male Bodies of the Bible*, London and New York: Routledge.

Pearse, P. (1996 [1915]) 'While Ireland Holds These Graves', Funeral oration over the grave of O'Donovan Rossa at Glasnevin Cemetry, Dublin, August 1, 1915, in M. McLoughlin (ed.) *Great Irish Speeches of the Twentieth Century*, Dublin: Poolbeg.

Pippin, T. (1992) *Death and Desire: The Rhetoric of Gender in the Apocalypse of John*, Louisville, KY: Westminster John Knox.

—— (1994) 'The Revelation to John', in E. Schüssler Fiorenza, with A. Brock and S. Matthews (eds) *Searching the Scriptures*, Vol. 2, *A Feminist Commentary*, New York: Crossroad.

Rajak, T. (1997) 'Dying for the Law: The Martyr's Portrait in Jewish-Greek Literature'. Paper presented at the Annual Meeting of the *Studiorum Novi Testamenti Societas*, University of Birmingham, 4–8 August, 1997.

Schaberg, J. (1992) 'Luke', in C. A. Newsom and S. H. Ringe (eds) *The Women's Bible Commentary*, Louisville, KY: Westminster John Knox.

Shaw, B. D. (1996) 'Body/Power/Identity: Passions of the Martyrs', *Journal of Early Christian Studies* 4: 269–312.

Washington, H. C. (1997) 'Violence and the Construction of Gender in the Hebrew Bible: A New Historicist Approach', *Biblical Interpretation* 5: 324–63.

NAME INDEX

Achtemeier, E. 17, 18, 24
Aichele, G. 5, 9, 53, 64
Alcoff, L. 4, 7, 9
Alter, R. 9
Anand, K. J. S. 74, 85
Anderson, J. C. 3, 9, 24, 64, 96, 106, 109, 128, 140, 200
Anzaldua, G. 126
Aquino, C. 60, 63, 64
Arendt, H. 20, 24
Arndt, W. F. 67
Auwers, J.-M. 104, 109

Bach, A. 126
Bass, E. 178, 181
Bassler, J. M. 109
Bauckham, R. 185, 186, 190, 191, 192, 193, 200
Beatles 80, 83
Berger, M. 200
Berlin, A. 126
Betti, E. 130, 140
The Bible and Culture Collective 10, 16, 24, 97, 110
Blount, B. K. 9, 96
Boesak, A. A. 130, 140
Bonhoeffer, D. 8, 12, 16, 17, 21, 24
Boring, M. E. 55, 64
Braund, S. M. 8, 9
Brenner, A. 181
Brett, M. G. 4, 9, 37, 108
Brock, A. 200
Brown, R. E. 96, 109
Bultmann, R. 12, 24, 106, 108, 109, 130, 142
Butler, J. 200
Buttrick, G. A. 37
Byrne, B. J. 97, 105, 109

Camus, A. 14
Cannon, K. G. 181, 182
Carson, D. A. 96
Caws, M. A. 5, 9 181
Cherry, C. 35, 37
Clements, R. E. 181
Clines, D. J. A. 186, 200
Coleridge, S. T. 8
Collins, M. 92, 96
Coloe, M. 108
Cooke, M. 186, 200
Cousineau, P. 126
Crafford, D. 144, 145, 153, 155
Croatto, J. S. 6, 9, 39, 43, 50, 52
Crüsemann, F. 43, 52
Culpepper, R. A. 9, 96, 106, 109, 126

Davies, G. I. 39, 52
Davis, L. 178, 181
Deem, A. 175, 181
De Gruchy, J. W. 131, 132, 140
Denniston, G. C. 85
de Pury, A. 52
Derrida, J. 76, 83–4, 85
Dickson, K. 155
Donaldson, L. E. 4, 9
Dormeyer, D. 136, 140
Dube, M. W. 4, 6, 9, 11, 22, 24, 141
Duke, P. D. 88, 96, 104, 109

Easthope, A. 9
Ebeling, G. 130, 140
Eilberg-Schwartz, H. 178, 181
Elisabeth (empress) 115
Ellingworth, P. 155
Enzeanya, S. N. 144, 155
Exum, J. Ch. 126, 177, 178, 179, 181

SUBJECT INDEX

Aaron 44, 49
Abraham 47, 65, 72, 135; descendants
    of 134, 135, 136; sons of 135, 136
Abram 175
abuse 177, 178, 179, 194; child 177;
    childhood sexual 178; physical 178;
    sexual 177; verbal 178
abusiveness 176
Acts (book of) 161
Adam 138
adulterous 174
adultery 174, 177
advocacy scholars 13, 15; *see also*
    feminists
aesthetic approach 87
Afrikaans 131
African: Christians 148; Christianity
    149; people 142, 150; religious
    culture 143; religious ethos 143;
    traditional communities 142;
    traditional family 151
Afrikaner: nationalism 131; people 132
Afrikaners 131, 132
African traditional religion (ATR) 143,
    144, 145, 146, 148, 149, 150, 151,
    153; narrative 144
Akkadian 172
'alternative world' 136, 137
ancestors 119, 143, 144, 145, 146,
    149, 150, 152, 153; ancestor
    veneration 151
ancient Near East 171, 173, 188
androcentrism 22
androcritical perspective 22
anti-colonialism 132
anti-Semitic/Semitism 16, 19, 20
'anti-structure' 136
apartheid 131, 135; apologists 135;

ethics 133; exegesis 133; exegetes
    132; perspective 128, 129, 133;
    philosophy 134; policy of 132;
    principles 133; protest against 134;
    reading 129, 133; system 131;
    thinking and theology 132; *see also*
    post-*apartheid* reading
Apocalypse 165; *see also* Revelation
apostle *see* Paul
application 29, 137, 159, 163, 164,
    166, 167
appropriation 14, 15, 128
archaeological 132; tendency 134;
    thinking 133, 135, 136 (*vs*
    eschatological)
argumentation 134
argumentative: situation 134; text 134
Australian culture and society 105
Austrians 115, 124
authority/authorities 163, 165, 166,
    195; governmental 165, 167
autobiographical 16, 26, 63, 77, 86,
    97, 98, 106, 111
autobiographical (biblical) criticism/
    reading 3, 4, 7, 8, 53, 97, 106, 107,
    128, 129
autobiography 26, 78, 97, 105, 106,
    107, 108, 130

Baal 171, 175; *see also* Hadad
Babel 132
Babylon 47, 188, 189, 190
Babylonian Talmud 171
baptised 100
baptism 99, 154
'beloved disciple' 105
Benedictine: monastery 116; nunnery
    116

BIBLICAL INDEX

213